"Let's Face It, Men Are @$$#%\¢$"

What Women Can Do About It

Joseph W. Rock, Psy.D.
Barry L. Duncan, Psy.D.

Health Communications, Inc.
Deerfield Beach, Florida

www.hci-online.com

Library of Congress Cataloging-in-Publication Data

Rock, Joseph W.
"Let's face it, men are @$$#%\c$": what woman can do about it /
Joseph W. Rock, Barry L. Duncan.
    p.   cm.
    Includes bibliographical references.
    1. Men—United States—Psychology. 2. Man-woman relation-
ships—United   States. 3. Women—United   States—Attitudes.
I. Duncan Barry L.   II. Title.
HQ1090.3.R64   1998   98-34228
306.7—dc21   CIP

©1998 Joseph W. Rock and Barry L. Duncan

ISBN 1-55874-625-0

Publisher: Health Communications, Inc.
               3201 S.W. 15th Street
               Deerfield Beach, FL 33442-8190

Cover design by Andrea Perrine Brower.
Barry Duncan's photo courtesy of Dale Brown of Stuart Photo, Inc., Stuart, Florida.
Joseph Rock's photo courtesy of Today's Photos, Rocky River, Ohio.

To all the women who privileged us with their stories and inspired this book.

Contents

PART ONE: FACING THE TRUTH ABOUT MEN

TABLES AND FIGURES

Preface

Although women have won many battles in the courtroom and workplace, equal relationships between men and women are the exception rather than the rule. An inspection of this unfortunate reality reveals what many women know only too well: *Let's face it, men are assholes.*

This book, unabashedly and without apologies, zeroes in on men who act like assholes in relationships. We've heard about these men from conversations with countless numbers of women and seen this reality in action in men we've known. This book organizes those experiences into categories that make it easier to comprehend the dazzling array of troubling male behaviors women typically run across. Our insider's view as men combines with our clinical training and experience to give you practical methods for recognizing, avoiding and coping with these problematic men you inevitably encounter. While it should provide some chuckles along the way, it is not intended as a parody of self-help books. Nor is it a deadly serious, self-important, "scientific" report on a newly discovered social "disease."

Why should you bother reading this book? First

of all, to help you realize that you're neither alone nor crazy in your perceptions of how truly difficult, immature, controlling, etc., a lot of guys are. We intend to confirm your gut feelings by allowing you to look at assholes when they don't think anyone else is looking. You'll be able to see these guys for what they really are and deal with them on *your* terms, not theirs.

As a broader goal, we hope our controversial position about men raises not only eyebrows but also awareness. For too long, women have shouldered the responsibility for relationships, while negative male behavior in relationships has virtually been swept under the carpet. Analogous to how the O. J. Simpson trial burst the country's denial bubble about race relations and domestic violence, we hope this book will open some eyes regarding gender equality, or lack of it, in close relationships.

Acknowledgments

Any endeavor of this kind reflects contributions by many, and to them we are deeply grateful. We are most indebted to our female clients. They generously shared their tragedies and triumphs—their painful, humorous and enlightening experiences with men of all shapes and sizes—and we are far better for it. All the examples in this book are real, although identifying information and specific details have been drastically altered to ensure confidentiality. In addition, some of our examples represent combinations of many different true stories, to further guarantee anonymity.

Several people deserve special mention. We owe a great debt of gratitude to Barbara Janus, Sue Posada, Susan Gouveia, Douglas Flemons and Pat Cole for critiquing the manuscript and strengthening its message. Feedback from Jo McDermott and Jacqueline Sparks was particularly useful in helping us consider more thoroughly the gender implications of this book.

We are especially indebted to Marny Nedlin, who provided many suggestions, designed the tables

and was someone to count on during last-minute pressures. Clare McManamon also provided invaluable help in preparing this book for publication. Joe's colleagues, especially Sharon Wiza, Catherine Sheehan and Sylvia Herd, gave direction and input at opportune times. We are grateful to Barry's colleagues at Nova Southeastern University's Department of Family Therapy, especially Shelley Green, Chris Burnett and Lee Shilts, for providing an unusually open, friendly and supportive environment in which to work. In addition, we thank Dean Ron Chenail for his encouragement of this endeavor, and the students, too many to mention, who make every day of Barry's work a stimulating, challenging and delightful experience.

Barry is also grateful to Scott Miller and Mark Hubble, his friends and coauthors of many other books, whom he depends on to stretch his thinking, make him laugh, and keep his passions about psychotherapy ignited. In addition, Barry owes a great deal to his wife, Karen Adler, for her almost endless support of his almost endless work.

We are also grateful to Allison Janse of Health Communications, for her skillful editorial help and enthusiasm for this project. Finally, we feel especially indebted to Christine Belleris, editorial director at Health Communications, for giving a book with such a provocative title a chance.

Introduction

While this book does not take a sympathetic position toward men, we do not believe that all men are assholes. Neither do we doubt that there are reasons that explain the ones who are. We're just tired of these reasons being used as *excuses* for unacceptable behavior.

Women have been far too willing to give men the benefit of the doubt, to be patient and understanding, and to wait for "potential" to sprout in the soil of unconditional love. So, to help women compensate for those tendencies, this book will pull no punches in describing *certain types* of men. It will explain what common types (and subtypes) you typically see, and offer ways to spot them early and avoid them. Next, for the woman already involved in a destructive relationship, we examine the issues involved in her dilemma and provide tips on how she can make the decision to stay or go. If women decide to leave, this book offers practical steps. If women decide to stay in their relationship, they'll find down-to-earth suggestions on how to cope with (and maybe change) their specific type of man.

While we try to have some fun with these subjects, we are serious about what we are saying. As you know already, men can be assholes—big ones—and getting involved with these noxious men can make women's lives impossible. We hope that our humor not only helps make a serious topic more palatable, but also makes it more likely that you will do something about the situations you find troubling. Sometimes laughing at our foibles opens new ways to look at things and different methods to try.

We hope to help you: (1) be more selective in choosing the guys on whom you lavish your understanding and support; (2) seriously consider your prospects for the future if you are with a toxic man; and (3) employ your inherent strengths to sabotage his manipulations and control, explore a better life for yourself, and in the process of taking charge of your own story, set the stage for him to change.

Facing the Truth About Men

1

Who Are These Guys?

*I was so happy. He was everything
I always dreamed of—sensitive, kind,
intelligent, passionate. Yes, he was a real
class act. The only problem was,
that's all it ever was—an act!*

—Gail, thirty-five-year-old Realtor

Connie came into the therapist's office distraught. Her husband acted as if he didn't love her anymore. She was afraid he might be having an affair and that her marriage of fifteen years was on the verge of ending. She was willing to try whatever it took to save it and was able to talk her reluctant husband into seeing the therapist one time.

Her husband, Michael, insisted on coming in alone. He cut right to the chase. He was having an affair with his twenty-two-year-old secretary and

felt no guilt about it. His wife was overweight, sexually inhibited, too wrapped up in the kids and uninteresting to him. He felt he deserved better and had no qualms about seeking it. He was only staying with Connie for financial reasons, and expected he'd leave her once their youngest child reached eighteen and child support wasn't an issue. Michael threatened the therapist that if he told any of this to Connie, Michael would sue him for violating the confidentiality of the doctor-patient relationship. Then he got up and abruptly left.

Nice guy, right? Well, he's not alone—not by a long shot.

Men can't commit. Men hate women. Men can't communicate. Men "don't get it." Men want to be Peter Pan. Men are from Mars.

You see it on TV talk shows, you read about it in women's magazines and self-help books, you hear it from your friends. Men are doing lots of things that make it hard for women to relate to and understand them, much less prosper in intimate relationships with them. Yet they don't seem to care. It's mostly women who read articles and self-help books, who talk about relationship problems with their friends, who seek counseling.

Even so, "asshole" is a pretty strong label to hang on someone. To a certain extent, we use the term with tongue in cheek. We started out joking with each other that the direction self-help books and talk shows were taking would inevitably lead to the conclusion stated in this book's title. We were kidding.

Then we began running the idea by our female friends and clients. The response was overwhelming. Virtually all agreed men *were* assholes, and, for the most part, they weren't kidding. Sure, they acknowledged that not *all* men were bad and that even those who were had their good points. But still, there was clearly a vein of anger, resentment and frustration the statement tapped into.

Do We Have to Use the "A" Word?

Using the word "asshole" may put many people off, dissuading them from reading this book and perhaps even leading some to protest its being carried in bookstores and libraries. It is not meant to be offensive or profane. Nothing about the word or this book's orientation is in any way sacrilegious. There are no descriptions or even suggestions of any acts people would find objectionable or morally depraved.

It is vulgar, of course, to call men assholes. But that vulgarity is only dimly reflective of the behavioral and emotional damage these men perpetrate, often unwittingly, on the women with whom they get involved. We could find no better word that was both vague enough to mold into our own definition, and at the same time emotionally consistent with the anger and frustration women increasingly feel in their relationships with men. It's the only word that does justice to the kind of men that we have heard countless women describe.

The irony in this discussion is that the people least likely to be offended by our use of the word are those very men to whom it applies. Guys call each other the "A" word all the time, and even wear that appellation with pride. Treating women badly, short of frank abuse, rarely causes a man to be shunned by his peers. More often, it is overlooked or even viewed with some perverse respect—after all, real men don't take any crap from women.

Everyone Knows It— Why Harp on It?

A reasonable criticism of this book's approach is that it does a disservice to women by highlighting men's negative qualities and not mentioning nice guys, making women even more pessimistic

than they already are about men. *Women who are with nice guys will never pick up this book.* For the rest of you, this book is intended to validate some of your perceptions, clearly label the types of men who complicate your life, and give you some specific ideas on how to deal with those men.

The average romance novel does women a far greater disservice than a book like this ever could. Romance novels are extremely popular, and that popularity is almost exclusively with women. The magnitude of that popularity is astonishing. According to a 1997 *Newsweek* report, "The Queen of Hearts Gives Up Her Throne," romance novels accounted for $1 *billion* dollars of sales in 1996 alone. And more than half of all paperbacks aimed at the mass market were novels from the romance genre.

Romance novels, like mysteries and other genres, follow formulas. One such formula is that the male romantic interest starts out being a rogue—unprincipled, untrustworthy, rough around the edges, but exciting and desirable. The perfect asshole. However, eventually the love of a good woman straightens him out and tames him, and at the end they ride off into the sunset.

Now, *that* is some dangerous propaganda. First of all, it glamorizes the rogue and contributes to the dangerous (and very seldom accurate) belief that he can be changed. Romance novels aren't the only place women are fed this nonsense. It's an uplifting, optimistic story line, and women not only want to believe it, but are conned into buying it by societal myths about relationships. So, the plots of many movies, television shows and even popular novels outside the romance genre deliver it. As a result, a lot of women keep kissing frogs and waiting for the transformation into princes.

This isn't surprising. Women want to see Prince Charming when they fall in love, so they overlook some things. Men often believe the things they tell women early in relationships (despite evidence in their past relationships to the contrary). They want to see themselves as nice guys. So, you have two people colluding to delude themselves as a relationship begins.

There are lots of books that will give you a balanced perspective on men. This one won't. This book will convey to you what many men are really like—what they say, think and feel about women when they are among their own kind. As men, we have been privy to the unedited and non-politically correct ideas in our offices as well as in locker rooms and at sporting events. We hear men refer to women as "D cups," "bimbos" and the "C" and "B" words regularly, and not just by the unwashed and uneducated. These uncensored viewpoints paint an ugly picture of the average guy on the street. Seeing men as they are can only help to forewarn and forearm you as you enter or maintain a relationship.

More important than these uncensored conversations with men, we have been privileged to listen to women's stories about men for a combined thirty-five years in our psychotherapy practices. We have been enriched by those experiences. Thousands of women have taught us about male behavior as well as female resilience. This book relies heavily on the expertise of those women.

There are many (well, at least, some) kind, reasonable, sensitive men out there. This book describes the ones who aren't. What proportion of men they represent is not known, but it's not a small number. We hope to send a strong message to women that if they are dealing with these Princes of Darkness, feeling sorry for them, showing understanding and being patient won't work. According to the many women interviewed for this book, frogs stay frogs, rogues stay rogues and assholes remain assholes. Let's start with identifying who these guys are.

What Makes Someone an Asshole?

Everyone has an opinion about what makes someone worthy of wearing the scarlet "A" (and we're not talking about "adulterer," although that will be addressed in chapter 4). Let us clarify the

characteristics we refer to when we use that term:

1. **Insensitivity to their partners.** It doesn't seem like much to ask to pay a little attention to what a woman likes and dislikes, and what makes her feel good or hurts her. These men don't.

2. **Selfishness.** Another key to a decent relationship is the ability to put the other person's needs, wants and desires first a reasonable proportion of the time. These men lack that ability.

3. **Inability to take responsibility for themselves.** When things go wrong between two people, both are at fault. These men either don't recognize their contributions or contend they can't help what they do. They somehow figure out a way to blame you.

4. **Making their partners' lives harder, not easier.** One reason people get into relationships is to have someone to share things with and lighten life's burdens. These men add to those burdens in many different ways.

5. **Competition, not cooperation.** Ideally, a relationship involves sharing and working together. These men compete, as if winning and being right are more important than getting along.

6. **The need to control.** The best relationships occur between equals, who deal with each other out of mutual respect and division of responsibilities. These men need to call all the shots.

A disturbing number of men meet many of these criteria. While the way they became this way may capture your intellectual curiosity, whether or not you are with one is of more immediate importance. To give you a general idea of what you're dealing with, take the quiz that begins on the following page.

If you answer "No" to all questions, clone him. You could make a fortune. If you answer one to five questions, "Yes," you are with someone who has definite "A" tendencies. If you respond with "Yes" to six to ten questions, he is a jerk, without a doubt. If you answer eleven to fifteen questions, "Yes," he is an enormous asshole, with characteristics of many of the varieties discussed in subsequent chapters. If you answer sixteen to twenty questions with "Yes," you are in hell.

	Table 1.1 IS HE OR ISN'T HE? A QUIZ	YES	NO
1.	Did you think, at first, he was too good to be true . . . and it turns out he was?		
2.	Do you find yourself doing more than your share in many areas of the relationship?		
3.	Do you have to pry thoughts and feelings out of him?		
4.	Does he live with his parents (or did he when you met him)?		
5.	Are you ashamed or embarrassed to tell friends and relatives what he's really like?		
6.	Do you defend and explain yourself to him a lot?		
7.	Do you often feel like a child being talked to by a parent when he talks to you?		
8.	Does he get close, pull away, get close, pull away?		
9.	Do you wonder what you did to make him stop caring?		

Table 1.1 *(Continued)* IS HE OR ISN'T HE? A QUIZ		YES	NO
10.	Does it seem to you that he has no feelings at all (except maybe anger)?		
11.	Does he ever tell you to quit acting like his mother?		
12.	Does he openly flirt with other women when you're around and then tell you you're hyper-sensitive when you point it out?		
13.	Do you find yourself frequently saying, "I'm not allowed"?		
14.	Does he make you feel as if you can't do anything right?		
15.	Does he make you feel guilty when he wants sex and you don't?		
16.	Do you wonder, sometimes, if you're living in a fraternity house (beer, sports on TV, his hanging out with his friends)?		
17.	Does he feel entitled to things—whether or not he's done anything to deserve them?		
18.	Do you have trouble recognizing the man you met as the one you're with now?		
19.	Does it feel like you have another child in the house when he's there?		
20.	Do you believe he can't, or doesn't want to, understand when you tell him how you feel?		

Listen Carefully . . .
He Doesn't Want to Change

Many women get into or remain in relationships, based on their hopes that the men they are involved with will eventually change. Some believe it will happen due to his growing up. Others hope loving him will make him love himself. Regardless of the specific reason, hope fuels a woman's determination to stay in a relationship with a man who is not keeping up his end.

Years ago, a series of "lightbulb" jokes made the rounds. The straight line was always, "How many _____ does it take to change a lightbulb?" The punch line for how many psychologists it took was, "Just one, but it takes a long time, and the light bulb has to really want to change."

Women who are involved with grade "A" men (as this book defines them) need to realize that most of them don't want to change. If they did, *they* (not you) would be reading self-help books, going to therapy, asking friends and family members how to make things better. The person who comes to a therapist's office or reads self-help books regarding a relationship problem isn't the "crazy" one; she is the one who is hurting more, who is more uncomfortable with the way things are and who is trying to work for change.

Just because you're uncomfortable, don't assume he is, even if he moans and groans a lot about you and the relationship. People who are truly uncomfortable either do something about it or leave. If he's doing neither, a reasonable supposition is that he's fairly satisfied with the way things are.

As you read the descriptions of different kinds of men and the relationships they get into, their relative lack of discomfort won't be hard to understand. They set up relationships so they have most of the power or they get things their way. Or they are incapable of functioning in mature, intimate relationships and aren't even

aware of what's missing (they just don't "get it").

If you make the assumption, for whatever reasons, that he wants to change when he doesn't, you can spend a long time banging your head against a wall of resistance. On the other hand, recognizing that *you* are the motivated person gives you a far more hopeful, accurate and helpful perspective.

Men Who Write Self-Help Books: A Class of Their Own

While we're on the subject of men's motivation to change, let's look for a minute at self-help books about relationships. The sheer number of books on this general subject is overwhelming. Your local bookstores are teeming with books on how to salvage, spruce up, enhance, give deeper meaning to or bring back the magic in your relationship. A lot of these books—including this one, of course— have been written by men.

No doubt, the male "experts" writing these books have good intentions that go beyond a desire to make money off people's misery. However, a lot of what is written by both men and women on the subject of relationships is not only unhelpful, but downright counterproductive.

The vast majority of the people who read these books are women, for reasons described in the previous section, and for other reasons as well. Our society encourages women to take responsibility for the emotional maintenance of relationships. Women also tend to place more emphasis on the quality of their relationships than men do.

Romance novels are not the only dangerous source of relationship propaganda confronting women. Self-help books about relationships tend to tell women what they want to hear—that men

can change. When this message comes from male authors, it has even more of an impact. Women think they are getting inside information. After all, the authors are not only "experts," they are also men. They know how men think and what motivates them. These ideas can be dangerously misleading.

As an example, let's consider John Gray and his enormously popular book, *Men Are from Mars, Women Are from Venus*. Dr. Gray's book is full of genuinely insightful material that resonates with the experiences of huge numbers of people (mainly, from what we have seen, women). His ideas validate a lot of women's feelings and help them understand common problems they have with men in intimate relationships.

Many men, as well, can relate to his ideas such as "going to the cave." Unfortunately, most of what he writes about men is read by women. They get what we believe is false hope that their partners could change if they would just read the book. The problem is that most of these men DON'T WANT TO CHANGE.

If we had a dollar for every woman we've talked to who has tried to get her husband/boyfriend to read that book (and failed), we'd be retired in the Caribbean rather than writing this book. One section of *Men Are from Mars, Women Are from Venus* is "101 ways men can score points with women." One of those 101 suggestions is to "give her four hugs a day." Yeah, right. Can you picture some of the men you've been involved with reading that and following through with it? If a guy is willing to read a self-help book, take it seriously and follow advice like the "four hugs a day," he's an unusual guy who probably doesn't need to be reading the book to begin with.

The problem with this kind of advice is that it implies to women that there is a realistic possibility the average guy will seek it out and follow it. This feeds their delusions that men can, and want to, change. Consequently, women continue beating their heads against brick walls, trying to get their partners to change via

straightforward, simplistic methods.

This book's point of view is quite different. We believe that if you have made several sincere attempts to get your partner to work on the relationship with no success, you need to step back and look more carefully at him. Is he a "four hugs a day" kind of guy, or someone who is content to leave things the way they are regardless of how uncomfortable and unhappy you are? We think a more accurate book title would have been *Women Are from Earth, Men Are from Uranus.*

So What's a Woman to Do?

He's a jerk. He doesn't want to change. Doesn't that make the situation pretty much hopeless?

Not necessarily. First of all, women get involved with problematic men when they don't see them coming. Prevention is always preferable to cure, and if you can avoid dealing with a difficult guy, you're way ahead of the game. By delineating both general categories and specific types of these men, this book will enhance your awareness of the salient factors to look for as you begin a relationship. What are the warning signs? What characteristics do you have that may make you vulnerable to a certain type of man, or what kind of man is especially toxic for you, given the way you are? Attending to things you may not have thought to look for could keep you out of an emotional quagmire.

Even if you're already involved with a man who has the "A" traits *and* he's not motivated to change *and* you want to try one more time to make it work, all is not lost. There is hope for motivated women who want to improve relationships with unmotivated men.

A relationship isn't just two independent people interacting

with each other; it is a system. In a system, the parts are dependent on each other. When one part (person) acts, it influences the other, who reacts. If one person in a relationship system can find *truly different* ways to handle relationship issues, the other person's reactions will change. You can't be certain which direction, but they will definitely change. A helpful analogy is that of a pair of dancers. If they have been doing the same steps for years, each anticipates the other's moves, and they operate automatically, instinctively. However, if one partner radically deviates from the usual routine, the other partner can't maintain the old pattern, at least not without feeling very awkward and unsure of his or her own steps.

The same holds true for old patterns in relationships. However, women typically make the mistake of thinking they are trying new approaches, while their partners see their actions as slight variations on the same theme. For instance, women often try reasoning with their partners. This sounds like a valid approach, but it isn't when dealing with someone who is unreasonable. When rational, straightforward discussion doesn't produce any change, most women try approaching the situation from a different direction. The problem is, they still use reason and rationality. Their partners see the same old pattern and respond the same old way.

This book helps you to recognize harmful patterns and break out of the rut with a radically different approach that puts *you* in charge of your emotional destiny.

In trying to describe and understand problematic men, a good place to start is to examine how they got that way. The next chapter looks at how evolution, genetics, cultural factors and family influences conspire to produce these traits in men, and how society doesn't encourage them to change.

2

How They
Got That Way

*From the moment I met him, I thought
he was great. Unfortunately, so did he.*

—Theresa, twenty-eight-year-old occupational therapist

I n her award-winning science fiction novel, *The
Left Hand of Darkness*, Ursula Le Guin envisions
a society of human beings that are completely
equal. On the planet Gethen, there is no such thing
as sexism, prescribed sex roles or rules for appropriate gender conduct. The following passage is from
the field notes of an Earthling male visiting this
alien culture.

*Our entire pattern of socio-sexual interaction is
non-existent here. The Gethenians do not see one
another as men or women. This is almost impossible for our imaginations to accept. After all,
what is the first question we ask about a newborn*

baby? Yet you cannot think of a Gethenian as "it." They are not neuters. They are potentials; during each sexual cycle they may develop in either direction for the duration of the cycle. No physiological habit is established, and the mother of several children may be the father of several more. There is no division of humanity into strong and weak halves, protected/protective. One is respected and judged only as a human being.

Le Guin's classic invites us into a world of no gender differences, where individuals are free to develop identities separate from their sex at birth. Unfortunately, it is just science fiction. Differences between men and women do exist. Consider the following.

Researcher and family therapist Dr. Judith Myers Avis reports that the proportion of women who have experienced sexual abuse before the age of eighteen is 37 percent, and the percentage of abusers who are male is 95 percent. The number of women abused by men they live with is one in six; the number of male college students who coerced sex from an unwilling partner is one in four. The overwhelming percentage of perpetrators of violent crime, sexual assault and abuses of power are men. Perhaps the most frightening statistic that Dr. Myers Avis reports is that 20 percent of male college students said they would commit rape if guaranteed immunity from detection or punishment.

Consider male therapists such as psychologists, marriage and family therapists, psychiatrists, mental health counselors, pastors, etc. These men are supposedly more sensitive than the average male and are professionally socialized to help rather than abuse. Yet it's well known among therapists that 99 percent of therapists who sexually exploit their clients are male. This is indeed sad commentary on the state of masculinity. But why are men abusive to women, and why do men appear to be controlling, dishonest, immature and emotionally inept? What accounts for

the differences between men and women and the striking but inevitable conclusion that men can be big assholes?

Genes and Evolution

Anthropologists and evolutionary psychologists say that contrary to popular belief, men are not the way they are because they want to be; rather, they have been genetically programmed that way to ensure the survival of the species. As humans evolved in a hostile environment, men hunted, killed food, and were ever ready to defend family and tribe against any physical threat. Men are indeed still driven by thousands of years of evolution toward aggression, defensiveness, dominance and control, and protectiveness—even though these qualities in today's world are not necessarily useful, especially in close relationships.

Unfortunately, some men are rediscovering their hard-wired masculinity with a vengeance. The resurgence of the "bad boy" image depicted in programs like Men Behaving Badly is evidence of a male backlash against criticisms of their Neanderthal nature. Regrettably, these programs encourage men to get in touch with their inner assholes. In the movie Swingers, a man likened meeting woman to a bear trapping and killing a bunny. A Newsweek piece depicted male sensitivity as wimpy and not what women really wanted. It asserted that men were tired of being bashed by feminists and apologizing for their masculinity.

From an evolutionary perspective, the bottom line is that there is genetic wiring for many negative male characteristics. Men "remember" primitive impulses to defend, control, dominate and suppress weakness, thereby subconsciously acting out their genetic programming.

Psychological Influences and Family Training

Boys are pressured to demonstrate toughness in sports, to stay away from girls and to not hang out with Mother. The underlying message is, "Don't be a sissy or wimp, and whatever you do, don't act feminine." Ultimately boys learn that they should demonstrate contempt for the female world, which, paradoxically, includes the mother they love. The result is psychological confusion and paranoia about women. Boys solve these problems by repressing whatever is feminine within them and denigrating whatever is feminine in the outside world. Boys grow up to be men who are filled with extreme ambivalence toward women. From this perspective, men seek power and control in relationships with women to manage their ambivalence and avoid feelings of confusion and danger.

Not only does psychological confusion sow the seeds for troubling male behavior, but families also offer fertile soil for assholes to grow and flourish from the very moment of birth. Parents of newborn male babies describe them as firmer, larger, more alert, stronger and hardier. Parents play rougher with boys than girls and encourage "gender-appropriate" play. Boys are directed toward sports and other physical activity, while girls are steered toward reading and other less aggressive options. The parents describe females as adorable, softer, smaller, prettier and more delicate. Parents place more demands on boys and expect them to take more risks. Parents expect girls to respond to other children's needs and affiliate more. Parents push boys to be independent and give less comfort to boys when they are frightened or injured.

Boys are taught to control emotions and to not express their feelings. Girls are taught to express emotions, to solve their concerns verbally. Girls, in effect, are socialized for sensitivity to others, to desire collaboration and a sense of community, while boys are socialized to disregard others in service of their own goal

attainment. Although this is changing to some degree, the family couldn't plan to train men any better to become assholes.

Cultural Expectations

Popular culture only adds to male confusion about masculinity, femininity and relationships. Men are indoctrinated, virtually brainwashed, into wanting female beauty—everything they want is decorated with attractive women. Unfortunately, it is the type of beauty that is not only one-dimensional, but also woefully misrepresentative of women. Naomi Wolf, author of *The Beauty Myth*, tells us that it is the fantasy beauty that only exists in magazine ads and television commercials. As women are flimflammed into pursuing this impossible beauty at any cost of money, time or self-esteem, men are bamboozled into the desire to acquire, own or win such a trophy. Anything else becomes second best—an object of contempt that is expendable if a woman closer to the ideal appears on the horizon.

Men are therefore conditioned, according to Dr. Warren Farrell, author of *Why Men Are the Way They Are*, to want the unattainable fairy-tale beauty of women, while holding nothing but disdain for all that is feminine. To win the trophy, they must perform and compete. Whatever it takes, whatever it costs, men must be successful to win the prize. Men learn that the ticket for female attention is bought through obsession with success at the expense of everything else— especially relationships. This is indeed a paradoxical situation. The reward for success is a prize that is devalued as soon as it is won.

Competing for the trophy of female beauty, men risk rejection time after time. While desiring the fantasy woman with all their souls, men ultimately resent the competition and rejection. They protect themselves by objectifying women, trading open

communication and a desire for intimacy for dishonesty and a need
for conquest.

Our culture in general, and the media in particular, program
men to desire women as decoration rather than relational companionship; ornaments to adorn their environments and reflect
their success. Similarly, the first cultural representation of sex that
many preadolescent boys see is pornography via magazines, videos
or personal computers. Women are denigrated not only as objects
of beauty who are bought with success, but also as sex objects to be
used and abused for selfish satisfaction.

Recent history is replete with high-achieving men whose repu-
tations plummeted from sexual scandals. Boxer Mike Tyson was
convicted of rape; actor Hugh Grant and political consultant Dick
Morris both hired prostitutes; and former Senator Robert
Packwood left office under sexual harassment charges. (Actually,
none of these four fared too badly. Grant's acting career barely
stumbled; Tyson was paid millions to fight again, and Morris and
Packwood moved successfully into the private sector.) The list goes
on and on.

Of course, the most shocking news in recent years has been the
sex allegations involving President Clinton: the leader of the free
world accused of having a sexual relationship with a woman half
his age (yet, interestingly enough, retaining an unprecedented
approval rating with both genders).

Men who engage in this kind of behavior have been socialized
to objectify women. Some men in power find they suddenly have
access to attractive women they hadn't had before. They can
finally compete for and acquire the previously unattainable reward
for their hard work and sacrifice. Or worse, because of their positions of wealth and power, they feel entitled to take or buy what
they want.

Although gender roles are loosening and media depictions of men are changing, the majority of programs and commercials still portray the "real man" as strong, cool, unemotional, in control and afraid of nothing. By being a "real man," he adopts the qualities that make him a perfect jerk.

Women Enabling Them

"Enabling" does not mean "causing." Women are not *responsible* for negative male behavior, but rather, have an *influence* on it.

Women enable men to behave badly in a variety of ways. The first way is by treating men like children (although their assessment of their men's emotional development is likely correct). Women make the assumption that men can't take care of themselves and are not capable of running their own lives. They are too helpful and do things men can and should do for themselves. This enabling behavior allows men to ignore responsibility for their share of the load. They wind up *expecting* women to shoulder the burden of running everything.

Second, women enable men by making them the center of their universe—making themselves less important *consistently*. They give up their own power and competence. They give up hobbies, friends and family members. Most important, they give up their dreams and aspirations. When men are treated as the source of everything important in the relationship, it is virtually certain they will behave accordingly. As such, men are trained to dismiss women's concerns as insignificant whining—because anything of value only comes from them.

Third, women enable men by being attracted to their potential, who they can *become* rather than who they are. Women often romantically believe that the "rogues" they fall in love with will

change with the benefit of their love and nurturing. Women, there-fore, ultimately accept and even condone unacceptable behaviors because of the possibility of changing their man. Many women hold on to this hope despite no evidence suggesting that a miraculous transformation is forthcoming. Because their inappropriate behav-ior is accepted, men become indignant when women begin to com-plain—"You knew this about me when you met me."

Finally, women enable negative behavior by treating men like "success objects." Women are attracted to and value men who are successful and can provide the accoutrements of achievement. No one wants a loser. Men who are less "successful" but offer a "kinder, gentler" choice are rarely considered. Women, then, inadvertently reinforce the qualities required to achieve success. There is noth-ing wrong with liking successful men, but unfortunately, many of the qualities that it takes to be successful are not the same attri-butes that contribute to intimate relationships.

A Collective Fantasy: Things Are Changing

Despite recent changes in attitudes, gender inequality in rela-tionships remains in full force. In fact, believing that things are changing is a dangerous fantasy that will leave you ill-prepared to defend yourself against the type of man described in this book—the same guy you may find yourself with now.

You may be saying that of course things have changed. Women have successfully fought for legal and workplace equality, and have excelled in virtually every area previously considered male domi-nated. This is true. But things have not changed regarding gender stereotypes of relationships. Men's behavior toward women hasn't changed. You can't legislate attitudes; they merely become covert.

Evidence for this pessimistic view is all around us. Family

therapy scholar Dr. Shelley Green points to incidents like the Spur Posse, a group of Southern California males in the mid-1990s whose initiation rite was to rape preadolescent girls. When caught, some of the boys' fathers defended them publicly, minimizing their violent behavior by trotting out the old "boys will be boys" excuse. Were the fathers secretly pleased their sons were not gay, or did they witness their own fantasy lives in action? These kids were not raised in the '50s or '60s. One might think that newer attitudes would prevail, but they have not.

Consider a cartoon called *Tiny Toons*, a program supposedly targeted toward young children. In one episode, Buster and Babs Bunny offer tips about dating. Babs is depicted in a Spandex outfit, revealing a shapely, adult-like figure. In response, Buster goes crazy and eventually takes a cold shower to cool off. Babs replies that a girl should never underestimate the value of Spandex. In the same cartoon, Buster frets over the money required to take Babs out and has a nightmare of a judge sentencing him to pay for everything. What is the message here?

As much as we hate to say it, perhaps things are getting worse. Now that men know it is politically incorrect to say and do certain things, they have merely gone underground and become more proficient at hiding their views or else camouflaging them in more socially acceptable forms. As men, we know all too well that changes in men's attitudes toward women are much less dramatic than we would like to believe.

For example, in a *Time* magazine article, Barbara Ehrenreich explains that some men are becoming less invested in long-term relationships. Some men used to seek out the companionship of women, if only for clean clothes, ironed shirts and hot meals. But with the advent of wrinkle-free clothes and prepared food, it is possible for anyone to manage on their own—and they are. The age of first marriage is up. Men, with their growing separation

from women, are learning to be better jerks—more efficient and effective.

Even in families, men are often in worlds of their own. There used to be just baseball, basketball and football. Now there's a parade of sports, sports and more sports twenty-four hours a day, seven days a week. Men can watch all the traditional forms of combat, and now can also watch bikini-clad, beach volleyball players and pubescent girls in gymnastic tights. Their prayers have been answered. Who says there isn't a God and he's not a man—*thank you Lord, thank you Jesus, thank you* (fill in the deity of your choice) *for ESPN and CNNSI.*

Ehrenreich also points out how male publications only reinforce male isolation and difference from women. GQ, for example, tempts guys with all the cool things they can have without having to share their paychecks: spring training, fishing and golfing vacations, and hot babes galore. The masculine ideal life is no longer the dutiful family man in the gray flannel suit, coming home to a beautiful wife and a beautiful home. Instead, today's man is the yuppie bachelor with a taste for microbrewed beer, autographed sports artifacts and several female "friends" who have sex with him without expecting a commitment. The New Millennium Man is a lean, mean, asshole machine.

All this talk about the forces that conspire to make men difficult can be depressing. As a humorous antidote, consider the following explanation for troubling male behavior.

Masculinity: The Neglected "Disease"

*The evidence is strong that masculinity
is a common mental disorder that, like other
stigmatized and hidden disorders in the past,
may be ready for discovery and demands
for treatment on a large scale.*

—*Psychoproctology Today*, 1998

The pervasiveness of negative male behavior has led some to conclude that masculinity is a disease, an illness in need of treatment. Masculinity is a syndrome that only recently has begun to receive serious attention from mental health professionals. Despite this history of neglect and ignorance, it has been estimated that 50 percent of all Americans have experienced and are still experiencing masculinity directly. In fact, statistics show that there are more persons stricken by this pernicious disease alive today than in any other time in history.

The significant features of masculinity are:

1. Congenital onset
2. Physical abnormalities: a penis, excessive body and facial hair, excessive height and weight, loud body noises
3. Delusional faith in own abilities and knowledge, "legends in their own minds"
4. Pathological concern for control, dominance, winning and the remote control
5. Obsessive and inordinate attention to sports
6. Compulsive desire to "grill out" and
7. Emotional and social ineptitude.

Congenital Onset

Masculinity is almost always present at birth. This observation has led some researchers to speculate on a biological contribution to masculinity. Two different theories are under study. One group of researchers posits the presence of the abnormal Y chromosome to be the culprit, while another suggests that the evidence points to a biochemical imbalance involving a toxin called testosterone.

An early investigation has discovered that masculinity runs in families. In a survey of over 1,200 American families, over half were found to have the disease. Behind every person stricken is at least one parent sharing the affliction. Masculinity indeed is a family disease.

Physical Abnormalities: The Misunderstood Penis

Those suffering with the syndrome are afflicted with a tubular protruding anomaly known as a penis. The penis is certainly the most familiar clinical marker of masculinity that stands as hard evidence of the disorder. Some sympathetic scientists have ascribed positive attributes to the penis, especially its growth potential. However, the prevailing hypothesis holds that much of the disease is localized in this tumorous protrusion. This has led some to attempt surgery to relieve sufferers of their masculinity, such as in the case of Lorena Bobbit.

It is unfortunate that negative attributes associated with masculinity are often conveyed in substitutes for the word "penis." For example, we often label the afflicted ones "dicks, schmucks, pricks," etc. This continued use of degrading terms only stigmatizes the disorder and prevents the impaired from seeking help.

Legends in Their Own Minds

Indeed, those suffering from masculinity have delusions of grandeur. This symptom is manifested in afflicted individuals' propensities to believe that they are literally right all the time. In the face of direct evidence to the contrary, they will continue in their delusions and will die or suffer any consequence before admitting their mistakes.

The Three Cs: Control, Competition and the Clicker

Perhaps the most recognizable personality feature of the disease is the pathological concern for control. Many specific issues (what car to buy, where to go for dinner, who gets the "last word" in an argument) have at their root an attempt to gain control. Those impaired with masculinity make a big deal out of insignificant issues because the smallest issue symbolizes control—who wins and who loses. Their embarrassing possessiveness of the remote control is a case in point. They may have virtually no control over the rest of their lives, but these individuals will defend the remote control with their very lives because of the symbolic power it represents.

Stricken individuals thrive on competition. While competitive sports are favorite pastimes, they will compete with each other for virtually anything: for promotions at work, for affection and love, for bragging rights about the most sexual conquests or the largest penis, or for a good parking space at the mall. Nothing is too big or too little to be the object of a win-lose, competitive battle. Competition is at the core of the disease.

As far as the remote control is concerned, this relatively new, technologically facilitated manifestation of masculinity has already reached epidemic proportions. Those impaired can now control the TV, VCR and stereo *without moving*. Some begin to believe in their own magical powers or omnipotence. In these tragic cases,

they experience profound levels of anxiety at movie theaters, where the film and story unwind independent of their control.

Compulsive Desire to "Grill Out"

It is commonly accepted that those infected with masculinity have extraordinary talents for operating outdoor cooking devices. Since it is arguably one of very few, if any, positives, it is understandable that the impaired individual would ritualize the process. It has been hypothesized that the ritual serves to symbolically "grill" the dysfunctional person's enemies, thereby momentarily relieving paranoid fears.

Emotional and Social Ineptitude

While many of those diagnosed with masculinity have normal or above average IQs, almost all will have knowledge deficits or experience frequent episodes of cognitive lapses ("I just didn't think of it"). Anyone who has known a real person with masculinity has experienced the frustration of trying to discuss any topic that requires knowledge other than sports, TV programs and ratings of female body parts.

Perhaps because of this social ineptitude, the sad fact is that most stricken with this pernicious disease have few friends who are not themselves similarly afflicted. The following statements by those afflicted are excellent diagnostic indicators:

- How about those Indians?
- "You know how bad my memory is." It really means: "I remember the theme song to *F Troop* and the vehicle identification numbers of every car I've ever owned, but I forgot your birthday."
- "I was listening to you. It's just that I have things on my mind." It really means: "I was wondering if that redhead over there is wearing a bra."

Treatment

The overwhelming number of men suffering from this affliction has made government intervention inevitable. The nineteenth century saw the institution of what remains the largest single program for the treatment of masculinity—sports. Under this massive program, perhaps devised by those afflicted themselves, individuals are placed into group activities based on the severity of their condition.

For example, those most severely afflicted may be placed in a football group. Patients at this level are caricatures of the disease and extremely aggressive (at times yelling "KILL"), flaunting their disease with padding that accentuates their pathological size and mass, often regressing to strutting in front of large crowds like peacocks in full plume. The strategy here is merely patient management: keeping these animals off the street. Unfortunately, the sports intervention has not only failed miserably in decreasing the incidence of masculinity, but it has also perhaps inflamed it. Sports have regrettably been totally assimilated into the counterculture of the disease they attempted to control.

While other treatments such as surgical removal of the penis, antitestosterone drugs and psychotherapy have shown some promise, the most successful approach to masculinity is Assholes Anonymous. It seems that in many instances, the only way to break through the denial is for the afflicted male to hear it from the lips of another person who is recovering from the "disease." This program has no dues or fees, does not keep records or case histories, does not participate in political causes and is not affiliated with any feminist organization. Meetings are devoted partly to social activities but consist mainly of discussion of the problems inherent to masculinity. Recovering members give witness, contrasting their lives before the program and after they have found hope and

recovery. Support for the loved ones of those afflicted is provided by Assanon.

Chapter 3 begins our discussion of the different types of men to avoid, with a presentation of the most common one: the controller.

Types
to Avoid

3 Controlling Assholes

*It took me twenty years of
trying to please my ex-husband to realize
I never would. Being dissatisfied with
me was his way of keeping me down.
It didn't matter what I did, it never pleased
him because he didn't want it to.
How could I have been so stupid?*

—Marge, forty-one-year-old executive secretary

The need to control and be "one up" in a relationship may be the most common characteristic of the men we're labeling assholes. Some manipulation or control is present not only in the types of men described in this chapter, but also in virtually all the varieties of undesirables portrayed in subsequent chapters. The difference here is that control is the key defining characteristic of these men. It can be direct or subtle, passive or active. It

can be acquired through guilt, fear or insecurity. Regardless of how it manifests itself and how it is maintained, control is central to relationships with these men.

For control to exist, there must be a power disparity in a relationship. Theoretically, a marriage or other romantic relationship exists between peers. The partners are on equal footing, have equal say in decisions and share responsibility. That's theory, not reality. The vast majority of relationships have a power imbalance. Rather than being 50-50, they might be 60-40 or even 70-30 in terms of give and take. That isn't necessarily a problem. Some people are more competent and better able to do more things. Others feel good about giving and doing, and happily shoulder more of the burden.

However, the power disparity in a relationship with a controller *is* a problem. It does not develop out in the open, a product of a difference in abilities or dispositions. Instead, it is surreptitiously acquired through manipulation, intimidation and/or deceit. The equilibrium that is established in the relationship is not a comfortable one for both parties—only for the one in charge. And that is the key to recognizing these situations.

Despite differences in the types of controllers, they all have certain traits in common. They need to be in charge of the most important aspects of their lives to feel secure and comfortable. Ambiguity and unpredictability are poison to them. Many are out-and-out compulsive. Generally speaking, they think they are right, want things their way, can't handle closeness and intimacy (they might lose control over their emotions), and act to reduce discomfort rather than to seek pleasure.

The bottom line for these guys is that they need to determine what will happen in all-important areas of the relationship. If they don't, they feel very uneasy—and act quickly to get control back. In the movie *Sleeping with the Enemy*, the actor who played Julia

Roberts's husband was the poster boy for controllers. Everything had to be perfect, by his standards, or there was hell to pay. His control tactics also included violence. However, the fear women feel in relationships with nonviolent controlling men is also devastating. They find themselves just as manipulated and intimidated as the Julia Roberts character.

There are four types of controllers: the Boss, Mr. Helpful, Mr. Know-It-All and the Critic. On the surface, they look dissimilar, but underneath they strive for the same thing: to be in charge, not to be an equal partner.

The Boss

Gina came to see her therapist because he was within walking distance. She and Tony owned a car, but he wouldn't let her drive it. He didn't like her taking the bus, either, since guys might try to hit on her. He didn't like any of her friends, so she never saw them. She enjoyed working, but everywhere she had worked, he had become suspicious of her relationships with male coworkers and forced her to quit. Her health was not good, but he didn't like her to go to doctors unless it was an emergency—it was too expensive. He blamed her for their poor financial situation, even though it was he who discouraged her from working. He had never hit her, but if she disobeyed him, he yelled, screamed and threw things. Not surprisingly, she was depressed.

It's obvious why a guy like Tony is a "Boss." He aggressively takes over his partner's life and treats her like an underling. He expects obedience and is not interested in hearing her opinions. His wife's friends and relatives usually dislike him because they see how disrespectfully he treats her.

Characteristics of a Boss

1. **He acts like a parent, not a partner.** Like Tony, Bosses make rules, set limits and are generally dominant. They talk down to their partners and see nothing wrong with doing so. They expect to be obeyed, and punish if they aren't. Women in these relationships find themselves explaining a lot because they are questioned constantly and expected to respond. After all, a child *owes* an explanation to a parent (but an equal doesn't owe one to a peer).

2. **He is very direct in how he controls.** No subtlety here. If his control is threatened, he will use fear, guilt, withholding money or any other means he deems necessary to enforce his will. There is no pretense of equality. Women involved with these men find themselves saying, much too often, "I'm not allowed." Think about it—who is a partner to tell you what you are *allowed* to do?

3. **He can be a benign dictator.** If you do as you're told, the Boss can be very kind and generous. He can be deferential, complimentary and a pleasant companion as long as his dictates are being followed. Many women readily acquiesce to the Boss's expectations because they truly enjoy the kind of person he can be when he is content. However, it is always clear he is *giving* to you. What you own jointly is his to share with you or not, as he sees fit.

4. **There are two sets of rules—one for him, one for you.** He can go out with his friends, spend money freely, flirt with women, drink, gamble. Your options are much more limited. The implication is that he can be trusted with adult responsibilities, but you need to be "managed." That alone is a subtle, daily blow to your self-esteem, but a more direct one comes each time you don't live up to his expectations. He is then angry at and/or disappointed in you—and that matters to you. Not only does your self-esteem take a nosedive, but you also become vulnerable to further manipulation as you strive harder to please him the next time.

5. **He can be jealous and possessive.** At the core of this personality style is insecurity. He's both afraid you'll do something he can't control (or handle) and that you'll find someone better. He's not in charge because he's confident and secure, but because he's afraid of spontaneity and unpredictability. He secretly fears that he's no big deal and that you'll eventually realize that if you interact with other guys.

What It Feels Like to Be with a Boss

As must be obvious by now, a woman with a Boss feels like a child dealing with a parent. She feels "one down" and inferior. Even if she gets what she wants, she is not in control of her life. She feels helpless, emotionally and financially dependent, and generally disenfranchised. She has no sense of worth since she's not entrusted with any important responsibilities or decisions. Without any opportunity to accomplish meaningful things or to be treated as an equal, her self-esteem erodes more and more. After a while, attempts to assert herself are as futile as a ten-year-old's protests against her parents. She's unhappy, but feels more and more undeserving of happiness. That, combined with her feelings of dependence, makes her feel doubly trapped: she can't go on her own, and who would want her?

What Kind of Woman Is Vulnerable to a Boss?

Who in the world would want to get involved with a man like this? Remember, these leopards don't show all their spots right away. Initially, they can come across as strong and decisive—traits attractive to many women. There are women who like the idea of being taken care of, and these men also convey the ability to do that. "Old-fashioned" women who believe in traditional values (especially regarding male-female roles) fit right in with guys like

these. It also helps to be the kind of person who can yield, who doesn't need to get her way all the time.

Sometimes, as you might expect, women drawn to these men are passive, timid and unsure of themselves. However, others are quite different. They start out on more equal footing and give Bosses a run for their money when they try to take control. These women usually get worn down by a number of factors—his relentless drive to be in charge, societal pressures to be "feminine" and "a good wife," and/or constraints on her mobility due to motherhood. Or they get while the getting is good, and find someone who is secure and adjusted enough to want an equal partner.

Mr. Helpful

When Leslie met Herb, she thought, Finally, I've met a guy who might actually give something to me instead of taking all the time. *From her father on, men had been trouble for Leslie. Her first husband was a good provider but expected (demanded) that she do everything around the house and for the children. Then he ran around on her and flaunted it. Her second husband was verbally abusive, could not hold a job and treated her children badly.*

Herb was different. He did everything for her and didn't seem to expect anything in return. He was hardworking, successful and generous with her and her children. When they got married, Leslie believed she'd broken her old pattern with men and found a guy who would treat her right.

Leslie didn't come into therapy to deal with her relationship with Herb. She was depressed but felt "stupid" and "whiny" for saying so. After all, she didn't have to work outside the home, her needs were all met, and her husband never raised his voice or his hand to her.

As therapy progressed, Leslie revealed that she felt she had no meaning or purpose in her life. Not only didn't Herb make her do anything, he didn't let her do anything. Anytime she mentioned a project she was considering, he either did it or had it done before she had a chance. When they made plans, he always solicited her opinion, but it never ended up as she envisioned. If they were going to dinner, he would ask her what she wanted. If she said Chinese food, he'd say okay. Then thirty minutes later he'd say, "How about that new Thai place?" If she suggested 8:00, he'd agree but later on change it to 8:30.

Though neither of them saw what was going on, Herb had taken control by (1) doing everything and doing it his way, and (2) modifying—often just slightly—any ideas Leslie had about how things should go. She realized she felt like a spoiled child but wanted to feel like an adult.

Many would say that Leslie had it good and was just spoiled. But Herb was every bit as controlling as Tony from the previous example. He was just a lot nicer and more subtle about it. Mr. Helpful's partner also feels like a child, but in a very different way.

Characteristics of Mr. Helpful

1. **He is a nice guy who wants to please.** Of all of the men described in this book, Mr. Helpful is the hardest one to classify as an asshole. His intentions are good, and he does a lot for his partner. But he seems too good to be true, and he is.

Doing and pleasing are the ways he takes control. His underlying purpose is not to make his partner happy (though he believes it is), but to be in charge, do things his way and be appreciated along the way. What makes Mr. Helpful join the ranks of jerks is that he doesn't treat his partner as an equal. He robs her of the

opportunity to be a fully functioning, competent adult who can feel good about herself.

2. He is indirect and subtle in his control. He doesn't flaunt his control and one-up status as the Boss does. He controls by guilt and energy level. His energy is his greatest asset: He thrives on doing a lot and is happiest when busy. His partner usually lets him do things for her because she can see he enjoys it, and she doesn't have the energy to keep up with him anyway.

If he doesn't get his way, he turns to guilt. His partner is likely to hear, "Look at all I do for you, and this is the thanks I get?" Or "Can't we do it my way just this one time?" His partner is well aware that he carries a disproportionate share of the burden, and she feels somewhat guilty about that. So when she is called on it, she usually caves in and acquiesces to his wishes.

Mr. Helpful's subtlety is demonstrated by the fact that, like Leslie, his partner seldom recognizes she is being controlled. She thinks she has the upper hand since he does everything for her. While her agenda might seem to dominate the relationship, he decides what gets done, when and how.

3. He doesn't choose to help, he needs to help. Mr. Helpful can't *not* help. He thrives on being recognized as a good guy and has a very hard time backing off when presented with the opportunity to lend a hand (and be appreciated for it). Some therapists would call him compulsive and neurotic. Like the Boss, he needs to be in charge of key aspects of his life to feel comfortable and safe. Unlike the Boss, he also needs people to like him and to single him out as an especially good guy. This leads to relationship stress for Mr. Helpful's partner. His need to help everyone takes time and resources away from his marriage and creates conflict. His partner feels guilty and selfish for resenting him when he does things for other people instead of for her.

What It Feels Like to Be with Mr. Helpful

When she's with Mr. Helpful, a woman feels pampered and cared for. Not only is she not required to do much for herself, she is actively discouraged from doing so. While she feels better about herself than the wife of a Boss since she is treated well, her self-esteem is low because she doesn't feel competent and useful. She feels guilty about not holding up her end of the relationship and indebted to Mr. Helpful for doing so much for her.

She feels like a spoiled child, and Mr. Helpful is like a kind father. She doesn't believe she's done anything to deserve her special treatment, so it doesn't help her feel better about herself. And, like the Boss's partner, she is treated like a child, not an equal.

What Kind of Woman Is Vulnerable to Mr. Helpful?

Like women attracted to a Boss, these women are often traditionalists who want to be taken care of. However, they are drawn to "nice" guys, not aggressive, take-charge men. Often they have had experiences with men who have treated them poorly, and Mr. Helpful looks like the knight on the white charger. These women are generally not the dynamic, outspoken or "go-getter" types, but rather put more value on getting along in a relationship. They do know, however, what they want and are happy to find a man willing to meet their needs. Yet they feel guilty about getting those needs met without doing much in return and knowing their own abilities are not being challenged.

Mr. Know-It-All

Carol and Neil both had very busy lives. He worked long hours as an up-and-coming executive in a large firm. Carol took care of

*their three young children, managed the household and did tele-
phone solicitation work in the evening.*

*As you might expect, both of them felt stressed out much of the
time. The ways they dealt with it were very different. She tried to
put aside her frustrations as much as possible and be supportive of
Neil when he had a bad day. She worked to make the relationship
a priority and not let it get overrun by all the other responsibilities
she had.*

*Neil seemed to spend a lot of time letting her know when she did
something wrong, questioning her reasons and motives for doing
things, and pointing out the ways she didn't meet his emotional
needs. No issue was too small for him to have an opinion on, and
his opinion was almost always very different from hers. Arguments
were common, and Neil was a much better arguer.*

*Carol had never been a very emotionally expressive person.
Her parents were both reserved and undemonstrative. She worked
on making sure she expressed her feelings and showed affection.
Although Neil had no complaints about that when they were dating
and during the first few years of their marriage, he had begun to
harp on her being an "emotional robot." That was the main but-
ton he pushed when he needed to throw her off guard to win an
argument. Generally, Carol managed to stay in control throughout their arguments, but eventually, with enough prodding, she
would get angry or tearful.*

*When she disagreed with him, he criticized her in personal
ways. She felt guilty about not figuring out what he needed from
her emotionally. She continued to try to hold her ground and stand
up for herself, but it was clear he was more and more in control.*

What Carol couldn't see clearly, because she was too closely
involved, was that Neil didn't see his opinions as opinions—they
were gospel. He was always sure he was right, so arguing didn't

bother him because he knew he would prevail. Most people have at least some doubts about their opinions, as Carol did, and wither in the face of a Know-It-All's certainty.

Characteristics of Mr. Know-It-All

1. **Unlike other controllers, he shares responsibilities with his partner fairly equally.** In contrast to other controllers described in this chapter, the power disparity in this relationship does not result in one person's doing a lot more than the other. From the outside, this can look like a fair, equitable relationship. This is not, of course, true. Mr. Know-It-All does things his way with no second-guessing, while his partner is always looking over her shoulder, waiting for the inevitable questioning and criticism he bombards her with.

2. **He can look very rational and reasonable.** Unless people see him when his guard is down or challenge him, Mr. Know-It-All seems like a very reasonable guy. His partner, on the other hand, can come across to the casual observer as jumpy and defensive. What outsiders don't know is that she has been conditioned to be that way by Mr. Know-It-All's constant challenges of her every action. In public, a seemingly harmless question can provoke an emotional response from his partner because it symbolizes all the grief he gives her at home.

Mr. Know-It-All's Achilles' heel is easily exposed if someone challenges him. He can't stand it when someone disagrees with him and can't leave even the smallest issue alone until he's had the last word. Often, this comes across as excessive and inappropriate, but he can't see that. At these times, people get a glimpse of what his partner has to contend with daily.

3. **He fights dirty.** If Mr. Know-It-All feels he's in danger of losing an argument or not getting his way, he launches an irrelevant,

negative attack on his partner to put her off balance and gain control of the situation. For example, if Neil was trying to provoke Carol into an argument and not succeeding, he would accuse her of not having any feelings, of being insensitive. Then Carol, having had one of her hot buttons pushed, would defend herself even though she was the one who had been calm and reasonable up to that point.

4. **He uses "discussions" of "issues" as excuses for judgment and criticism.** One woman married to a Mr. Know-It-All described how once or twice a week, she and her husband would have a discussion about how to make their marriage better. Each and every time, her husband initiated the discussion and used it as a forum for his complaints about her performance as a wife: She was lousy in bed. She was unsupportive of his work. She was no fun. If she defended herself or told him he was unfairly picking on her, he would accuse her of being hypersensitive and refusing to work on the relationship. His performance as a husband, however, was out of bounds as a topic.

Since Know-It-Alls believe they are always right, they see their judgmental attacks as simple statements of fact: They are not mean, just truthful. They pride themselves on being logical and reasonable, but in reality, they are arbitrary and irrational. "Discussions" with them are pointless since their minds are completely closed to any ideas besides their own.

5. **He would rather be right than happy.** A successful, happy relationship involves compromise and give-and-take. Mr. Know-It-All won't do either one. Instead, he does whatever it takes to prove he's right and to bend the other person to his will. If that makes everyone in the house miserable, so be it. He remains smug in the knowledge that he proved his point and the truth prevailed. Of course, he has no idea that he's often, if not usually, full of crap. Since he never questions himself, he doesn't have the

opportunity to correct any of his inaccurate perceptions or to learn from experience. He's so sure he's right that he is more often wrong.

What It Feels Like to Be with Mr. Know-It-All

A woman with a Know-It-All is constantly on the defensive. He has an opinion about everything and is always right. So when she disagrees, she has to be wrong. He second-guesses her so much, she begins to second-guess herself. Her contributions to the relationship are never acknowledged or appreciated, and her feelings and concerns are never validated. She feels unsure of herself and unconfident. She is also angry and resentful. She is dealing with an argument machine and has no peace.

What Kind of Woman Is Vulnerable to Mr. Know-It-All?

These women like strong, verbal men. They enjoy challenges and being challenged; easygoing men bore them. They often come from families in which one or both parents kept the children "on their toes" by questioning their motives for doing things and encouraging lively exchanges of ideas.

They want men who are strong enough to accept them as equals and self-assured enough to hold their own in discussions and disagreements. That is how these men look at first, and it is how they see themselves. Eventually, it becomes clear that these men aren't self-confident, but rather, rigid and judgmental. Women who stay with them have enough self-doubt to wonder if they really know what they're saying and doing, and enough desire to please to be blinded to the fact that these men can't be satisfied.

The Critic

Lynn and Josh didn't have your typical marriage. She worked full-time in a professional capacity. He worked part-time and at a much lower pay scale. He took care of their two children when she was working and he wasn't. At night and on weekends, however, Lynn had full responsibility for the children. She also did the shopping and laundry, and handled the family finances.

Lynn was not unhappy with this arrangement. She liked being busy and liked to be in control of things. What bothered her was that Josh was never satisfied with anything she did. She worked too much, wasn't a good cook, didn't discipline the children well and did a poor job of managing money. He thought she was too career-oriented and neither affectionate enough nor a good lover.

While it might appear to the naïve observer that Lynn was in control in this relationship, such was not the case. By being relentlessly critical of Lynn, Josh kept her on the defensive and off balance. She spent so much time doing everything and trying to please him that she didn't see that things usually went his way. He won most arguments, made key decisions (even though she usually carried them out) and had a much easier life. Lynn had most of the responsibility, but Josh, the Critic, had the power.

Characteristics of a Critic

1. **He's more passive and less responsible than other controllers.** The Critic rarely initiates activities. He's an armchair quarterback. He lets his partner take risks and do most of the work, while he sits back and does little, if anything. When he does make decisions, he has trouble taking responsibility for their consequences. His game is blame. If his partner does something well, he says nothing. If she does something he doesn't like, he misses no

opportunity to let her hear about it.

The main difference between the Critic and Mr. Know-It-All is the Critic's passivity. Both are very critical of their partners, but Mr. Know-It-All actively vies for control and uses his enthusiasm to get his way, while the Critic lets his partner do the lion's share of the work, then sits back and tells her what a lousy job she did.

2. **He controls by keeping his partner on the defensive.** In response to his criticism, the Critic's partner defends herself. This does three important things that help give him control: (1) it gets her focused on what she is doing (not what he is *not* doing); (2) it encourages her to try harder to please him in order to avoid further criticism; and (3) it makes her doubt herself.

Let's look at these one at a time. By being relentless in his scrutiny of his partner's behavior, he keeps the spotlight on her and her presumed deficiencies. All her behaviors and decisions are fair game for second-guessing and negative judgment. The saying "The best defense is a good offense" certainly applies here. She stays so busy justifying her actions that his are rarely called into question. He gets a free pass to do (or not do) what he pleases, while she feels his critical eye on her whatever she does.

The Critic's partner needs to be a competent and responsible person, since she takes on the lion's share of duties in the relationship. She's used to being praised for those qualities, but she gets the opposite from him. So she tries harder to please. Approval is important to her. Little does she know that no matter what she does, it won't be good enough. He can't afford to be satisfied because once he stops harping on her shortcomings, his will be more obvious, and he will lose his power over her.

The final way the Critic keeps his partner on the defensive and gains control is harder to see. Most of us have mixed feelings about many things. We might believe we're right about something, but we're not totally sure. If someone challenges us, we defend

ourselves. But even as our verbal self-defense comes out of our mouth, our mental self-doubt grows. This is what happens to the Critic's partner. She spends so much time defending and justifying herself that she begins to wonder, *If I'm right, why isn't it obvious to him? Maybe I'm not right after all.* As her self-doubt increases, her self-confidence fades. This weakens her resolve and makes her much more susceptible to his influence.

3. **He hooks up with strong women.** The Critic's partner is usually strong and self-reliant. She needs to be. He does very little besides complain and needs someone to take care of all the messy details of being a responsible adult for him. It may seem strange that an intelligent, competent woman would get involved with a guy like this. There are many possible explanations. Perhaps she had a father she could never please and needs to win over a demanding husband to compensate. Or she could be wracked with self-doubt despite her obvious abilities, and his criticisms ring true for her. Or she could have rebounded from a Boss, and the Critic's passivity looked like a welcome oasis.

The reasons are unimportant. The fact is that strong women often wind up with Critics; and if they don't see the pattern of the relationship, they can go on indefinitely trying in vain to please them.

4. **He is insecure.** If the Critic felt good about himself, he wouldn't need to keep putting his partner down. Obviously, he's unsure of himself. He has to do his best to keep her feeling "one down" to him because he fears if she deals with him on equal terms, she'll see him for what he is and leave. He's probably right about that.

What It Feels Like to Be with a Critic

The Critic's partner carries the load in the relationship. She works, manages the money, and takes care of the kids, the house

and the relationship. Yet he's never happy with what she does. She does her best, keeps working hard and tries to please him. She explains, defends and justifies a lot, even though she does so much more than he does.

She feels overwhelmed, tremendously stressed and like a failure. Everything begins to feel like a job to her, even things she used to like to do. She feels guilty, abandoned and rejected. Her self-confidence gradually erodes, and she constantly second-guesses herself (in anticipation of his doing it). This self-doubt can spill over into work and create even more stress.

What Kind of Woman Is Vulnerable to a Critic?

Women who are achievers, hard workers and ultraresponsible are attracted to Critics. Unlike women who are attracted to the Boss or Mr. Helpful, these women don't want to be taken care of. They are independent and don't feel comfortable in a passive or dependent role.

Unfortunately for them, these women often combine tradition-ally "masculine" traits (independence, self-reliance, strength) with traditionally "feminine" ones (need for acceptance, responsibility for the emotional side of the relationship). The need for accep-tance makes them very vulnerable to Critics. They look outside for validation, and usually receive it by performing and producing. When Critics blame them, it echoes the doubts that they have about themselves. They keep themselves motivated by constantly critiquing their actions, so they can't "connect" with guys who adore them and fully accept them for who they are. Since they judge themselves on performance, it feels comfortable to be with guys who do the same.

Friends, family and even acquaintances say, "What the hell is she doing with him? She could do a lot better." She doesn't believe

that, because she's been listening to a litany of her faults and fail-ures for so long that she has an unrealistically low opinion of herself. This puts him in control in the relationship with her work-ing harder, only to get further and further behind.

How These Guys Think

As you will see when we get into ways to deal with these men, it is incredibly important to understand how they think. The biggest mistake women make when dealing with these guys is to put themselves in the man's shoes. Rather than actually thinking like a man, a woman usually winds up thinking like a woman try-ing to think like a man.

In other words, you think you understand where he's coming from, but in reality you don't. He realizes this, and two very nega-tive consequences follow: (1) he tunes you out, and (2) his auto-matic defenses go up so that what he does hear is strongly resisted.

On the other hand, if you can think like him, you can penetrate his defenses and get through to him. So each chapter on different types of men will include a discussion on how they think.

Everyone has two sets of thoughts that affect how they act and feel. One set is conscious and aware; the other is subconscious and automatic. Your partner's conscious thoughts are usually more acceptable to him and fit his self-image. His subconscious thoughts are more threatening and unacceptable to him, but they still have very strong effects on his actions.

Here are some of the key conscious beliefs controlling men hold:

- I know the right way to do things, and you don't.
- I don't like to admit it, but I believe I'm smarter, better or more skilled than other people.

- Since my way is the right way, if you don't do things my way, you are messing with or challenging me.

These conscious beliefs give controlling men a compelling rationale to run the show and become angry when you don't get with the program. However, their subconscious beliefs say more about why it is so important for them to be in control, and why they are threatened when they're not:

- *If I don't control everything I can, I'll lose control of my emotions (and become too angry or uncomfortably vulnerable).*
- *I don't really know what to do many times, but I'm afraid to show that, even to myself.*
- *I really believe, in my heart, I'm not as good as you are.*

These latter beliefs hold the key to dealing with controlling men. If you relate to their conscious beliefs, it appears you are dealing with strong, self-assured people. But when you explore the beliefs they're afraid to look at, you find they're threatened and insecure. Coming at controllers with logic and reason won't work because they consciously believe that they are right and you are just challenging them. They are not aware of how scared and insecure they are. If *you* are aware, you can see they can't afford to observe themselves as giving in. They need to be approached indirectly and in a nonthreatening way.

More on that in later chapters. Meanwhile, let's see what's going on with lying and cheating types.

4 Lying, Cheating Assholes

How do you know when a man is lying?
His lips are moving.

T he men in this chapter either lie (deliberately or inadvertently, but consistently) or cheat (with other women). Where control was key in the last chapter, here it is trust.

While no woman sets out to be with a guy who lies to her or violates her trust by cheating, countless women wind up with one. Why is that?

These guys can be very charming and engaging. They are adept at saying what women want to hear, so they have a way of worming their ways into their lives. In addition, since they are being dishonest about their (many) shortcomings, they tend to look better, at first glance, than a lot of other guys out there.

They are likable predators, if that's possible. Their numbers are not small, and most of you reading this book probably know one or more. Let's take a closer look at who they are.

The Great Pretender

Sharon met Dennis when she was on the rebound from a verbally and physically abusive boyfriend. Dennis lived in her apartment complex, and was a casual friend until she showed up at his door one night bruised and shaken after a fight with her boyfriend. She stayed with Dennis, at first for protection from her boyfriend. Gradually, they became lovers.

She didn't really feel attracted to Dennis at first but became very fond of him as she got to know him. He was very kind and understanding. She could be herself with him without worrying he would fly off the handle and get abusive with her.

Dennis was also a fascinating man. A few years older than Sharon, he had experienced a far more diverse and exotic lifestyle. He had been overseas, in Germany with the military, during which time he received electronics training. When he got out, he hooked up with a computer software company that took off rapidly and became a household name. He had recently cashed in his stock options and was in the process of starting his own consulting business. He had not had time for any serious relationships. Sharon was his first.

Well, not exactly. Sharon and Dennis agreed to move out of state to get away from her ex-boyfriend and get a fresh start together. She got a job, and Dennis began to "network" in preparation for starting his business.

Things began to get weird. Sharon realized that the more Dennis told her about his past, the more inconsistencies showed up. Then one day when she was home sick from work, an

overseas call came in. It was from a German woman trying to reach Dennis about money he was supposed to send for their two children. She also wanted to know when he would be sending for her and the children, and how his business (in which her father had invested heavily) was going.

As Sharon did some checking, the whole house of cards began to fall in. Dennis had been dishonorably discharged from the service after only a few months overseas. The woman who called was one of the three by whom he had children. None knew about the others, and all believed he was still committed to them. He had never worked for the nationally known software company, and his money had come from conning people—especially women.

It took over a year from the time of the initial call for Sharon to gather all of the information. During that time, Dennis denied everything. While she worked, he "networked" and never earned a dime (he had spent all the money he conned from other people). She constantly questioned her own sanity as evidence piled up, since Dennis very convincingly denied it all. Finally, when he could no longer explain away the inconsistencies, he confessed all (well, almost) and promised to turn over a new leaf.

Dennis is, admittedly, an extreme version of the Great Pretender, but his pattern is consistent with many others we have seen. One man took frequent "business trips" to New Jersey. His wife was surprised to get a call from an Atlantic City casino asking about payment of a $100,000 gambling debt he had incurred. Another woman got a call informing her that her husband of thirteen years had been supporting a child in another state for six years (the same age as their youngest).

Most lies are less flamboyant and audacious than these. But the men who tell them have a lot in common, as do the women they wind up with.

Characteristics of the Great Pretender

1. **He will say or do whatever it takes to get what he wants.** One thing this man understands is that people generally want to believe other people, particularly when he says what they want to hear. He wants a relationship, or at least something the relationship can provide (money, sex, shelter). He has a gift for quickly assessing what a woman is looking for and then becoming it.

2. **He lies easily and constantly.** The Great Pretender is a very convincing liar. He lies so much and so smoothly that he himself loses track of what's true and what isn't. There is no more convincing liar than one who actually believes his own lies. For instance, one man was mandated to enter therapy after he beat up an Asian busboy in a restaurant, with no apparent provocation. In his therapy group, he told long and detailed stories of his service in Vietnam and of how he still had flashbacks when he saw Asian men in uniforms. The therapist found out he had never even made it through basic training, much less gone to Southeast Asia. He seemed genuinely surprised when confronted with this fact. He had gotten so far into his fantasy that it took him a while to accept that none of it was true.

3. **He "fesses up" only when backed into a corner.** When the evidence mounts to the point that even he can't find a way around it, the Great Pretender confesses to his lies. Then he usually asks for forgiveness and promises to turn over a new leaf. However, be wary of his confessions. He admits only to what he thinks you already know and often lies even about some of that.

4. **He has no real ability to empathize.** While this guy has the ability to sense what you want from a man, he can't put himself in your "emotional shoes." That is, he has no sense of how his lies and deceit will make you feel, and when you have found him out, he cares only about saving his skin, not about the harm he has done

to you. This makes it easier for him to lie because the consequences for you don't bother him.

5. **He is narcissistic and self-centered.** As you have probably figured out, he cares only about himself and his needs. He sees the world from his perspective, no one else's. His perspective derives solely from his wants and needs, and they color his judgment and perception.

6. **He's very likely to cheat also.** Why shouldn't he lie about cheating? He lies about everything else. Cheating is not the key characteristic of the Great Pretender (as it is with Don Juan), but it is a very common occurrence. He thinks only of his own needs, and if his sexual ones aren't being met, he'll do something about it. He won't look at his part in any problem or work toward change. Instead, he blames his partner and sees the solution as finding someone else to satisfy his needs.

What It Feels Like to Be with the Great Pretender

At first, it feels great. He's everything a woman wants. But as his story begins to unravel, the woman feels disoriented, as if she's going crazy. Even though she finds more and more evidence that he's lying, he vehemently denies it. She's not sure what to believe, and begins to distrust her own perceptions and reasoning.

Then, when the evidence of his lies is clear, she feels frustrated, cheated and resentful. But he turns out to be a poor target for her anger. He apologizes, confusing the issue and subtly putting the blame on her. ("You wanted to believe me, or you would have seen it sooner".) She winds up feeling empty, distrustful and bitter.

What Kind of Woman Is Vulnerable to the Great Pretender?

Any woman is vulnerable to a convincing liar who knows what she wants to hear. Particularly vulnerable are women who are very

trusting and idealistic, and trying too hard to get their legitimate needs met (especially if the last guys they were with were also jerks). Being idealistic, these women tend to see the best in people and have a somewhat romantic view of relationships.

No one is safe, however. A lot of women have learned, by experience, to be cynical and wary of men who look too good too fast. They call them on their lies early on. Some liars appreciate this and see it as a challenge. Their approach with these women is, "I see I can't fool you. I'd better tell it like it is." Then, of course, they use a different set of lies, geared toward cynical women.

The Chameleon

Mary was twenty-eight when she met Darryl. She had two young boys, five and two, and had been divorced for a year. Her husband had left her for a coworker and was minimally involved with the children.

Darryl was thirty and had never been married. He had a good job and lived in an apartment by himself. Mary made it very clear to Darryl when they met that she wasn't eager to get into any relationship, but if she did, she wanted stability. She particularly didn't want the boys to get attached to someone who would not be around for long.

Darryl assured her he was ready to settle down. He loved kids and had always wanted a family. He came on very strong to Mary. He called several times a day, saw her every time her ex took the kids, and did things with her and the boys as soon as she was comfortable letting him. He was a good listener and agreed with her values in every important area.

She was thrilled. She had been leery at first, due to her past experience with men. Darryl really did seem to be different. In

fact, he seemed bent on showing her how different he was from other guys.

Then as soon as she became comfortable with him and saw them as a couple, things began to change. Darryl began to find fault with her, where he never had before. He admitted he missed seeing other women and that it began to scare him to think of the limitations that being in a family with children would put on him. He always let her know how terrible he felt about all this, and he was much quieter and moodier when they were together. Gradually the relationship deteriorated, and they broke up.

After a couple of weeks, he called Mary and said he missed her. Could they see each other occasionally? She remembered how he was at the beginning and missed that, so she agreed. For a year, they dated once a week and slept together, but had no other contact. Mary had wound up in exactly the kind of relationship she had sought to avoid. Darryl's relationship with Mary became the carbon copy of several others he had had before.

Many people would look at this story as a typical relationship that just didn't work, a woman who saw what she wanted to see or a man scared of commitment. Darryl was clearly not the blatant, lying jerk that Dennis was. A lot of readers probably have a hard time seeing that Darryl has any negative qualities at all. But like Mr. Helpful in chapter 3, the Chameleon is more subtle, and his intentions are good.

He really wants to be what a woman wants and convinces her and himself he is. His own identity is so weak and poorly defined that he can fit into her expectations—for a while. Once the "chase" is over and she has accepted him, it all falls apart. Then he begins to think more about what *he* wants, sees he isn't getting it and pulls away rather than work on the relationship or himself.

Characteristics of the Chameleon

1. **He has no clear sense of himself.** His life has little consistency. He bounces from one thing to another because he doesn't know how to focus on what he likes and wants. He eagerly adjusts to a woman's lifestyle and expectations to give his life some direction and clarity.

2. **He needs to be liked.** He doesn't lie primarily to get what he wants, but to be liked and appreciated. He has a hard time breaking up with a woman unless he feels she understands and accepts his reasons, and won't hate him afterward. Many Chameleons stay in relationships because the woman makes it clear she will hate him if he leaves. He can't stand that prospect.

3. **He's very sensitive to other people's feelings.** He picks up easily on what people want and need, and tries to provide it to them. This is not to say he puts their needs first. Ultimately, he winds up hurting whoever he's with. He can tune in to others' needs, but not his own, so he doesn't communicate what he wants (and feels dissatisfied).

4. **Underneath his desire to please are anger and resentment.** The Chameleon sees himself as bending over backwards to please his partner. When she doesn't reciprocate (because he gives her no clue as to how), he feels cheated and resentful. He can't see that he has set himself up. His desire to be liked prevents honest expression of that anger. It comes out indirectly, in annoyance at little things and in letting his partner know she's not making him happy.

5. **Guilt is a big issue for him.** The Chameleon is much more neurotic than the Great Pretender. He lies or misleads in order to please and be liked. When he doesn't please, he feels guilty, as he does when he ultimately breaks off the relationship. Grappling with the conflict between wanting to please and waiting to be

pleased creates a dilemma that often paralyzes him with indecision about whether to stay in a relationship. During that paralysis, he makes both himself and his partner miserable.

What It Feels Like to Be with a Chameleon

At first, it feels great. He lets you call all the shots, and whatever you like, he likes. You feel understood, appreciated and trusting. Then, as he settles into the relationship, he begins to let you know you aren't making him happy. You become confused. You don't know what you've done or what you can do to make it better. He gives you no guidance, so you question yourself and your worth. You get angry and frustrated at times, but you feel guilty because he's basically a nice guy, and he's obviously hurting too. When the relationship ends, you have vague feelings you've been set up, but you're not sure how it happened.

What Kind of Woman Is Vulnerable to a Chameleon?

Much as with the Great Pretender, a woman who knows what she wants from a guy is vulnerable, because that's what he needs to know to become it. She doesn't have to be obvious about it, though, because the Chameleon is very empathic and intuitive. Often, the Chameleon is drawn to women who are bitter and disillusioned about men and romance. He likes to win these women over by proving he's different from all the other guys. Unfortunately, of course, he isn't, and the women become more bitter and disillusioned.

Don Juan

Danielle met Pete in a rather unusual way. He was stopped next to her at a traffic light one Saturday afternoon and asked her

to join him for coffee. It was unlike her to do that with a stranger, but he seemed very nice and had a way about him, so she did.

Pete was a charming, easygoing guy. He was very flattering and attentive, and when she was with him, she always felt she had his full attention and interest. He was good-looking, but not strikingly handsome. He was very sensual, and sexual. She found herself being comfortable doing things sexually with him she'd never done before.

From the outset, Pete made it clear he was not interested in a long-term commitment or an exclusive relationship. Nevertheless, they began seeing a lot of each other and, after just a few months, Danielle moved into his house.

She liked the lifestyle they had. He liked to golf, play poker and hang out with his friends. Danielle had plenty of her own friends and interests, so both of them were happy to have plenty of time to themselves.

Pete also liked to gamble—not a lot, but often—and play the stock market. He was a salesman and carried a pager, on which he received all his personal calls. He didn't even have a phone at home, only a cell phone. At first Danielle was afraid he was dealing drugs. But she never saw him doing any, and he was able to assure her that he just didn't want any of his gambling contacts to have his phone number.

It took a long time, but Danielle gradually suspected Pete was seeing other women. He readily admitted he was. He didn't believe it interfered with their relationship since they were only sexual encounters. Pete reminded Danielle that he had been very up front with her about not wanting an exclusive relationship and had never told her anything different (he just stayed away from the subject).

Danielle couldn't believe he could think his promiscuity didn't matter, and was angry with herself that she had not even considered it as a possibility for so long. When she told him she couldn't handle that kind of relationship, he appeared genuinely

mystified that she could be so upset, but made no offer to change his ways. She moved out.

It is usually accepted in our culture that men find it easier than women to have sex without love. This case involved much more than that. Many people would probably call Pete a sex addict. Without question, he had a very strong sexual appetite and little compunction about satisfying it whenever he got the opportunity.

There is more to Don Juan than being oversexed. He cheats, usually lies about it and has a hard time understanding why it is a big deal to his partner (or partners). He enjoys not only the sex, but also the chase, the excitement of possibly being caught and the stimulation of having multiple things going on at once. All this makes him fun and attractive to many women, but also emotionally dangerous. His conscience is blind to the way many of his partners feel when they discover his infidelity.

Characteristics of a Don Juan

1. **He can be charming, funny and attractive.** It is not just looks that make Don Juan desirable; in fact, he is often fairly ordinary looking. It is more his energy, vitality and lack of inhibition that women find appealing. He has a sizable gap in his conscience (in the areas of fidelity and truthfulness, at least), and people unencumbered by strong consciences can be very spontaneous and engaging. A woman who has been with Don Juan often pines for the good times they had, even while feeling the pain of his infidelity and lies.

2. **He is insatiable and intense sexually.** While he seems fun and playful in bed, Don Juan is intense and driven sexually. He gets a tremendous high from sex and is not easily satisfied since he is a stimulation junkie. Many women take his unquenchable lust as a

flattering reflection of their desirability, which is part of what blinds them to the cheating.

3. **He is very good at talking to and being with women.** A big part of Don Juan's charm is his ability to connect with women. He is comfortable with them, confident of his attractiveness to them and genuinely interested in them (although not for all the reasons they might want to believe). Amazingly, he manages to remain friends with many of the women he becomes involved with, since they have fun with him, sense that he genuinely likes them and realize his promiscuity is not deliberately intended to hurt *them* but simply to satisfy *him*.

4. **He finds things in most women that are attractive and communicates that.** One reason Don Juan is so adept at convincing women he likes them is that he is attracted to a wide variety of women. Unlike some men, who zero in on a woman's slightest flaw, he uses his radar to detect her every physical and personality asset. In some way, every woman is beautiful to him, and he lets her know that. Women spend so much time around men who take them for granted or point out their shortcomings that a man like Don Juan, who sees only their assets, has a big advantage (and has a lot of his flaws overlooked).

We have a friend who is a very likable Don Juan. He's easy-going, completely nondefensive and sees the beauty in every woman he meets. In fact, between the two of us, we must have heard him say the exact same thing to at least twenty women: "You're the most beautiful woman I've ever seen." Not particularly creative, but it always sounds sincere because he believes it when he says it. One of us met a woman at a party, and it turned out she had dated our friend briefly. She told the romantic story of their first encounter. He sent a note to her table with the waiter. "You'll never guess what it said," she gushed. She was shocked to hear the reply: "Could it have been, 'You're the most beautiful

woman I've ever seen'?" Pausing for just a minute, she answered, "Oh, he must have told you this story." Not exactly.

5. **Sex and love are not linked for him.** It is hard to explain what love means to Don Juan. He sees something to love in every woman he's with, but that "love" is a shallow, superficial attraction (albeit sincere) that doesn't translate very well into a deep, committed relationship. His strong libido helps him see women the way he wants to, but it is not something he can easily harness. For him, love is attraction and desire, not commitment and emotional intimacy.

6. **He is a stimulation seeker.** Calling him a stimulation "junkie" is not far from the truth. He can't get enough of thrills and danger. Gambling, sports, fast cars—and often, drugs—attract him. He is not comfortable with predictability, stability and caution. He needs to be "doing," and preferably something with an associated risk. So cheating fills two needs: the need for sex and the need for danger (the possibility of getting caught). This thrill-seeking aspect of Don Juan seduces many women. It stands in sharp contrast to the relative predictability of their lives (and previous boyfriends). They just aren't made aware of all the risks going in.

7. **He is vague and hard to pin down.** Don Juan is not shy about saying kind, flattering or titillating things. It is much harder for him to be specific about his activities, intentions and past. He doesn't get defensive or angry (usually). He avoids subjects, makes vague statements or tells "white lies."

What It Feels Like to Be with Don Juan

As is the case with all these lying and/or cheating guys, it feels great, at first, to be with them. You feel attractive, important, the center of the man's universe. You might feel he brings out a never-before-seen side of you—sexy, uninhibited, spontaneous.

One woman who had been with a Don Juan described it as like being under a spell. He could bring out a side of her that she loved, and only he could do it. When he left her, she believed he had taken that part of her with him.

That is why it is so hard to let go. Even after you see his true colors, you fear you'll never find what you had with him. That fear allows you to believe his lies for far too long, to give him second and third chances, and to convince yourself he's just "screwing" *them* but that he loves *you*. Of all the men described in this book, none is missed more or remembered more fondly than Don Juan. Yes, he lies to you and cheats on you, but while he's with you, you feel special. Unfortunately, that negatively affects your ability to get on with your life, appreciate a decent guy who's less charming but more stable and accept reality rather than his fantasy.

What Kind of Woman Is Vulnerable to Don Juan?

Any woman who is looking for romance, adventure and excitement (and who isn't to some extent?) is fair game for Don Juan. If a woman is unsure of her attractiveness or sexual desirability, he can make her feel special—for a while. Still, as with the Great Pretender and the Chameleon, any woman is vulnerable to someone like Don Juan, who convincingly portrays himself as what he is not. Don Juan's unique gift is not his ability to be what a woman wants him to, but to help her to believe *she* is who she wants to be. Compared with the romantic dreams Don Juan inspires, most women's lives look boring and unfulfilled.

How These Guys Think

Men who consciously lie and cheat believe their own needs (for sex, belonging, acceptance) are very important, and that doing

whatever it takes to get them satisfied is justified. After all, they don't think they are being malicious or trying to deliberately hurt anyone. They say what women want to hear, and what women don't know won't hurt them. Their key conscious beliefs are:

- I have strong needs that must be satisfied.
- Everyone plays games in relationships; it's expected.
- I tell her what she wants to hear, and at some level, she knows it's not true either.
- I'm not being mean or vicious. My intentions are good.

It is clear that these beliefs are self-serving and involve overlooking or distorting the woman's point of view and feelings.

The subconscious beliefs show why it is crucial to consciously overlook and distort:

- *There is something about me that is weird, different and worthy of being ashamed of.*
- *If I show who and what I really am, I won't have a chance with a woman.*
- *I can't stand the feeling of being alone or celibate. I have to avoid that at any cost.*
- *Women are just objects to me. Thinking about what they need or how they feel is just confusing to me, so I don't.*
- *I can't feel connected to anyone except during sex, so when I'm without it, I feel terribly alone and alienated (for Don Juan).*

While control is not the main issue for these men, through deceit they achieve control in relationships. Underneath their facades are needy men who lack the skills to satisfy those needs within a mature, honest relationship. They have learned to acquire

by deception what they believe they can't get any other way. They convince women they can give them what they want, but these guys are pathetically unable to follow through on any real or implied promises.

5

Immature
Assholes

*I'm working two jobs to pay the bills,
and he just lost his fourth job in three years.
Then I find out he's spending money
on another woman. When I confront him,
he finally admits it but blames me!
It turns out I'm no fun—all I think about is
work. I'm working to support our family
while he's out screwing some bimbo.
When am I supposed to have fun?*

—Shelly, twenty-nine-year-old human resource specialist

Control and deceit were the primary weapons for the first two types of men described in this book. Immaturity is the distinguishing trait of the men—or boys—in this chapter. Their interpersonal development lags behind age, work skills and other areas. In chapter 3, the relationships between controllers and their partners

looked like parent-child ones, with the man taking the parent role. Here, the immature Peter Pan often appears childlike, which forces his partner into a maternal role she doesn't want. These guys can't handle mature, adult relationships and either shirk some key responsibilities or avoid committing to a relationship at all.

The Mama's Boy

When Joan met Donnie, he was twenty-seven. He had a job working construction and lived with his parents. She was a little put off by his living arrangement, but Donnie explained that he was only staying with his parents until he cleared up some credit card bills. He did move out on his own a few months later. By that time, he and Joan were seeing a lot of each other. She cooked dinner for him a few nights a week, and most other nights he ate at his parents' house. His mother still did his laundry for him, and when she stopped by to drop it off, she straightened up his apartment.

Joan thought this a little unusual but wrote it off to his mother's having a hard time letting go of Donnie, her only son. Joan found Donnie to be sweet and easy to get along with. He was very flexible and usually let her have her way if they disagreed. She liked to cook and was very particular about how her apartment looked, so when they got married, it seemed very natural for her to assume those duties. Theirs was a traditional relationship in which she handled household chores, and he the yard and house repairs. Both of them worked outside the home (Joan was a nurse) but agreed she would stay home when they had children.

They had their first child a year and a half after they married, and a second two years later. When the younger child was two, Joan went back to work part-time because she missed nursing. Donnie decided to strike out on his own and do general

contracting, and Joan was very supportive.

Gradually, Joan began to feel overwhelmed. She put in more and more hours at work to help out while Donnie's business got going. She also did his books and billing. She maintained primary responsibility for the house and the children. At first, she blamed herself for not being able to handle what a lot of other women were doing. Then she began to realize that Donnie was like a third child. He left his clothes lying around and never helped with the laundry, cooking or cleaning. The kids loved him because about all he did was play with them. Discipline was left to her, and he often undermined it by letting them out of her punishments or encouraging them to be disruptive and disobedient. His business never really took off, so she had to work full-time. When he worked, he worked hard, but he wasn't good at marketing himself or organizing his jobs. He was unable to save receipts, keep track of the hours he worked or bid jobs so that he made a decent profit. At home, he did chores only if she begged him or made a list. She handled the household finances and gave him an allowance for his incidental expenses.

This kind of situation is amazingly common. The details differ from one relationship to another, but there are a lot of Mama's Boys out there. They are dependent, disorganized and incapable of accepting equal responsibility in a relationship.

Characteristics of a Mama's Boy

1. **He was spoiled by his family.** The Mama's Boy never had much expected of him at home. His mother did most of the house-hold chores, sometimes with the help of his sisters. Often, he is the only son. His parents probably had a very traditional relation-ship, and his father didn't do "women's work." Regardless, he

learned that not much is expected of him and other people will take care of him.

2. **He doesn't know how to do simple, basic things.** As a result of having little expected of him, he doesn't know how to do many basic tasks (cook, do laundry or ironing, clean the house). Even if he is willing to try some of these things, he's inept. His partner decides that if she wants anything done right, she had better do it herself.

3. **He will do things if directed.** This is the kind of man whose wife gives him lists of tasks to accomplish or has a "job jar" for him. Left to his own devices, he putters around, has three or four projects going at once and never completes one. He's not unwilling to work, he's just disorganized and not a self-starter. However, if he feels his partner is making too many demands or being bossy, he can become contrary and defiant. He doesn't really assert himself, but rather comes across as "You can't make me," as he actively or passively refuses to keep up his end of the relationship. If this reaction sounds childish, it is.

4. **He is irresponsible.** Since he was not brought up to be responsible for himself, it is very natural for him to be irresponsible. He expects things to be done and doesn't find it strange or unfair that other people do more than he does. He doesn't shirk responsibility out of meanness or laziness. It just does not occur to him to do things unless he's asked (and usually prodded). His irresponsibility isn't total. Very often the Mama's Boy can be a hard worker, if expectations are clear and he has a lot of structure. His problem is recognizing on his own what he ought to be doing.

5. **He has a hard time being a parent.** Since in many ways he is still a child himself, parenting does not come easily to the Mama's Boy. He can be great at playing with the kids, but other parental duties elude him. Changing diapers, setting limits, teaching self-care and countless other tasks are foreign to him. In fact, it is

easy for him to feel left out and become resentful when his wife devotes time to the children.

6. **He lives at home for a long time.** This is not always the case, but it makes sense that a Mama's Boy feels quite comfortable staying where he will be cared for in the manner to which he's accustomed. If not, he usually finds a girlfriend who will step in and fill Mama's shoes (cook for him, pick out his clothes, get him up for work).

7. **He is narcissistic and self-absorbed.** Part of being spoiled involves learning that you are more important than other people. The Mama's Boy learns from a young age that he's special and his needs take precedence over the needs of others. He learns to look at the world as it relates to him, not in terms of how others might see it. Therefore, if he doesn't feel like doing something, it seems quite natural and appropriate not to.

What It Feels Like to Be with a Mama's Boy

It feels nice to be needed, and these guys are needy. A woman who is with him feels important and in charge. If he treated his mother well, he will probably treat his partner well also. That, too, feels good. Gradually, however, she feels the strain of the unequal distribution of responsibility in the relationship. This is amplified when kids come. The woman is likely to feel as if her husband is an extra child to care for. She feels overwhelmed and overburdened. She may get down on herself for being unable to handle all her responsibilities. She feels unsupported and, eventually, uncared for. As nice as the Mama's Boy can be to his wife, he has no clue how to meet her needs or be an equal partner.

What Kind of Woman Is Vulnerable to a Mama's Boy?

Women who are nurturing, who like to be in charge and who are hyper-responsible gravitate toward these men. Many of them

grew up with a lot of responsibility for the care of their younger siblings, or got a lot of reinforcement for being hardworking and responsible. It is not unusual for these women to automatically put the needs of others first. Some would call this kind of person "superwoman" or "supermom." Others would call her "codependent" or "enabling." A disproportionate number of these women work in helping professions (nursing, teaching, therapy, social work).

"Yessirree, kids, your mother is one heck of a gal!"

The Eternal Teenager

Tammy had never been the life of the party. She was quite attractive, but a little shy and introverted. She met Chad at a trendy singles bar, where she had gone after work with single friends. He told her he'd made a bet with his friends that she didn't know she was the "prettiest girl in the bar." As corny and obvious as that line was, Tammy was flattered he'd approached her. Soon she and her friends were drinking and laughing with Chad and his buddies. Before she left, Chad asked her if she wanted to go out on his boat sometime.

When they did go on Chad's boat, it was with a group of people, which was okay with Tammy. She liked being in a group because it took the pressure off her to be talkative and clever. It also relieved some of her apprehension at being on a boat alone with someone she barely knew.

She had a great time, and she and Chad began seeing a lot of each other. He always found fun things to do—parties, ball games, concerts—and they usually went with his friends and their dates. This was all very new to Tammy. She was used to going out with a girlfriend for a quiet dinner or staying home and reading. When she dated, it was usually with guys who took her to dinner and a movie—just the two of them. She found herself having a blast with Chad.

Slowly, it dawned on her that they really weren't getting to know each other very well. They did see each other three or four times a week and were sleeping together, but they rarely had a serious conversation. She didn't know much about his past or his aspirations for the future. She also began to miss quiet dinners and nights at home.

She approached Chad with these observations, and he was taken aback. It hadn't occurred to him to do things any other way.

He said he'd be glad to spend more time alone with Tammy and get to know each other better. But something "fun" always came up, and their time alone was postponed.

Tammy began to argue with Chad about spending so much time with his friends. The arguments always followed a similar course:

Tammy: "Don't you want to spend time just with me?"
Chad: "You know I do, but my friends are important to me, too. What do you have against them? They've always treated you well."
Tammy: "I know, but I have nothing in common with their girlfriends, and you and I are never alone until we get back to my apartment."

As things moved along, Tammy thought about a future with Chad. He said he didn't want to see anyone else. However, he just wasn't ready to think about marriage and wasn't sure he ever wanted kids. This was the complete opposite of what Tammy wanted, and she felt stuck and unable to make a decision. She enjoyed being with Chad, and her life was certainly more exciting than it had been. But she felt she wasn't getting anywhere and that there were important things missing in their relationship.

Chad is a good example of the Eternal Teenager. His life revolves around friends, fun and excitement. Adult responsibilities aren't a priority for him, and a girlfriend is nice to have for social occasions, but he doesn't crave intimacy.

Characteristics of the Eternal Teenager

1. **He hangs out with a group of buddies.** His social life revolves around his friends, and his actions, if not his words, clearly

demonstrate that they come first. He acts as if he's in a fraternity—sports, parties, drinking. If any of his friends are married, their wives are very understanding and nondemanding women since marriage doesn't diminish their loyalty to the group.

2. **To him, a woman is an accessory.** He likes having a girlfriend, especially a goodlooking one. In fact, looks tend to be the main criterion for him and his friends when choosing women. By the way, they aren't called "women." They are usually "girls" or "gals" or "chicks" (or worse when they're not around). The Eternal Teenager doesn't want a meaningful, adult relationship. He wants a perpetual date. Relating in an emotionally intimate way to a woman is not high on his list of personal skills.

3. **He is insensitive to his partner's needs and feelings.** It's not that he treats his girlfriends badly. He can be very generous, flattering and kind. He just doesn't get it when it comes to dealing with a mature woman in an adult relationship. When the Eternal Teenager is with his friends, it's as if they are in a high school locker room. They talk about sports, jokingly insult each other, play practical jokes and rarely talk about women other than as sex objects or party poopers ("My girlfriend wants me to stay home more and *talk* to her. I'm with her all the time. What does she want from me?").

If a woman tries to talk to him about what's missing in the relationship, he's mystified and hurt. Mystified because he's getting what he wants and figured she was, too, and hurt because he treats her well and feels she's criticizing him. All he has to compare his relationship to are his friends' relationships, and they're all doing what he is.

4. **He's not too motivated to succeed at work.** For the Eternal Teenager, work isn't a career, it's something he has to do to get money to have fun. Many of these guys are in sales, at which they are very good. After all, they like to be with other guys and drink

and talk sports. However, the Eternal Teenager is all too ready to leave work early to get to a ball game or come in hung over after being out until 2:00 A.M. Some jobs encourage a lot of schmoozing and socializing, and if the Eternal Teenager finds one of these, he can make good money. But it tends to be spent on vacations, sports cars, boats and bar tabs—not on houses, retirement plans or wedding rings.

5. **He drinks too much.** When he is with his friends, the Eternal Teenager hangs out in bars and restaurants, at concerts and ball games, and at parties. Alcohol is usually a part of these activities, and moderation is discouraged. Tickets for driving while intoxicated, bar fights, poor judgment and other signs of heavy drinking can be part of the package. Those things all put a strain on a relationship, as does his inability to have a reasonable, sober conversation when he is finally alone with his girlfriend after a night out with his friends.

6. **He lives for the present.** He knows how to have a good time and doesn't spend a lot of time worrying about tomorrow. It would help a lot of people to be able to do more of that. It would help the Eternal Teenager to do less of it. In his hands, living for the moment becomes aimless hedonism. He's not going anywhere or accomplishing anything, but he's enjoying himself.

Sometimes the Eternal Teenager grows out of this, but a lot of women have become very frustrated and disappointed waiting for it to happen. Given the right circumstances, the Eternal Teenager *can* achieve financial success and social status (and a subset of them are born into money, in which case the game is the same, but the money spent playing it increases drastically). Remember, however, that these things are not his primary goal, nor is a meaningful relationship. Having fun comes first.

What It Feels Like to Be with the Eternal Teenager

Tammy's experience is a good example of what it feels like to be with a guy like this. He brings the party with him, and all she has to do is show up. It's exciting and fun. She goes out a lot, he spends money on her, and she gets exposed to a new circle of friends. If her life before the Eternal Teenager was a little on the boring side, it gets kicked into high gear when she meets him.

After the initial rush of excitement, however, she begins to feel empty. She doesn't know who he is or just what he does, and he doesn't really know her. Nor does he want to. Things are fine with him the way they are, and if she asks for more, he makes her feel demanding and ungrateful. She feels unimportant compared with his friends, and needy of real emotional contact. Most women end up jumping off the roller coaster after going along for the ride for a little too long, but others get used to the lifestyle and have a hard time giving it up. The price they pay is feeling unfulfilled.

What Kind of Woman Is Vulnerable to the Eternal Teenager?

Women who are quiet, shy and lonely are prime targets for the Eternal Teenager, especially if they are attractive. They are not overly excited about their own lives, so they are happy to live his vicariously. These women need to be tolerant since he is with his friends a lot and may not be all that sensitive to what she wants. Like most women who are with assholes, they hope he'll change over time. And like most women who are with these guys, they are usually wrong.

The Fence Sitter

A friend of hers fixed up April with Dan. They seemed to hit it off very well, and he asked to see her again. He moved fast. Dan

called her every day, saw April as often as she would let him and pushed to get more involved. She had some reservations about how fast things were going. But she did like Dan a lot, and his obvious interest in her was very alluring.

Within a month, they were a serious couple, going out several times a week, sleeping together, seeing each other exclusively. Less than one month later, Dan began to back off. He said they were going too fast, and that he needed to get some space and clear his head. Well, April had heard that before, and so she broke up with him.

Initially, he seemed almost relieved. It didn't take long, though, for Dan to begin to pursue her again. He missed her. He realized he didn't want to see other women, and he couldn't bear the thought of her being with other men. April was very skeptical. But he was persistent, and she did like him. She relented.

This time it lasted longer—almost six months. Then he started to backpedal again. He had doubts. It just didn't feel right to him. He wasn't sure he wanted to settle down. She was crushed. She couldn't believe it was happening again. They broke up—again.

You'll never guess what happened next. Surprise—he wanted her back!

She was much more reluctant this time. He pursued, pleaded and finally, proposed. As ridiculous as April knew that idea was, part of her wanted to do it. Finally, she relented and accepted his proposal. She was shocked when Dan set a date right away.

The plans were made, the hall was rented and the wedding dress bought. In retrospect, it seemed inevitable, but at the time, April didn't see it coming. Of course, he called off the wedding.

Dan couldn't stay away from April, nor could he stay with her. April let it go on too long. She kept taking him back despite well-founded reservations. Still, it was Dan's inability to know

what he wanted or commit to a relationship that kept this ridiculous charade going.

Much has been written about men who can't commit. Many writers have advanced theories as to why they can't and how society contributes. Although this book will touch on those things, the focus, as with all the men described, is on what they are rather than how they got that way. Granted, these men are unhappy and uncomfortable. But this book isn't written for them. It's written for the women they ensnare and then emotionally victimize.

Characteristics of the Fence Sitter

1. **He is hopelessly ambivalent.** He wants a relationship, but he doesn't. He loves his girlfriend, but he doesn't. He always finds himself in what psychologists call an "approach-avoidance conflict." The closer he gets to something he thinks he wants, the more he sees its flaws. So he backs away. The more distant he gets, the more he sees its attraction, and he closes in again.

The biggest mistake a woman can make when she sees this process is to try to figure out what she is doing that drives him away (or makes him come back). This is *his* problem and *his* pattern. He can't see that, so you had better.

2. **He is indecisive.** In addition to his chronic ambivalence, he is unable to make a decision. This is similar to, but somewhat different from, his ambivalence. His indecision flows from deepseated fear of making a mistake, of doing the wrong thing. The Fence Sitter has a really hard time being happy for very long. So he treats every decision in his life as if his happiness and satisfaction depend on it. He can make a big deal out of the most insignificant things. You might see this guy standing paralyzed in the supermarket, trying to decide which brand of beer to buy.

3. **He is a perfectionist.** He has very exacting standards for

himself and the people he is with. Those standards are arbitrary and meaningless, but he can't let go of them. He's very judgmental and has trouble accepting anyone or anything as it is.

This triad of ambivalence, indecision and perfectionism brands the Fence Sitter as one of the most neurotic of all the men described in this book. He has a lot of internal conflicts, doesn't know how to make himself happy, and repeats the same relationship mistakes over and over.

4. **He looks outside for happiness.** Since he doesn't know how to make himself happy, he looks to other people to do it for him. He's a searcher—for the right person, the right job—who never finds what he's looking for. If he's alone, he needs to be with someone because he can't be content with himself. When he's with someone and unhappy (which he inevitably is), he holds her responsible.

5. **He doesn't know what to expect from a mature relationship.** He understands and craves the passion of the early stages of a relationship. This briefly makes him happy, and he expects to feel that way all the time. As a relationship progresses, he reads the diminution of passion and lust as a sign that something is wrong, as opposed to the opportunity for intimacy and growth it can provide. He can't look at himself and what he needs to do to help the relationship progress. Instead, he feels dissatisfied with her and sees what *she* should be doing. This makes him feel justified in leaving. But then he feels the pain of being alone and can't tolerate it. So he needs to have her back.

6. **If he ever makes a commitment, he can't decide whether to stick to it.** Believe it or not, the Fence Sitter does, occasionally, get married. Once he does, he immediately begins to debate whether he has made a mistake. Here, it's his indecisiveness that keeps him in the relationship. Since he can't decide if he should leave, he stays. He's miserable, and makes sure you know it and are too. In

short, if you think he gets off the fence once he's married, guess again.

7. **He never feels ready to take on the full responsibilities of adulthood.** As with all these immature guys, the Fence Sitter isn't ready to grow up. He hides this fear from himself by focusing on the pros and cons of serious relationships. He distracts himself from the realization that while he's obsessing about whom he wants to be with, he's putting his life on hold. At some point, he wakes up to the fact that he's middle-aged but has no wife, children or direction. His solution to this midlife crisis is to try even harder to find the "right woman."

What It Feels Like to Be with the Fence Sitter

After a brief honeymoon period when they are close and passionate, the woman with the Fence Sitter quickly finds him to be maddeningly frustrating. She wants to slap him and say, "Grow up already." She is a mature adult looking to move on with her life. At first, she thinks he is too. He looks mature and talks a good game, but beneath the pseudo-adult exterior beats the heart of a neurotic Peter Pan. He won't grow up, and you can't make him.

His vacillation causes a lot of conflict as the couple breaks up (or pulls away at least) and reconciles. After a while, her feelings begin to dull. As the relationship winds down, she feels disconnected from herself and her feelings, and she experiences herself just going through the motions. She's frustrated and bitter, but numb.

What Kind of Woman Is Vulnerable to the Fence Sitter?

A woman who is looking for a commitment and is impatient about getting it is most vulnerable to the Fence Sitter. It is ironic, of course, because that is what she is least likely to get from him.

He comes on strong and fast, and his intense interest leads her to believe he thinks she's the one. She has reservations about how fast things move at the beginning, but deep down this is what she wants: to be in a close relationship *now*. Her needs drown out her misgivings. It also helps if she is accepting and uncritical, ready to take him as he is. When his ambivalence shows itself, she can overlook it and take him back. Someone more demanding would be rid of him the first time he backed away.

How These Guys Think

Each variety of immature man has his unique way of thinking. What all three have in common is that they *don't* think too much about what they're doing (except the Fence Sitter), and hardly ever about the future.

The conscious thoughts of the Mama's Boy are:

- I do my share *(because he has no idea of all the things that are left for the other person to do)*.
- She likes doing things for me.
- If she wants something, she'll ask.

The Eternal Teenager's conscious thoughts are:

- Life is short, so live for today.
- Why not do what feels good?
- If I'm having fun, so is she. (If not, what's her problem?)
- Girlfriends come and go. Friends are forever.

The Fence Sitter consciously believes:

- I really want a committed relationship. I just can't find the right person.

- I try to think too much about women's feelings and don't take care of myself.
- If I settle for less than the right person, I'll never be happy.

As you can see, what all these guys believe and what they are actually doing are very different. They allow their personal, selfish needs to distort their actions so that they can see themselves as good guys rather than the self-absorbed, immature people they are.

While the conscious beliefs and thought patterns are different in the specifics for these three types of men, their subconscious beliefs are essentially the same:

- *I'm not ready to be grown up. I have no idea what I'm supposed to do.*
- *There is something missing in me. I need someone else around to make me happy and take care of me.*
- *I don't know what there is to life beyond what feels good (or bad) today. I can't look ahead. It's frightening.*
- *Once I accept being an adult, I will have to come to grips with aging and dying. I can't begin to grasp or cope with those concepts.*

While none of these guys think much about it, all are afraid of what lies ahead for them. They distract themselves from their fears of being inadequate to handle the next stage of life development by staying children, staying teenagers or searching futilely for the perfect partners to take that step with them. Staying immature is a primary defense mechanism for them. It shields them from their fears of what comes next.

6

Emotionally Retarded Assholes

*In twelve years of marriage,
he's never been wrong. He second-guessed
everything I did and kept me constantly
walking on eggshells. I never had a
legitimate complaint, let alone a righteous feeling.
So I finally left him. He says he wants me back, but
he has no clue what to change. He refuses to go to
therapy because I'm the one with the problem.*

—Beth, thirty-seven-year-old homemaker

Well, here he is—the hero of the romance novels many of you read as you fantasize about what love could be. He is strong and steady, but quiet and guards his feelings. You know that locked inside that cold, hard exterior is a passion that is just waiting for the right woman to ignite. It's not his fault he's distant. Something about his childhood, his station in life, his drive to be

someone has made him the way that he is.

That's the fantasy. In romance novels, part of the formula is to have a strong, silent, unapproachable man as the object of desire. He needs to be a blank screen on whom women can project all their dreams and illusions. He needs to be a challenge to win over so that the victory is sweeter when it inevitably occurs.

In reality, we have the Emotionally Retarded Asshole. Doesn't sound too romantic, does he? What, in fantasy, is the object of women's desires becomes, in reality, the object of their universal complaints. "I can't get him to talk." "He never shows me what he's feeling." "I can't get any reaction out of him." The internal workings of these men are not what romance novels portray. Instead, they tend to be guys who have not evolved emotionally to the point where they can access and express the full range of their feelings or meaningfully communicate within an intimate relationship. Women enter relationships with men like these hopeful that what they first see is a bud ready to bloom with the right care and feeding. Gradually they realize that the flower had fully opened when they first saw it. There is nothing waiting to bloom.

The silent, unemotional men presented in this chapter are not just idealized in women's romance novels. Westerns have traditionally given men the message that a "real man" has these traits as well. The characters portrayed by John Wayne and Clint Eastwood in Westerns were not, as a rule, talkative or emotional. Their actions spoke louder than their words, and about the only emotion they showed was anger at injustices they set out to put right.

Jerzy Kosinski created a wonderful parody of this type of man in Chance, the protagonist of *Being There* (played by Peter Sellers in the movie). Chance was a simple-minded gardener with no education and no knowledge of anything but gardening. He said little because he had little to say. He wound up in contact with

influential political figures. They read what they wanted into his silence and took his pronouncements about gardening as profound metaphors about life—when in fact, they were just simple, obvious statements about gardening.

The point is that we are culturally prepared to see uncommunicative, unemotional men in a positive light. We give them the benefit of the doubt by assuming that still waters run deep, and that inside these inscrutable men are profound reserves of passion and wisdom.

These assumptions blind many women to the obvious flaws in men such as these and allow a lot of Emotionally Retarded Men to go undetected. They are silent because they have little to say and no skills at saying it. They don't show feelings because their experience with them is limited, as is their ability to express the little they do feel.

The area in which the romance novels are on target is that these men use their reticence and emotional reserve to attain power and control in relationships. The romantic heroes are reluctant to show how they really feel (passionate and loving) for fear of being controlled by the women they secretly desire. The men described in this chapter seldom have that depth or purity of emotion, but they still enjoy the power they gain by revealing little of themselves, making their partners do all the work and take all the risks in the relationship. To speak openly and feel deeply is to be vulnerable.

The Strong, Silent Type

Byron was a friend of Georgia's older brother. She found him attractive and had a slight crush on him, but didn't think he had any interest in her. Her brother told her that Byron was really attracted to her but was painfully shy with women. When they

finally went out, Georgia took the frequent silences as evidence of that shyness. She was used to it (her dad was that way), and she didn't mind doing more than her share of the talking. In fact, it felt pretty good. Byron seemed to be a good listener, genuinely interested in what she had to say.

Georgia was very comfortable with Byron and continued to be physically drawn to him. After dating a couple of times a week for a year, they got engaged. After they married, either he got even quieter or his silence bothered her more. What was comfortable on a short-term, part-time basis became virtually intolerable day to day. He could park himself in front of the TV or sit with a book all night without speaking to her at all. He would buy things or make plans to go hunting with his friends without even consulting her first. He didn't seem to be doing it meanly. It was just his style. Still, it drove Georgia crazy.

She tried whatever she could think of to draw him out. It started with her asking him in detail about what he did each day. Single-word or brief-sentence answers were the best he would do. She tried to understand his interests better (sports, hunting and fishing, libertarian politics) but still couldn't get him to open up. Eventually, Georgia got tired of trying, threw in the towel, and resigned herself to a marriage bereft of meaningful communication and mutual understanding.

The most extreme example of this pattern we have seen was a man who literally did not speak to his wife for up to six months. They communicated through notes left on the refrigerator. He looked at her, usually, when she spoke, but gave no reply. He talked to his family, friends and coworkers, but never to his wife. She didn't even know why he stopped.

That example is an exaggeration of the common pattern, but the passive-aggression and deliberate intent to punish is often

present in more subtle form. A more amusing illustration comes from a 1960s TV show, *Captain Nice*. The hero's father was in many scenes, but you never saw his face or heard his voice. All you saw were his lower body and his hands holding a newspaper. Parodies like these are funny because they remind people of similar situations in their own lives.

Characteristics of the Strong, Silent Type

1. **He doesn't say much.** Obviously, this is the defining characteristic of the Strong, Silent Type. He's more comfortable with silence than conversation. He can sit in a room or a car with you for hours without speaking, and it doesn't necessarily mean he's angry. It's just how he is.

2. **When he does talk, he still doesn't say much.** He rarely talks about how he feels or what he believes. Conversation is utilitarian for him—to get or give information necessary for daily functioning ("What time is dinner?" "I need to use your car."). On those relatively rare occasions when he does talk about what he's thinking, he doesn't elaborate much and doesn't reveal all he's thinking.

3. **He isn't a good listener.** Since the Strong, Silent Type doesn't say much, he rarely interrupts. It is easy to assume that if you are talking and he isn't, he's listening. That is not always the case. He's often not paying attention, and his lack of response indicates he's not actively trying to understand what you are saying. He might appear forgetful, but there is a good chance he didn't forget—he didn't listen to you in the first place.

4. **He doesn't consult you regarding decisions.** Part of his not telling you what he's thinking involves not sharing with you his intentions to go places, make purchases or do things. He isn't necessarily trying to be secretive, he just doesn't see the need to bring you in on what he's planning. Speaking of his doing things, he is

likely to prefer quiet, solitary pursuits—hunting, fishing, camping. Even though he goes with friends, a lot of their time is spent in silence.

5. **He provokes you through his silence.** After being with him for a while, you become desperate to get a response, any response, out of him. You may find yourself in anger or hysterics as he sits by passively, looking at you as if you've lost your mind. It's bad enough when this happens at home, but it can spill over into malls, restaurants, friends' houses. In those settings, you wind up looking like a shrew or a crazy person, and people feel sorry for him. What they don't see is the constant deluge of silence he bombards you with that has driven you to distraction.

6. **Silence becomes a weapon for him.** As his lack of responsiveness gets to you more and more, he is able to use it to indirectly express anger at you and punish you. He can choose to stay quiet in the few situations in which you can usually get a response. You both know what he's doing, but, of course, he won't admit it. And make no mistake, he is very likely to be an angry guy. The "strong" in Strong, Silent Type is meant to be ironic. He is far from strong. His social skills are weak. His verbal skills are weak. His ability to handle an intimate relationship is weak. Men can get away with a lot by not talking since society equates silence with strength and self-control. For the Strong, Silent Type, it provides camouflage for a myriad of weaknesses.

7. **He is distrustful.** Silence is not just a weapon, it is also a means of control. If information is power, he holds on to his, while you pour yours out to him. He knows your vulnerabilities, your hot buttons. You know little about him, and that keeps him safe. He has a hard time believing that people can be trusted not to hurt him or try to "beat" him, so he reveals very little about himself to most people.

8. **He isn't just shy.** Being quiet and shy is not enough to put a

man in this category. A shy person will open up more when he gets close to someone, not less. He doesn't use his silence as a weapon, but as a defense against embarrassing himself. A shy man doesn't like to provoke because he's uncomfortable with conflict.

What It Feels Like to Be with the Strong, Silent Type

A woman with the Strong, Silent Type can feel a little uncomfortable and self-conscious at first. Then she can get to like it. She talks, he listens (or seems to). He doesn't tell her what to do or second-guess her decisions. His lack of intrusion into her thoughts and activities feels like respect.

But soon it begins to feel as if he is holding back. She tries to draw him out, but every time she approaches, he withdraws. She feels alone and isolated even though she is in a relationship. She doesn't really know what he thinks, feels, believes. She feels left out of his decisions, and he appears uninterested in hers. He won't discuss issues or even argue. She feels unimportant, insignificant, unloved.

What Kind of Woman Is Vulnerable to the Strong, Silent Type?

A woman who is tired of egocentric guys who can't stop talking about themselves, who equates reticence with strength and self-assurance, and who hates to be told what to do is fair game for the Strong, Silent Type. Many of these women have fathers who were distant and unexpressive. A woman who is outgoing and talkative doesn't have to compete for airtime with a guy like this. A woman looking for stability and dependability might see it in this kind of man. Any woman looking a little too hard for her dream mate can make the mistake of projecting the traits she desires onto the mute, blank slate of the Strong, Silent Type.

The Ice Man

Monica's wild days were behind her when she met Walter. She was ready to settle down. She was used to guys who were spontaneous, uninhibited, fun. Unfortunately, they were also irresponsible, self-absorbed and uninterested in commitment (Immature Assholes?). Not Walter.

She met him at work. He impressed her as very bright, very professional. She was more than a little surprised when he asked her out, since he hadn't flirted with her or shown any apparent interest. They went out once or twice a week—dinner, art films and classical music concerts. Here was a man who knew what he wanted. Walter's career was a priority, but he also wanted the stability of family life. He needed a mature, committed partner who shared his goals and was willing to work with him to achieve them. His proposal was more like a business proposition, but she was ready. She said yes.

There wasn't much romance, but that wasn't as important to her as it used to be. Monica was ready for a family, and they wasted no time. Within three years, they had two children. Walter did a lot of research on child rearing. He made sure the children were exposed to activities that would stimulate their intellects and hasten their development. He wasn't very good at just playing with them, but Monica compensated for him.

Their relationship was short on what Walter saw as frivolous activities—time with friends, parties, eating out. When they were in social settings, he often said tactless, insensitive things to people. After all, he was right, and he really didn't care what they thought. Still, Monica would get embarrassed. Sex became even less romantic and more mechanical (Saturday night, ready or not).

The only roles Monica saw herself filling were mother and homemaker. Walter didn't really want or need a partner or wife. He had

no friends, while she became more and more involved with and dependent on hers. They were her only social outlet. She also became very involved with the children, who at least showed her some emotion and appreciation.

The Ice Man prides himself on being logical and rational. More than one of our female clients have accused their husbands of being like Mr. Spock, the *Star Trek* character who was totally logical and had no feelings (or at least tried to pretend he didn't since he was only half human). Their Ice Men husbands take no offense at this comparison.

Think about what that means. These men see *not* having feelings as an asset, and having them (which most women do) as a liability. Unlike Mr. Spock, they are completely human, so a lot of their energy is spent pushing down or redirecting the normal feelings we all have. That process of ignoring or denying feelings is so natural to the Ice Man, though, that it looks as if he just doesn't have the feelings at all.

Characteristics of the Ice Man

1. **He sees himself as completely rational.** As we just discussed, the Ice Man believes he deals only with facts and logic. He is not encumbered by emotion or sentiment, so he can be detached and objective. This allows him to be utterly rational, unlike you, who are burdened with emotional baggage and subjectivity.

While he truly believes himself to be logical and rational, the Ice Man is really pseudological. He does not realize that he has opinions, prejudices and reactions that color his thinking. He is blinded to the fact that his assumptions about people and situations are as arbitrary and subjective as anyone's.

2. **He needs to be right and believes he is.** Since the Ice Man

deals only with facts and logic (or so he thinks), he is usually, if not always, right. It is maddening to him for someone to disagree with his opinions, which he sees as facts that can't be disputed. Arguing with him is a monumental waste of time since he is not open to opinions different from his own. Often, he doesn't even bother to argue. He says his piece and shuts up, giving off the superior air of someone who knows he's right and can't be bothered discussing it with someone of obviously inferior reasoning abilities. The only time he changes his mind is when someone calmly exposes him to new information that leads him to see a situation differently (new facts, not opinions or feelings).

3. **He is judgmental and critical.** The Ice Man sees things in black-and-white terms. It is one way or the other, no gray area. Someone is right, the other is wrong. Since he believes he's right, he can be matter-of-factly critical of people who hold positions different from his (including you). Moreover, he often expresses his critical judgments tactlessly, not caring what the idiots who disagree with him think. This can cause you a lot of embarrassment if it occurs in a social situation. People who like the Ice Man admire how straightforward he is, how he doesn't beat around the bush. Those who don't like him think he's insufferable and snobby.

4. **When he talks, it can have a lecturing quality.** Unlike the Strong, Silent Type, the Ice Man will talk. In fact, at times you wish you could shut him up. But his speech has a didactic, lecturing tone. He talks at people, not to them. He doesn't often have conversations since he doesn't care what other people have to say. He's very much like Mr. Know-It-All in this way. However, he is not nearly so controlling. He doesn't try to force you to do things his way, he just knows you're wrong if you don't.

5. **He doesn't like most people.** Being judgmental and feeling superior, the Ice Man has a definite misanthropic quality to him. Most people fall short of his standards, and he has little use for

them (and doesn't try to hide that fact). As a result, he has few friends, doesn't like to socialize and puts people off. It may seem as though he doesn't like you much of the time, and he probably doesn't.

6. **He sees emotionality as a senseless loss of control.** Emotions are useless and irrational. They lead people to behave in foolish ways, and the Ice Man wants no part of them. He is not interested in controlling other people as the Controllers described in chapter 3 do, but he's very interested in controlling himself. A burst of emotion can interfere with his logic and reason, on which he bases his life.

This excessive self-control is horrible to be around on a daily basis. You can get no emotional response from him, and he makes it clear he thinks you're an idiot if you feel and express emotions yourself. As with the Strong, Silent Type, the Ice Man's partner is often driven to emotional outbursts by his lack of responsiveness.

7. **He has no capacity for empathy.** Empathy, the ability to understand and relate to what other people feel, is the basis for all closeness in an intimate relationship. It is based upon feeling things yourself, being aware of those feelings and recognizing them in others. Naturally, the Ice Man has no capacity for empathy. He is unaware and intolerant of most of his own feelings, and can't understand how others feel (nor does he care to). This rules out any true intimacy and makes him come across as robotic and uncaring.

8. **If he shows any emotions, they are not "soft" ones.** The Ice Man is not totally bereft of emotion. He lets himself feel anger, frustration and disgust. He believes he's justified in feeling these things because of his critical and judgmental nature. He expresses these feelings in a measured, controlled way. He doesn't let the emotions consume him. He feels them, shows them (or not) and moves on. Softer emotions—sympathy, hurt, love—don't have any place in his view of the world. So

he doesn't feel them (or at least let himself consciously realize that he does).

What It Feels Like to Be with the Ice Man

She starts off respecting him for his mind. She sees him as a challenge in two ways. First, he's bright and doesn't like people who aren't, so she believes she needs to be sharper than she would have to be with other guys to keep up with him. Second, she thinks she can get through to him emotionally. Sure, there's a big wall there, but if she breaks it down, all the pent-up emotion and passion will come cascading out. Just like the romance novels. In the meantime, she admires how he doesn't lose his cool. There is no passion, but there is a safety and predictability to him.

The fantasy begins to fade as she realizes that he is getting even less emotional as time goes on. It turns out he was giving her more than usual when they began dating and then fell back into his unemotional true self. She craves some kind of response. She's afraid she's losing her own passionate, playful side. She feels judged and put down when she shows her own feelings. She tries to draw him into arguments just to get a reaction and gets more frustrated when she fails. She then appears, even to herself, shrill and hysterical.

She is very vulnerable to having an affair with anyone who shows a little empathy and understanding. But she's afraid to do that because she realizes she's desperate and probably not making good choices. Meanwhile, the relationship feels wooden and artificial. She realizes she feels numb, emotionally dead.

What Kind of Woman Is Vulnerable to the Ice Man?

The Ice Man looks good, initially, to a woman who is ready to settle down and sees his lack of emotion as strength and self-control. Other factors that make a woman vulnerable are a

personal crisis (death of a loved one, job loss, breakup of a relationship) that leads her to seek out stability and predictability, or bad experiences with guys who are the opposite of the Ice Man (spontaneous, unreliable, passionate, fun). A woman who is uncomfortable with her own emotions or who grew up in a household where emotional expression didn't happen may see nothing unusual about the Ice Man for quite some time. A woman who is intellectual, and who likes a guy who is willing to discuss ideas and not afraid to take a stand, can also get reeled in by the Ice Man.

How These Guys Think

The Strong, Silent Type and the Ice Man have their significant differences. For instance, the Ice Man believes in the paramount importance of the workings of the mind—of ideas, intelligence, logic. The Strong, Silent Type doesn't care much about those things. His silence is defensive, whereas the Ice Man's coldness is his proactive choice.

Still, there are a number of conscious beliefs they share:

- Talk and emotion are wasted energy in most cases.
- Relationships serve a purpose (having a family, division of labor, regular sex), not a need.
- Strength is in self-control (this is the key for both types).

As suggested earlier in this chapter, men like this are easily seen in a positive light by society's standards. Their apparent self-control looks strong and manly. Subconsciously, they are afraid of who they are and what will happen if their self-control wanes.

- *There are things a real man shouldn't do, and if I loosen up and act spontaneously, I'll do them.*

- *I can't find a way to reconcile my idea of what it is to be a man with emotions.*
- *Emotions confuse and scare me. I don't want to feel them (or express them if I do).*
- *I don't trust people. If they see who I really am, they will use it against me.*
- *If I show who I really am, I will be ridiculed and embarrassed.*

The irony is that these quiet, unemotional men, who are glorified in genres as disparate as romance novels and Western movies, have fundamental doubts about their own "manliness." Their ideas about masculinity are so narrow and constricted that they can't fit feelings and intimacy into them. As a result, they shut those experiences out and live partial, incomplete lives.

7   Mixed Breeds and Other Special Cases

*He kept drinking and verbally abusing me.
But I stuck by him because I knew, underneath it
all, that he had a good heart. But eventually the
drunken tirades and middle-of-the-night police
calls became too much for me, and I left him.
Still, it took a hell of a long time, and I feel
pretty bad about it from time to time.*

—Liz, fifty-two-year-old retail buyer

Mixed Breeds

It is frequently the case that the dog you are dealing with will not be a "pure" type, but rather, a
mixture of traits exhibited by a couple of different
types—a complex breed. Perhaps this is obvious to
you already, since rarely does real life mimic the
clear-cut definitions given in books. Nonetheless,

the point is worth emphasizing, so that when you get to the chapters on how to recognize and deal with difficult men, you will be sure to attend to all the categories relevant to the man you are or may soon be with.

Fortunately, most complex breeds combine traits of certain types that are fairly similar to one another. If you look at our four main categories of men to avoid, you will see that two could be described as overcontrolled (Controlling and Emotionally Retarded) and two as undercontrolled (Lying/Cheating and Immature). The guys who are overcontrolled have overriding needs to control themselves, their partners and all aspects of their lives. They do it in quite different ways, but the key variable is being in charge, or one-up. They tend to turn their partners into children in one way or another. Undercontrolled men possess inadequate abilities or are unwilling to control their appetites, impulses, lives and selves. They tend to do either what they want to do or are comfortable doing and leave it to their partners to be the responsible ones. So their partners usually end up acting like mothers in the relationship.

Many laypeople and mental health professionals alike would say that heavy drinkers deserve a major category of their own in this book. We disagree, but not because we don't see alcohol abuse as a tremendous problem both for individuals and relationships. Rather, we see men who abuse alcohol in all of our categories, and we choose to focus on their relationship behavior instead of the drinking. That does not mean the drinking should be taken lightly.

Heavy Drinkers

When you consider some of the effects alcohol has, you can see how its use is likely to affect different types of people. Among

other things, alcohol tends to impair judgment, decrease impulse control, reduce reasoning capacity and cause changes in mood. So, a cheater who drinks is more likely to cheat, and a liar more likely to lie. Immature Men who drink can use alcohol both as an excuse for their irresponsibility and medication for their "pain" when you criticize them. Controllers are prone to be less subtly controlling when drinking, and emotionally retarded men withdraw into themselves even more.

Some women find that alcohol use is the straw that breaks the camel's back. They can handle the myriad of character flaws their partners have, but when alcohol enhances them, it is just too much. Another common scenario is that alcohol use diverts the focus away from the man's emotional and behavioral liabilities and onto the drinking. It can become an explanation that excuses irresponsible relationship behavior. Alcohol becomes the focus, and everything else is overlooked. This is a very seductive process since it is tempting to simplify a complex network of problems into a single problem (alcohol).

This is not to suggest that you ignore a drinking problem and just focus on the issues. If you think he has a drinking problem, he probably does. A thorough discussion of alcoholism is beyond the scope of this book, and bookstores are full of books devoted exclusively to it. Al-Anon is a wonderful program for women (and men) involved with people who have problems with alcohol. It provides support, feedback from people who have been where you are, and ideas on how to pull back and see more clearly what is happening, without necessarily having to leave the situation altogether.

The main thing is not to suffer in silence. There are many different approaches to drinking problems. Find a way that makes sense to you. If Al-Anon doesn't fit for you, then look at other ideas—for example, Dr. Scott Miller and Insoo Berg's book, *The Miracle Method*. If the problem is serious and seems to be the

primary cause of your relationship problems, don't be afraid to consult either an alcohol/chemical dependency counselor or other therapist yourself, even if your partner won't go. A poor strategy is to cross your fingers and hope it will go away. It won't.

Abusers

As with alcoholics, men who are physically and verbally abusive span the entire spectrum of the men we describe in this book. Controlling men can turn to violence in order to consolidate their power when they are challenged. Immature guys often lack the ability to tolerate frustration and frequently express it through physical abuse.

Whatever the reason for the abuse, it is an extremely serious problem that under no circumstances should be overlooked. While this book deals with serious, widespread interpersonal problems and ways to recognize and address them, it often adopts a light-hearted tone in describing those problems and their perpetrators. We want to be very clear that there is nothing funny about any abusive situation. Abusers need to be dealt with differently. As soon as physical abuse becomes a part of any relationship, get outside help—whether it is from a mental health agency, a shelter for battered women, a women's advocacy group, a private therapist or the law.

All too often, women use the explanations of abuse as an excuse for the behavior. It becomes too easy to minimize the seriousness of the abuse if you understand why he is doing it, especially if he is apologetic and remorseful afterward. If abuse is a part of your relationship problem, make sure you treat it as the primary, most urgent aspect of the problem. Go to someone who is well versed in dealing with abuse immediately. Don't try to handle it yourself,

and don't keep it to yourself. Conspiring with the abuser to keep violence a secret allows him to maintain to himself and the public a veneer of civility he doesn't deserve. Getting help is the best thing you can do for yourself, your relationship and perhaps especially for the abuser, because he knows, at some level, how miserable he really is.

You will be well served when you deal with difficult men if you keep the main types in mind (see table 7.1) and realize that they can exhibit traits of each category. Recognizing problematic men as early as possible and avoiding them like the plague is far and away the best strategy to employ.

Table 7.1 TYPES OF MEN TO AVOID	
Controlling	**Lying, Cheating**
The Boss	The Great Pretender
Mr. Helpful	The Chameleon
Mr. Know-It-All	Don Juan
The Critic	
Immature	**Emotionally Retarded**
The Mama's Boy	The Strong, Silent Type
The Eternal Teenager	The Ice Man
The Fence Sitter	**Mixed Breeds**

Early Detection and Avoidance

8 Recognizing Them Early: An Ounce of Prevention

*I seem to meet the same asshole
over and over again. He looks different every time,
but I start getting these twinges of recognition.
I ignore the warning signs, hoping they will go
away, but they don't. The twinges slowly turn into
side cramps, but by the time I realize it, it's too
late—I'm doubled over and can hardly
breathe from the pain.
He fooled me again.*

—Susan, twenty-four-year-old aerobics instructor

Despite our earlier protestations, after reading the past several chapters you might think that we believe most, if not all, men are assholes. Not at all. There are plenty of nice guys out there. We just suspect the proportion is somewhat low.

Also, being worthy of the "A" appellation is not an either/or proposition. The characteristics that

make some men unworthy of a woman's time and energy fall along a continuum. Some guys have none of the traits described in this book; others have them to a moderate degree; and still others have personalities defined by those traits. So one issue this chapter addresses is how to differentiate "normal" guys from noxious ones.

There are some key signs—red flags that should serve as early warning devices for women that a guy is not worth their time. Think back to guys you've known and how obvious it is, in retrospect, that they were jerks from the get-go. Yet at the time, you didn't see it. This chapter will help you take those blinders off.

On the other hand, not every guy shows his true colors right away. Most guys are capable of putting their best foot forward and covering up their most blatant deficiencies. We are aware of only one man, in our combined years of clinical experience, who came into therapy and admitted, flat out, "I'm an asshole. I've been one for our whole marriage. It's all my fault." Still, that unconditional admission would have been even more refreshing and impressive had he not still been having an affair with his wife's best friend. The point is that what you see early on might be *marginal* signs. You're not sure if he's enough of a problem to worry about. Try running the tests presented in this chapter to flush out the Mr. Wrongs and to ease your mind about the guys who might be right for you.

Theoretically, once you know what to look for, it should be easy to avoid problematic men. In reality, it isn't. Our rational, logical minds might understand things that our emotional, needy minds find ways to distort or miss. Even if you do see all the signs early on, you can still begin to get pulled in. This chapter will explore ways you can pull out before you get in too deep.

Quick ASS

Before we get serious about how to recognize and avoid problematic men, in table 8.1 we present a highly unscientific

but nevertheless reliable device that allows you to detect Mr. Wrong immediately. The Quick Asshole Screening Survey saves you the pain and inconvenience of spending too much time with these guys. The test is called "Quick ASS," for obvious reasons: If a man meets any of its criteria, get away from him.

	Table 8.1 **QUICK ASS**
1.	He has a "Born to Lose" tattoo.
2.	He wears more jewelry than you.
3.	He organizes the clothes in his closet according to color, date purchased and/or fabric.
4.	He checks himself out in every reflecting surface he passes (mirrors, car windows, toasters, etc.).
5.	He has his credit card cut up when he tries to pay for dinner and says, "Damn, not again."
6.	He has several ex-wives, all of whom were "incredible bitches."
7.	He asks you to marry him on the first date.
8.	He either drives a "muscle" car or one held together by large amounts of duct tape.
9.	He has a nickname for his penis—and works it into the conversation.
10.	He doesn't laugh when you tell him the title of this book.

Normal Guys vs. Noxious Ones

There is a saying among mental health professionals that on many personality tests, a normal teenager scores about the same

as a fairly crazy adult. In other words, the norm for teenage behavior is weird by adult standards. So a natural question to ask is, How do you sort out "normal" male behavior from abnormal behavior? There are a number of factors to consider.

As noted in the introduction to this chapter, being a jerk is not an either/or proposition. To determine how far along a guy is on the continuum, you need to assess how much of a given trait he has and how often it shows. For example, concerning selfishness, does he always seem to get his way (or need to), or does he do so only occasionally? Does he flirt with the waitress after he's had a few drinks, or is that the way he ordinarily interacts with women? Do numerous aspects of his personality make your life more difficult (irresponsibility, frequent temper outbursts, trying to control everything that you do), or does he merely leave his dirty clothes lying around and come home late every once in a while?

Not every situation is as clear-cut as the ones just described, and you will almost always be forced to make a judgment call. When doing so, be aware of any "hot buttons" you have—areas of extreme sensitivity that can affect your judgment. With that in mind, go with your gut instinct. The biggest mistakes you can make are over-thinking and giving him the benefit of the doubt. If certain things stand out and don't feel right to you, trust your gut. Thinking back on past errors in judgment about people, most of us regret ignoring our instincts and intuition.

Another issue involved in separating the normal guy from the noxious one is whether negative characteristics are predominant or only a minor part of his personality. Is a guy who is controlling insistent on taking over every aspect of your life, or is he just adamant about managing the money? Is he a full-blown, out-of-control Eternal Teenager, or someone who knows how to loosen up and have a good time in ways that don't disrupt your lives or your relationship?

Sometimes it can be helpful to put it in writing, to lay it out on paper so you can see it, touch it, experience it. One way to do this is to list the things that bother you about him and evaluate, numerically, how much of a problem those behaviors are and how much you care about them. For example, let's say you list selfishness, flirting and insensitivity as problems. On a scale of one to ten, how much of his behavior does each characteristic represent? Further, on that same scale, how important is each problem to you? His selfishness may only be a three, but yet is very important to you, an eight; or his flirting may occur frequently, a nine, but it is no big deal to you, a two. "Seeing it in print" is sometimes a useful way to organize and evaluate perceptions and experiences.

Change and its direction also differentiate normal guys from problematic ones. A normal guy will realize he's spending too much time with his friends and cut back. A normal guy will sense that his need to control is inadvertently affecting his relationships and will work on going with the flow more. A normal guy will admit it to himself when he wants to change and can't, and will seek out help. Noxious men don't see anything wrong with what they're doing. In fact, they are more likely to get worse instead of better once they go off their best behavior (saved for the early stages of a relationship).

There are a couple of more ways to sift through the Neanderthals to find normal, reasonable men. First, look at male friends and relatives you know pretty well and respect, and use them as points of comparison for the guys you meet. Don't expect every man you get involved with to be like your late father, for instance, whom you have put on a pedestal. Instead, pick a few areas and see how a potential partner stacks up to men you like and respect. A second way to involve your friends, male and female, is to ask the ones who know a particular guy fairly well to give you an honest appraisal. Don't ask if you aren't prepared to hear any negatives.

Make it clear to your friends that you really want honest feedback, not just an insincere confirmation that he's a great guy.

Key Signs (and Why You Ignore Them)

Chapter 1 discussed the general characteristics of men who are worthy of wearing the "A" moniker. It is from those general traits that specific key signs derive. These constitute the "red flags" which you need to attend to. But keep in mind that if he's aware of them, he will try to hide them early on in a relationship.

Insensitivity

- He listens, but you don't ever feel he really understands how you feel.
- He does what he wants to, even if it bothers you, and makes little effort to change as he gets to know you better and learns what your really sensitive areas are.
- He repeatedly makes remarks that embarrass you in front of people.

Selfishness

- He's like a kid. He does what feels good to him, without regard for what you want.
- He can't or won't compromise.
- It doesn't even occur to him to consult you about matters that have a direct impact on you.
- He thinks only of his pleasure sexually.
- He sees the world in terms of how it affects him (he acts as though he is the center of the universe).

Inability to take responsibility for himself

- He has trouble with relatively simple things, like being on time for appointments/dates, paying bills, keeping jobs.

- He can't accept blame if he makes mistakes.
- He can't make decisions (he tries to get you to do that for him) because he can't prioritize or accept the consequences of bad decisions.
- He criticizes you (to deflect blame/responsibility from himself).

Making your life harder, not easier

- You are always doing things for him (cooking, running errands, making excuses) and he seldom does anything for you.
- There is a lot of emotional turmoil in the relationship (and this roller-coaster from anger to passion can be quite exciting and distracting—for a while).
- He demands all your time and attention, so you find yourself having little time for basic, day-to-day activities like laundry, bill paying, reading and seeing your friends.
- If he is a liar or cheater, you waste a lot of your time playing detective.

Competition, not cooperation

- He creates situations in which you feel like adversaries, not members of the same team (especially with a Know-It-All).
- His way is always better, and his needs more important.
- He considers only what is "right," not what is best for the two of you (and only he knows what is right).
- You defend and explain yourself a lot.

Need to control

- He calls the shots, makes the decisions.
- He can't "go with the flow" or take suggestions.
- He wants to tell you what friends to be with, how to dress, how to spend your money and your time.

- You find yourself asking permission to do things (as if he is your father or boss, not your partner).

Why Do You Ignore These Signs?

Most of these red flags are fairly obvious, at least in retrospect. So what is it that makes you overlook these warning signs?

- As we've said before, guys put their best foot forward and hide whatever flaws they're aware of.
- It is natural to feel lonely, and to really want him to be okay. So you delude yourself into seeing him as you want him to be rather than how he is.
- You have blind spots and vulnerabilities. Guys who play on those get under your radar, and you miss what might be obvious to others. Sometimes you grow up around a particular kind of man (controlling father, spoiled and immature brothers), so a prospective partner like that doesn't stand out. In other cases, you play a role in your family of origin (caretaker, peacemaker, scapegoat) and fall easily into a similar role with a man in an adult relationship. Regardless of where these blind spots came from, learn from past mistakes and get to know yourself so you can compensate for them in the future.
- You compare a current guy with past partners, and he doesn't look that bad. It's great to give a guy the benefit of the doubt and appreciate how he is very different from your previous partner. However, do a reality check here. Is he really okay, or would Atilla the Hun look like a teddy bear compared with your last boyfriend/husband? Try to be sure you are basing any diminished expectations on sound reasons, and not on comparisons to past mistakes or to men at the extreme end of the spectrum.

- You probably have heard things like "A relationship is work," "It takes two," "You have to make sacrifices" and "Real life isn't like Hollywood; be realistic." Many black women say that a message they often receive is "Society beats down the black man, so you must support him even more than white women do their men." Those are all fine things to keep in mind. Just don't let them become excuses for putting up with clearly unacceptable behavior.

- Perhaps the worst and most pervasive reason women overlook warning signs is that they believe they can change men, or that men will change for them. If you suffer from this unfortunate delusion, refer back to the "Listen Carefully . . . He Doesn't Want to Change" section in chapter 1.

Prince Charming or Prince of Darkness? How to Test Him

For many reasons, it may not always be apparent right away if a guy is a jerk, even if you know what to look for. You have blind spots. He can hide his flaws for a while. And, of course, men and women play games early in relationships. Some do it deliberately and enjoy it. Others subconsciously or automatically reenact patterns from childhood or past relationships. Maybe some of these games are part of a natural mating dance couples do in order to get to know each other.

Regardless of the reasons, neither partner in a potential couple shows his or her true colors right away. Even if you are able to be patient and wait some time before getting involved, it might not be clear whether or not your prospective mate is a jerk. So run some experiments. Set up situations to test him in key areas about which you have doubts or questions. This "field research" puts you

in charge of your relationship destiny by recognizing trouble before it's too late.

When to test

- **If you have blind spots.** You need to do a historical review of your bad relationships. Does this guy resemble them in any way? Consult with friends who have seen you operate in relationships before. They may see things you don't. They probably see through your blind spots and can be helpful in deciding what specifically you should test for. If you have any doubts about whether you are repeating any of your previous negative patterns with your new guy, run an experiment.

- **If you feel driven to be with him.** Perhaps it is a physical attraction, your own loneliness or desperation, or an undefinable "something" about him. Whatever it is, if you feel you just *have* to be with him, look out. There is a good chance something is operating in you that will make you overlook his faults, and it is a good time to back off, cool down, and search for a way to be objective.

- **If you get irrational intuitive twinges that make you a little uncomfortable with him.** A lot of what goes on in our brains is not available to its conscious part. We respond to patterns. Danger signals can be automatically activated if we pick up a combination of factors that we can't put our fingers on but that caused us pain in the past. Don't ignore intuition. It's not always accurate, but it's valuable and worth checking out.

What to test for

- **Key signs.** Look back at the earlier section on key signs that a guy might be an asshole. If it's obvious he has a number of them, no test is necessary. Get out. But if he's on the

borderline on one or more, or if you're not sure and want to be, set up an experiment to test him on those specific indicators.

- **Past relationship mistakes.** We do tend to repeat mistakes. Celebrate your previous bad choices. Use them as resources that provide useful information. Not every guy shows his flaws in exactly the same way, and if you're not aware of your tendencies, take no chances. Look at pitfalls in previous relationships and test for them in this guy. Better to be safe than sorry since, if he passes the test, you feel that much more comfortable with him.

- **His problems in dealing with other women.** He might treat you well but be controlling, abusive, or immature with his mother, sister, female friends, or past girlfriends. If that is the case, set up experiments (in ways we will shortly describe) to see if he's capable of the same with you. There is an old saying that if you want to predict how a man will treat his partner, look at how he treats his mother. There is some wisdom in that.

- **Things you have been choosing to overlook.** Look very hard at aspects of his behavior about which you say, "That doesn't really bother me," "That's not so bad" or "Maybe I'm just being picky." Also, attend to criticisms your friends and family have of him and that you defend. They may well be more objective than you.

Running experiments

An experiment is a situation in which the majority of variables (things that could happen) are controlled, but one key element is left to chance, or more specifically, to his choice. In other words, you engineer a situation in which he can do one of two things in a given circumstance, and the one he chooses gives you information

on what he's really like. It may be helpful to think of yourself as a detective gathering clues to solve a crime. Each encounter with the "suspect" allows the opportunity for you to uncover evidence to prove or disprove his guilt. Women have told us that running experiments helps them feel in control and stay tuned in to what they know is best for them.

There are a few things you should keep in mind as you prepare to run your experiments. Try to stay detached—to look at the situation as gathering data. If you go in with a strong emotional stake in one outcome or the other, you will affect both the results and how you interpret them. Don't try to test for everything. Pick one or two areas about which you have doubts and set up a *series* of experiments to test him in those areas. If you try to test for too many things, you wind up confusing yourself and losing focus. On the other hand, if you just run one test, the results might be a fluke, and you could draw the wrong conclusion. With those conditions in mind, let's look at some examples of the kinds of experiments you could initiate.

Controlling Assholes

1. If he expects to do something specific at a certain time, surprise him and change the plans (for instance, change the restaurant and reservation time) and see how he reacts.
2. If he usually drives when you go out, suggest you drive this time.
3. Pick a "suggestion" he's made to you (what clothes to wear to an event, how much time to spend with a certain friend, what menu item you might like at a restaurant) and don't follow it.
4. Initiate sex, if he usually does, and be clear about what you would like him to do.

These are trivial and arbitrary situations, but they exemplify the kinds of things that controlling guys don't handle well but other

guys deal with just fine. If he gets obviously uncomfortable or pressures you to do it his way, you are probably seeing clues that you are with a controlling man.

Lying, Cheating Assholes

With these guys, the good news, according to Dr. Dory Hollander, author of *101 Lies Men Tell Women*, is that if you show a little patience, his true colors will shine through. He can't hide who he is for very long—his lies will eventually catch up with him. So the idea here is not to set up specific experiments, but rather, to be a "scientific" observer for warning signs. Dr. Hollander suggests that you should beware if he:

1. **Misrepresents his marital or relationship status in any way.** For example, he says he is separated or has just broken off contact with his girlfriend, but later you find that this is not the case. He then tells you that he meant he was emotionally separated or about to break it off.

2. **Distorts his current situation—his residence, job, finances, etc.** For example, he tells you he is manager of the bookstore in which he works, and you find out he is a cashier.

3. **Lies about basic personal things like his age, weight, ethnicity, nationality, etc.** For example, he tells you that he is a child of a Czechoslovakian immigrant, and you find out that his parents, while of Czech heritage, were born in Cleveland.

4. **Tells obvious lies that seem to serve no purpose.** For example, rather than just apologizing for his lateness, he says that he had a flat tire or encountered a bad accident on the freeway.

5. **Is inconsistent in his stories about his past or current personal, financial or professional circumstances.** For example, he says he owns a vacation cottage on the beach, but on another occasion it's a cabin in the mountains.

6. Makes absurd and/or extreme statements about you or the relationship that seem too soon or too good to be true. For example, he tells you that you are the only woman who really understands him, when you've known him for two weeks, or he talks about moving in together after the second date.

The main thing with these guys is to look beyond the words for the facts. Do whatever it takes to find out the truth about them. Avail yourself of public records like marriage licenses, birth certificates and divorce decrees, to refute or confirm your suspicions. Remember things he has told you and ask his friends questions that provide evidence of his honesty or lack thereof. Be skeptical and take your time. One incidence of a lie is no big deal, but several are.

"My, oh, my! What a fascinating guy you are, Vincent! But now, if it's not too much trouble, I'd like you to take my order."

Immature Assholes

1. Pick one or two things that you usually do, don't do them and see if he picks up the slack.

2. Ask him, in a genuinely curious and nonthreatening way, what his dreams and plans are for the future. Then see if he has any and if they have any basis in reality.

3. Subtly direct the conversation to a past relationship of his that went sour, and see if he can acknowledge his contribution to the problems or if he blames it all on her.

4. Gently criticize one of his friends and see how he responds.

5. If you suspect a Fence Sitter, pick a couple of situations in which you allow him to make a decision with no input from you. If he changes his mind, go with the flow and tally up how many times he flip-flops.

Emotionally Retarded Assholes

1. If you think he is a Strong, Silent Type, choose a few situations and "outsilence" him. If he is just shy, then he will not be uncomfortable with that. If he gets frustrated, then silence is likely a control maneuver for him.

2. With a possible Ice Man, make a point to say nice things about several different people on separate occasions. Notice how often he quietly accepts your compliments of others as opposed to pointing out their flaws.

3. Share with him situations in which you felt hurt, angry or sad. Then look for two things: Did he say anything that indicated he really understood? Whether he said anything or not, did you leave the conversation feeling better or closer to him? If no on both counts, look out.

Similar examples can be found to test other qualities. None of the situations presented here are relationship-threatening, life-or-death ones. They are trivial but telling. You can have some fun

doing them. Remember, you are testing a hypothesis, a guess, about him and trying to stay detached while you do it. Keeping the mood light makes that easier. Try to be clear with yourself about what you're looking for and how you'll know if you see it. Once you run the experiment and have the results, don't make excuses for him or second-guess what you saw. On the other hand, don't set him up to fail by picking a particularly sensitive area for him that may not be representative of how he usually is.

Probably the most important aspect of running experiments is to keep yourself in the rational part of your brain and to prevent the side of you that really wants things to work out from dragging you into a bad situation. This isn't easy. You don't have to be cold, distant, humorless and robotic while testing him, but you do want to make sure it's safe before you let your guard down and become emotionally vulnerable.

How to Avoid Getting Involved

Once you're reasonably certain the guy you've been considering as a relationship possibility is an asshole, it would seem simple not to get involved. You had your suspicions, you tested him, and he failed. Walk away and look for a better prospect. Of course, it's not that simple. Just beginning to interact with him has created somewhat of a connection between you. If he knows how to push your buttons, breaking even that fragile connection can be difficult.

Most of what can help you avoid involvement will be obvious, common-sense knowledge. However, just because you know what to do doesn't mean you will do it or that it will be easy. Use the following strategies to discipline yourself to follow through on your own common sense.

- **Take your time.** If you try but can't seem to avoid him, *slow down.* Don't get more deeply involved (by spending more

time with him, making plans into the future, etc.), and don't pressure yourself to act quickly if that hasn't been working. When he sees you trying to pull away, he will try to clean up his act and/or push your buttons to manipulate you into staying. Once he senses you are not trying to pull away, he will likely go back to being his usual asshole self. If you have stayed somewhat emotionally detached, you will see even more clearly what a jerk he is, and leaving will become easier.

- **Wait to have sex.** Maybe this is obvious, maybe not. Some people believe they can be sexual with someone and keep all emotional intimacy out of it. That is rarely true for most women in our culture. Even if it is for some of you, sex has subtle ways of changing a relationship. No matter how detached and unemotional you have remained, being naked with someone and exploring each other's bodies can't help but make you somewhat more vulnerable and connected to him. In addition, most of us attach subconscious (if not explicit) significance to sexual activity, and the relationship takes on added importance.

Besides, what do you have to lose? If you wait, and he turns out to be a decent guy after all, sex is still an option. If he turns out to be an asshole, it's hard to feel good (or even neutral) about having been sexually intimate with him. And once you've been intimate with him, the temptation to see his good points and overlook his faults can't help but increase.

- **When in doubt, back off.** The consequences of missing out on a potentially okay guy are not as bad as winding up with a jerk. If he were a *great* guy, you wouldn't be wondering about him and would have no reason to back off.
- **If you have a bad relationship history, get help.** Do some honest self-evaluation. Solicit candid feedback from people in your

support network, and allow yourself to lean on them. Get therapy if you feel yourself being pulled into what you know is another bad relationship and aren't confident you can fight the urge to dive in regardless. Therapy need not be long-term; a little therapy can go a long way in helping you access your inherent strengths. It is, frankly, a fallacy that therapy requires a lengthy examination of your faults for change to occur. The fact is, therapy is most often brief and is most effective when it enlists your existing strengths to empower change. (For other mental health myths, see appendix A.)

Once you decide you want to break away, feel strong enough to do it and have no serious doubts it's what is best for you, there are certain specific do's and don'ts we suggest:

1. **Pick the way that is easiest for you.** Don't feel compelled to do it the "right" way, whatever that is. A face-to-face meeting isn't mandatory. Make a phone call. Leave a message on his answering machine. Write a letter. Change your phone number. It doesn't matter how you do it. What matters is picking a way you can realistically follow through with.

2. **After you break it off, have no contact.** And we mean *no* contact. Don't have lunch with him. If he calls, say you don't want to talk and hang up. If he calls back, just hang up. Don't get sucked into believing you owe him an explanation. Any contact puts you at risk for getting pulled back in. Any contact creates a connection, however slight, and every connection brings you a little closer (while you're trying to get farther away). Be rigid (yet kind) with yourself about this rule. Don't make exceptions.

3. **If he continues to pursue, be as cold and unemotional as possible.** Being nice is obviously a bad idea. Getting angry and defensive isn't much better because that creates an emotional connection. Remember, the opposite of love is not hate, it's apathy. If his pursuit begins to feel like harassment (even if he's being pleasant), don't be reluctant to take legal steps to keep him away. That may sound harsh, but dealing with these men can be a serious business.

4. **Don't try to stay friends.** If you choose to ignore the last two suggestions, please don't let it go this far. There are no good reasons to stay friends (in fact, you probably never were to begin with), and plenty of reason not to. He's an asshole, and who needs one of those for a friend? Even if you were just slightly romantically involved, it's hard to take a step backward to friendship and make it stick. Finally, you're probably just doing it out of guilt or pity or because you don't have the guts to risk looking like a cold, uncaring person. And those are lousy reasons to maintain a friendship.

5. **The earlier the better.** Don't push yourself if you're not ready, but once you are, do it right away. The longer you're around him, the more buttons he will have pushed, the more manipulation you'll have been exposed to and the more things you'll have connecting yourself to him (common friends, shared activities and interests, secrets you've shared).

Throughout this early recognition and disposal process, keep the experimental/testing approach in mind. Early in any relationship, you are gathering data. Maybe that sounds cold and calculating, but it isn't really. In many ways, you are just intensifying your intuition and internal warning devices. You can always get closer and less "scientific" when you decide it's safe.

9

Do I Stay, or
Do I Go Now?

He had an affair a while back,
and we drifted apart. I got depressed
and then had an affair myself. Stupid,
I know. When my husband found out, he was
indignant, he was devastated, he was suicidal,
he was homicidal. I was miserable. He was also
merciless with me. He never let me forget
the affair, constantly saying vulgar things
about what I had done with the other guy.
This went on for months until I found out
he was seeing the other woman again—
and had never stopped seeing her!
Now I don't know what to do.

—Katherine, thirty-nine-year-old attorney

Detecting destructive men early and avoiding them like the plague is clearly the best way to deal with them. However, many of you

reading this book probably are already involved with one. Your decision whether to stay with or leave him is much more difficult to make, especially if the relationship is of long duration or involves children. Recognition and testing are still very relevant for you but need to be applied differently. It is also important to understand that what keeps women involved with difficult men differs considerably from what leads them to get involved initially.

This chapter addresses the woman who is caught in the dilemma of staying vs. leaving. This is obviously a tough spot to be in. We begin our discussion with a brief overview of all that is involved in such a gut-wrenching but incredibly important struggle. We then look at determining how bad he really is: what kind of changes he has made to date, how much better he's likely to get and reasons you have stayed with him this long. All this leads up to preparing you to make a decision to stay or to go.

"Baby Steps"

Some of you may recall the movie *What About Bob?* Bill Murray played a wacky patient of a pompous psychiatrist portrayed by Richard Dreyfus. Dreyfus's character wrote a book called *Baby Steps*. One of the funnier scenes in the movie depicted a quite literal translation of "baby steps" by Bill Murray's character. While this is not to suggest you take baby steps, you should take things slow and easy. This is probably the most critical decision of your life. A lot rides on it. The process of making the decision represents an important struggle and therefore offers a profound opportunity for change. It requires attention and time so that you can live comfortably with the outcome for years to come.

To make an intelligent decision, it is important to go through the process one step at a time. Our minds tend naturally to look ahead. While you're trying to determine if you are with a jerk, it's

easy for you to worry about whether you are ready to leave him if he is. Being afraid to leave, or being ambivalent about it, can cause you to avoid your first task—deciding if he is really an asshole. If he is, you can *then* decide whether to stay or go.

It's not a foregone conclusion that you have to leave just because you recognize your partner as one of the men in this book. Many of you will choose to stay, and we devote several chapters to learning to cope better if you do.

Similarly, it is important not to confuse making a decision with carrying it out. Many women are afraid that once they decide to go, they won't have the guts to actually do it. Or they begin to imagine how hard it will be and all the ways he will try to make it even worse. Not making a decision allows them to avoid, or at least postpone, that discomfort.

Take one step at a time. Just because you decide to go doesn't mean you have to do it immediately, or any particular way. You can think about the best time and the easiest way later. This may all sound obvious, but getting ahead of yourself by looking forward to the next step of the process is the most common reason why women stay stuck in bad relationships.

How Bad Is He?

By the time you've been with a man for a while, you already have a pretty good idea of whether or not he's a jerk. What is left to determine is how big of one he is, and what you are realistically willing and able to put up with. As you evaluate your situation, there are compelling reasons to look at your blind spots since you may have a motivation for self-deception. Children, time devoted to the relationship, financial considerations and a plethora of other factors that weren't in the early stages of the

relationship now come into play. Ironically, just when you need objective, outside feedback from friends and family, it becomes harder to get. They have probably dropped hints, or even made direct negative statements over the years, but you have chosen to ignore or discount them. So the people in your immediate support system may be gun-shy. Not only has their input had no impact in the past, but they also fear that they will alienate you if they say bad things about your partner and you choose to stay with him.

Still, the opinions of the people close to you are invaluable. You have been in a crazy situation for so long that you're not sure whether or not to trust your own perceptions and intuition. Make sure you're ready to hear whatever your friends and family have to say and are prepared to not let those opinions push you away from them. Then pick a few people whose judgment you trust the most, and give them your most persuasive argument that you're finally ready to hear their honest, unvarnished opinions about your partner. Those will be key pieces of data in deciding how bad (and what kind) your partner is.

Another source of information is a retrospective assessment of how he's acted in a variety of situations over the years. You've probably seen his whole repertoire by now. But you might not have let yourself see it for what it really was. Take this step when you are calm; both anger and apprehension can lead you to draw conclusions that are inaccurate and difficult to stick to later. When you're ready, look at the key signs described in chapter 8, zero in on the ones you believe he displays and think back over situations in your past in which he had the opportunity to show those signs or not. Then ask yourself the questions from chapter 8. How controlling (irresponsible, etc.) is he? Does he display the behaviors most of the time, or just occasionally? Are his negative qualities key chapters of his personality, or just annoying footnotes?

Finally, to remind yourself that having "A" traits is not a

black-or-white proposition, but instead falls along a continuum, find a variety of people to compare him against on the key traits. Look at people you admire, people you despise and people in between. Make your thoroughly subjective and personal decision as to where he stands (Mr. Wonderful, average guy on the street or absolute asshole).

Clearly, this process is not an exact science, nor is it meant to be. Your judgment will be colored by your feelings for and experiences with him, as well as your personality style (forgiving, judgmental, easygoing). For some women, the longer they are with guys, the more tolerant they are of their flaws since they have so much invested in the relationship. Other women become progressively more irritated, resentful and intolerant.

Where you fall on that spectrum is of at least equal importance to his position on the continuum. Your choice to ultimately stay or leave has to be made in the context of your realistic ability to tolerate what he displays. Keep in mind that troubling behavior is in the eye of the beholder. An average to slightly above-average jerk may be impossible for an angry woman who has grown intolerant to endure, since the time spent with him has poured kerosene on the flames of her annoyance and resentment. On the other hand, a bad-to-the-bone, extreme asshole may be someone an easygoing, forgiving woman could live with, if other factors such as children, finances and personal values regarding marriage motivate her to stay.

Has He Changed?

People continue to grow and develop (or perhaps regress) throughout their lives, so it is a mistake to look at how your partner is acting now without considering changes in him

over the time you've been together. A good way to begin is by doing a time line representing the ups and downs of his behavior over the course of the relationship (using the indicators of his behavior you identified while determining how bad he is). Draw the line with months and years marked off representing the time you've been together. Then think back and rate his behavior at intervals that stand out in your memory. You can do it graphically (draw a curve with high points in the relationship above the line and low points below) or describe in words what he was like with you at various times.

It may also be a good idea to mark in key events (marriage, birth of a child, moves, job changes), both to jog your memory and to see how he responded to transitions. A typical pattern might look like this: first six months, best behavior; next year, gradually got worse; hit bottom after one and a half years together; improved slightly when you threatened to leave; then leveled off and stayed about the way he is now.

"Damn it, Gwendolyn, you knew when you married me I only moved one square at a time."

Mischa Richter. ©1991 from The New Yorker Collection. *All rights reserved.*

A key element in this process is looking for movement. Some ways it manifests itself are:

1. **Progress**—Did he start off terrible but gradually improve? Is the improvement continuing?

2. **Deterioration**—Did he look pretty good at first but steadily go downhill? Has he reached bottom yet?

3. **Pace**—Were changes rapid or gradual? Did he get worse slowly and subtly, change for the better quickly but briefly, then get worse slowly again?

4. **Ups and downs**—If a clear pattern emerges in which good and bad times alternate, has the overall quality of his behavior deteriorated? This kind of vacillation can keep some excitement and passion in the relationship, while masking a gradual deterioration in how he acts with you.

While considering how things have changed, look at yourself as well as him. Assess what you are realistically capable of tolerating, and don't assume your tolerance has remained static. How do you feel when you are apart? Has that changed, and why? Are you getting so used to his crap that it doesn't really upset you anymore? Or does it feel like he's stomping on your last nerve every day now?

Look also at your level of avoidance. Do you have to distort or deny more of what you see in him to allow yourself to stay? Do you spend more time away from him to reduce your discomfort? Are you walking on eggshells more and more to try to provoke less of his obnoxious behavior?

Again, putting it in writing can be helpful. First, list what you want from a relationship. This is a lot harder than it sounds. Many times it is easier to say what we *don't* like; we get so caught up in our complaints, we don't think about what it would be like without them. Next, compare your list of wants with what you are actually receiving in the relationship.

Consider how you feel about the ways you've had to adapt for him. Are you proud of yourself for having learned how to cope better with a difficult situation? Or do you feel your self-respect slipping away as you see yourself putting up with more and more things that you believe to be objectionable?

The final and most difficult is predicting his *realistic* potential for future change. Women are notorious for seeing boundless positive potential in the most unlikely candidates. Whether that is based on an optimistic view of mankind in general, motivated self-delusion, fear of moving on or susceptibility to his empty promises of better times to come, you want to avoid that common pitfall.

Look at specific factors so that you base your predictions on some concrete evidence. First, consider what is the best he's ever been. A reasonable guess regarding the best he can do is the best he's done. Expecting him to behave in ways he's yet to show you is reminiscent of that old joke about the man who asks his doctor after hand surgery, "Doc, will I ever be able to play the violin again?" The doctor replies, "Yes, I believe you will." "That's funny, I never could before." If your partner's never played the violin, don't expect him to start now just because he says he'll learn.

A second factor to consider is his motivation. Does *he* want to change, or is it just that *you* want him to? If he does profess a desire to reform, is it based on his disgust with his behavior or the fear of your leaving? Have you heard this from him before, and if so, what did he do?

Another aspect to consider in assessing his potential for change is his openness to accepting help (from family, friends, a therapist). Has he rejected it in the past? Does he tell you he doesn't need help, he can do it himself? If so, his credibility goes way down, along with the chances of his changing.

Many women have told us of the difficulty inherent to evaluating their partners. Because of many factors, women have the

uncanny ability to see in their men not only virtues and potential that others don't see, but also ones that aren't there. Going through the process described can help keep you on track and allow you to evaluate him for what he is and will likely be, and what is best for you.

Why Are You Staying?

Once you've gone through the process of determining that yes, your partner is one of the men described in this book (or worthy of his own chapter), the logical conclusion would seem to be that you should leave him. Of course, it is not at all that simple. There are a lot of realistic factors you have to consider before leaving any longer-term relationship, and the fact he meets our criteria doesn't automatically mean you're a fool to stay. On the contrary, there are many reasons why you would be a fool to leave. As we said earlier, this is an excruciating decision. It affects virtually everything and everyone in your life, and is not to be taken lightly. Some of the pragmatic factors that keep women with toxic men are:

Children. The presence of children who are a product of your relationship represents the most obvious, complex and gut-wrenching complication when it comes to making a decision. There is no anguish quite like parental guilt. Naturally, what is best for a child is to be with two parents who love each other (and the child) and treat each other well. When that is not the case, things become more confusing. If there is frequent arguing in front of the child, or abuse of you or the child, the decision to leave is more easily made since it is hard to argue that the child is better off in that situation.

Where it becomes sticky is in a situation in which you appear (to the child and other adults) to get along, but you know it's only

a facade. Are your discomfort and unhappiness sufficient causes to break up the family? Is a child going to suffer subtle effects of being around people who are pretending and whose interpersonal tension could be transmitted to him/her?

The answer to these questions is far from clear. Research generally says that kids of divorce do okay unless: one parent does not fare well after the divorce (gets depressed, doesn't go on with life); one parent fades into the woodwork and the child essentially loses a parent; or a chronic hostility perseveres between parents. However, any decision you make has to be based on your individual value system and your personal assessment of your situation. Other factors to consider are:

- **You are a role model** for your child. Do you want him or her to stay in a bad relationship for the kids when he or she is an adult?
- By staying, you may be teaching your child to **handle adversity passively,** by doing nothing.
- By discounting your own happiness and personal needs, you transmit to the child the value of **putting others first** (which can certainly be valuable but can also be a recipe for guilt and being manipulated).

Finances. Many of you have opted either to stay home and raise your children or sacrifice your career for your partner's. When the time comes to consider leaving, those decisions could leave you in a very weak financial position.

If you really want to go, but finances are a key consideration, make sure you get accurate, reliable information from an attorney as to what kind of support you can expect. Some men often threaten that you'll never see a red cent if you leave, but they aren't judges or legislators. Those threats are often one more way to control you. Still, you need to be realistic. Is he bitter enough

to refuse to pay support or to quit a job just to spite you?

Even if leaving is financially feasible, it will almost always involve a scaling down of your lifestyle (and your children's). This might sound petty or superficial, but you have probably sacrificed a lot to get where you are, and giving it up is not always easy or the best decision. Let's face it—money is very important, and it is romantic nonsense to say that it isn't.

Emotional ties. Just because a guy is a jerk doesn't mean you don't love him. Or pity him. Or feel pangs of jealousy at the idea of him being with someone else. You could also have strong ties to his family that an acrimonious split could rupture.

Time invested. Most of you have put a lot of valuable years into your relationships. It's not always easy to say that staying is like throwing good money after bad by wasting even more valuable time with him. You could decide instead that taking steps to learn how to cope with him and be reasonably content is preferable to throwing away the time investment you've made.

Fear. Here we refer to what he might do if you leave. You know him better than anyone. Is he capable of violence against you? Could he stalk or harass you? Would he sacrifice your children's best interests to get back at you? These things aren't necessarily likely, but neither do they only happen in the movies.

Inability to leave. A number of factors, both personal (guilt, fear of being alone) and interpersonal (manipulation, being trapped in a role you can't easily shake), immobilize women who are trying to get out. The next chapter will look at these in more detail.

Making the Decision

The equation for deciding whether to stay or leave looks clear-cut on a surface level. You weigh how bad he is against the realistic factors keeping you in the relationship and make

allowances for changes he's made (depending on the positive or negative direction of those changes).

On a rational level, that is pretty much what the decision involves. The most important variable however, is very likely to be the least rational one—namely, how you feel. The next chapter deals with the situation in which your head tells you to go but you can't get yourself to do it. For right now, consider the opposite condition. You may lay all the factors out and decide it is best to stay, but find that you feel despondent at the conclusion you've reached.

If this is true for you, be aware that the ability of our conscious, rational mind to override our less conscious, less deliberate, less rational feelings is limited. Should you try to act against your feelings, you could find yourself so emotionally shut down and nonfunctional that you and your family will suffer (and make your decision to stay the "wrong" one after all).

So, add the emotional variable to your equation by "trying on for size" any decision to stay. See what it feels like to live with that decision for a while before you go public with it or commit yourself to it. The despondency could pass, or it could settle in and take over.

A specific way to try the decision on for size is the "odd/even day decision ritual." It allows you to explore and compare the emotional consequences of both sides of your decision before you actually make it. This can be particularly helpful if your rational decision making has reached an impasse, or if the pros and cons of leaving seem pretty equal. In this instance, your decision looks like the choice between death by hanging or death by firing squad.

The odd/even technique requires you to split the week into odd and even days. On odd days (days one, three, etc.), you live your life as though you have decided to leave. On even days (days two, four, etc.), you go through your daily activities as if you have chosen to stay.

The idea is to fully experience emotionally your decision by carrying out the behavioral routine it implies. On odd days, do things
separate from him and explore the ramifications of a single
lifestyle. On even days, totally immerse yourself in the relationship, and behave the way you believe a good partner should. What
feelings does each scenario bring up? Compare your daily levels of
energy, satisfaction and self-esteem on a scale of one to ten. Paying
attention to the emotional consequences of a decision ahead of
time can save you from making a big mistake.

However, don't test how the decision feels until you've gone
through all the steps of making the decision. Remember, if you
think about how hard it would be to implement your decision
(pragmatically or emotionally) while you're making it, you will
likely encourage yourself to avoid the decision and passively allow
the status quo to continue. You *can* decide to stay, even if you
determine he has all of the "A" traits, and if you do decide to
leave, you can wait until the timing is right for you (and do it in
whatever way is easiest for you).

The actual process of decision making goes like this:

Define the decision to be made. Are you deciding whether to
leave or stay? Or do you know you want to go and are deciding how
to get better prepared to do so? While it is obvious that you have
to know what decision you are making before you make it, people
often confuse themselves by overlooking this step.

Evaluate and weigh the relevant factors. Decide how bad he is.
Look at changes in him (and in you). Look closely and objectively
at the things that are making you consider staying. Check your
emotional pulse. Do you love him? Can you endure much more?
Then weigh these variables based on your values (happiness vs. stability, personal fulfillment vs. obligations) and your knowledge of
yourself (mentally you might value stability, but emotionally you
know you can't stay).

Look at the pros and cons you just evaluated, and decide. This sounds simple, and it can be. The hard work is done in the previous stage. Here, what is involved is the courage to look at what you have concluded and accept the results.

Decide how and when to implement your decision. If you are leaving, are you ready yet? Do you need to give yourself time to adjust emotionally, to prepare financially, to let your kids finish the school year? If you decide to stay, do you want to give him some time to stew in his juices, wondering if you'll leave (perhaps giving him some motivation to change)? In short, look at all the ways to go ahead with your decision, and pick the one that both meets your needs and feels most comfortable.

Follow through. Trust yourself. It's hard, but don't tolerate second-guessing. Put one foot in front of the other. Take it a day at a time. If you leave, remember that transition is always hard (even if it is also a relief), and don't confuse the pain of the transition with having made a bad decision. If your decision is to get out of the relationship, this implementation stage is fraught with many potential pitfalls. In the next chapter, we'll look at what they are and how to avoid them.

10

Making the Break

Those who wish to sing always find a song.

—Swedish proverb

A s many of you have undoubtedly already discovered, deciding to end a relationship and successfully doing it are two vastly different things. There are lots of reasons women feel stuck and find it hard to go, even when they are certain it is the right thing to do. This chapter begins by looking at the obstacles that prevent women from breaking off relationships.

Once you become aware of what is holding you back and find ways to deal with it, deciding *how* to leave is your next task. It sounds simple and straightforward, but, of course, it usually isn't. You have to accommodate your own strengths and limitations (not everyone can be direct, forceful

and decisive) and his likely attempts to sabotage your exit.

Finally, once you go, you don't want to renege, go back and have to leave again. Sticking to your guns can be very difficult. You'll have mixed feelings. Transitions are hard, and he'll pull out all the stops to get you back. Avoid caving in to this temptation. Many women say that leaving a second time (or third or fourth) is usually harder, not easier, than the first.

What Keeps You Hooked?

The last chapter looked at realistic, practical factors that need to be considered when deciding whether to sever a relationship. Here, we consider largely irrational, impractical reasons women remain in relationships they know are bad for them.

Fear of being alone. When you have spent every day for several years with an insufferable jerk, the idea of being alone looks pretty attractive. However, when push comes to shove, that prospect tends to lose most of its luster. Remarks made by single friends bemoaning their loneliness, which you used to sympathize with but not take personally, begin to hit home. Many women wind up settling because being with virtually anyone looks better than a life of projected miserable solitude. The negative memories of those pre-relationship times can come flooding back as the reality of leaving sinks in.

Even if you are able to break off the relationship, you are far from out of the woods. The idea of being alone is quickly replaced by the actuality of it. At first, it can be quite a relief. But most women don't have a support system ready to step into the breach and be available when they want to be with people. Building that support takes time, and its absence during a time of difficult transition can heighten the pain of loneliness, making it easy to imagine it will always feel this way. At this point, you become very

vulnerable to reconciling, for no real reason other than to reduce your immediate (and projected) discomfort.

The most effective weapons in fighting this fear are perspective and support. Work hard on putting your situation into perspective. You *will* feel lonely at times and long for company, any company. But you won't always be alone. Even if no man comes into your life soon (assuming for some reason you want one to), friends, family and interests you have put on the back burner can be cultivated. Along those lines, begin to put into place before you leave (if at all possible) a support network. Get in touch with friends you've neglected. Reconnect with your family. Start doing things you've put off but wanted to do. Women have often told us that the worst thing you can do to deal with loneliness is to give yourself too much time to sit and think about it.

Feelings of unworthiness. Perhaps you have been put down so long and so often that you believe the negatives he's told you about yourself (you're stupid, ugly, a bitch). Just by being with someone who treats you badly, you send yourself the message you don't deserve better. So, do you deserve happiness? Will anyone else ever want you, even as a friend?

The sooner you surround yourself with people who appreciate you, treat yourself well, actively challenge the negative beliefs you've internalized about yourself and remind yourself repeatedly of your new mantra—"*He's the asshole, not me*"—the sooner you can overcome this obstacle.

Feelings of responsibility for him. Despite the fact that he has controlled you, lied to you, cheated on you and/or taken advantage of you financially, sexually and emotionally, you worry if he'll be all right. Many would hang the all-purpose catchword "codependence" on this tendency. To the extent that it means you revolve your life and decisions around someone else's happiness and comfort, the term is accurate.

As improbable and wimpy as this tendency sounds, we hear it a lot. You need to prepare yourself for this possibility. Losing you will probably hurt him, but people live through that. Your leaving is a natural consequence of his behavior—not a cruel, unfeeling act on your part. He's a big boy. He can take care of himself (despite what he might have shown you in the relationship). If not, he's very likely to quickly find someone else to take care of him.

Guilt. A by-product of hyper-responsibility is guilt. You might feel you are doing something bad to him and deserve to suffer. Even if you know this is irrational, that doesn't stop it. Keeping in mind that most people feel guilty not because of what they've done, but because they are good at feeling guilty can help put it in perspective somewhat. Separating the experience of the pain of guilt from the need to atone for it (by going back, not getting your fair share in a divorce, continuing to see him after you've broken up) is crucial. If you can't make the guilt go away, do your best to not let it control your actions. The guilt will fade on its own, or you can get professional help to reduce it. On the other hand, the misery resulting from staying with him will go on and on.

Inertia. As bad as a situation is, on a day-to-day basis it is easier to stay in it than to end it. You are in a pattern (rut) that has its own momentum and is self-sustaining. It takes effort, determination and the ability to surmount his attempts to make you stay to change things. If you are already depressed, burned out and worn down, the task can seem impossible.

Keep your eyes on the prize. Put one foot in front of the other. Do what you can today, and worry about tomorrow *tomorrow*. (Have we left out any clichés?) Seriously, you need to anticipate this obstacle, discipline yourself to fight it daily, and build in rewards and encouragement for yourself along the way.

All the barriers to leaving are based on patterns of interaction that have been established over a long period of time. These very

patterns often define your relationship. You adopt roles—caretaker, dependent, rescuer—that are as hard to give up (often because you learned them in your family of origin first) as they are, ultimately, unrewarding. Still, you are good at the role and aren't sure you can effectively fill another one.

Giving relatively short shrift to the ways of handling the various obstacles to getting out is not meant to minimize their strength or to oversimplify the ways to effectively overcome them. Giving them their due probably entails writing another book. What we hope to have accomplished here is to increase your awareness of the pitfalls that are lurking as you try to leave, because once you are aware you can muster your coping resources to fight them. The suggestions made are merely jumping-off points to give you ideas as to how to begin attacking these obstacles as they present them-selves. Therapy, divorce support groups, and friends and family can help lighten your burden in dealing with any or all of these.

How to Get Out

Many of us got our first exposure to relationships vicariously through books, movies and music. Popular music has a particularly strong impact since in a lot of our early romantic experiences (dances, parties in someone's rec room), music is playing. Pop music certainly changes from generation to generation, but there are a lot of consistent themes. Unfortunately, most of those give us unrealistic ideas of what relationships are like. People fall in love at first sight. Boys are closet romantics waiting for the right girl to come along. Love is all that matters, and you'll know it when you feel it. What may be a more realistic expression of boy meets girl are the popular songs about breaking up. For instance, the 1960s and early '70s featured such titles as "Hit the Road,

Jack," "Just Walk Away, Renee," "(Keep on Walking) Don't Look Back" and "(If You Gotta Go, You Better) Go Now."

Sure, these ideas are simple and superficial—but keeping it simple is key to getting out and staying out. Walk away; don't look back; go when you're ready; and let him know that it's over—these are keys to getting this task done right.

The first thing you want to do is to look at the things that keep you stuck. See which ones are keys for you, and do whatever work you need to—awareness, support networks, therapy—to break free of those hindrances.

Even if you can't or don't know how to really resolve all the issues, making sure you find the easiest and most permanent way to get out can help compensate, and get you out in spite of yourself.

You don't have to "talk it out" first. Somehow, many women are saddled with the unhelpful belief that they have to clear the air, be direct and open about their intentions, and let their partners know exactly why it is they are leaving. This is often not only unnecessary, but also a very bad idea. Once he knows what you can no longer tolerate, he can solemnly promise to change it. Giving him your reasons for leaving implies that if those reasons are flawed, and he can "prove" that to you, you should stay.

This is not to say that you have to skulk out under cover of darkness, but if you do want to let him know why it's ending, make it a statement by you and not a discussion. If he doesn't know by now why you're leaving, he is really clueless anyway.

On the other hand, some women do need to leave fairly surreptitiously. Letting him know what is coming and when gives him the opportunity to sabotage it (physically, financially, legally). You know the man you are with. Will he "play fair" with the information you give him? If not, don't give it. Remember, he's had plenty of chances to make it better and didn't.

He doesn't need to "cosign" on your decision. Women tell us

that another problem with having an in-depth discussion once your mind is made up is that one or both of you might assume you have to both *agree* it's a good idea to end it. Hogwash. You may not realize you are sabotaging yourself by explaining to him all your reasons for leaving. If he refuses to agree or accept them as valid, that could immobilize you. If he doesn't agree with your assessment of the relationship, that's fine. Don't argue. Just leave, and let him believe it's your fault.

Look for "windows of opportunity." Even after your mind is made up, you can wait until the situation somehow makes it easier for you to go. You might need to see one more example of what you can't stand to give you the strength to leave. Getting settled in a job, expanding your support system and just getting used to the idea of being apart from him can make you feel strong as well. Perhaps you will need to wait for some of those factors to kick in before you're ready.

Other situations require different kinds of "windows." Some women wait until he goes out of town or leaves for work. Others wait for his raise to come through so child support will be adequate. Some women wait until they are involved with someone else before they leave. While we don't endorse this strategy or suggest you do this, neither do we condemn it. You may be the type of person who needs "a soft place to land" when you jump out of a relationship. Conventional wisdom (and many therapists) says quick, "rebound" relationships are always a bad idea. That's just not true. Sometimes they are, but we've also seen women stay happily in long-term relationships with the men they leave their partners for.

Find out what your rights are and what you can expect when you leave. Threats like "You'll never see a dime from me" and "I'll prove you're an unfit mother and take the kids" are the rule rather than the exception in breakups involving married or cohabitating couples. Talk to an attorney. See what you can expect in terms of

alimony, child support, custody and visitation. This may seem like obvious advice, but many women don't do it and are cowered by the idle threats of their partners. Knowing what to expect allows you to both prepare for it and to blow off attempts to manipulate you that are really just so much hot air.

We don't pretend to have exhausted all the aspects of "doing it the easy way" with what we've just discussed. Our intent was to let you know that you get no points for doing it the "right way." If you play fair, do what you "should," and remain unfailingly open, honest and direct, you are counting on his either doing the same or not taking advantage of you if he doesn't. Wake up! We're talking about lying, cheating, unreasonable men here. Manipulating, taking advantage, being selfish and not playing by the rules are what they are about. You don't have to compromise your morals—just be rational and realistic (and kind to yourself). For a lot of these guys, the longer they talk you into staying, drag out a divorce or do what they can to make life miserable for you after you've split up, the greater they believe the chances are that you'll return. Often, they are correct. So make leaving as easy on yourself as you can. And don't go back.

Don't Do It Twice

Changing your mind after you've left, going back and then realizing all over again that you need to leave becomes a living nightmare. Yet this is a very common occurrence—so much so that we warn our clients who are in this situation to beware of the temptation and its consequences. There are a few common reasons that account for the majority of the situations in which this (leaving, going back and trying to leave again) happens:

Mixed feelings. Very few women are able to make a decision to leave a relationship without having mixed feelings. Their

ambivalence becomes strongest at the points where a decision is made and where it is carried out. Ambivalence is, basically, an internal debate. One side points out the advantages of staying, the other of leaving. As emotional as this internal debate can be, it remains intellectual and hypothetical until one side "wins" and, in this case, you end the relationship.

Now the issues debated become very real. The part of you that lost the debate and wants to stay becomes stronger. The consequences of your decision loom larger, and the temptation to renege and stay with him is tremendous.

This self-doubt and mental back-and-forth is common to any situation in which a tough decision is being made. The hard part is keeping it in perspective. Remember, had you decided to stay with him, your doubts would be pushing you in the direction of leaving. Whichever decision you make, you are very likely to suffer pangs of remorse. Try to keep some emotional distance from this discomfort and see it for what it is—a natural period of transitional discomfort that *will* pass. If you act to relieve that discomfort and reconcile, you will still feel emotional pain, only now it will be despondency about being back in a bad relationship.

Pressure to return. As we have said before, now is when he will pull out all the stops. If he knows you are guilt prone, he will play on that. If he believes he can intimidate you, that will be his plan. Cutting off money, putting the kids in the middle, anything to get you to cry "uncle" and take him back will be fair game. This is a situation in which many men excel. Should you return under these circumstances, it will certainly be for the wrong reasons.

Emotional distress. You will hurt emotionally for a variety of reasons, and reuniting will end the immediate pain—but only briefly. Soon the misery you have been suffering for years will all come back to you—but you are so used to that that it will seem easier to cope with than the new challenges you face without him.

Whenever a client of ours leaves a toxic partner, we say, "If you decide to reconcile, talk to me first. I won't put you down or abandon you, and I will support your decision because you ultimately know what's best for you; but I would like to remind you of why you left and what to expect if you return to the relationship."

That sounds like a reasonable request, but some women who go back don't honor it. A part of them knows it's a bad idea, but another part just wants the discomfort of indecision, being pressured and feeling guilty to end. Usually, the worst that happens is they wind up back where they started (but also feeling stupid about having spent so much time, energy and emotion, only to accomplish nothing). Other times, things go downhill fast.

Anne was sure she was doing the right thing when she left Billy. Her husband was verbally abusive, emotionally unsupportive and left her with all the work of caring for the kids (in addition to her working more hours). His own family members kept telling her he was an asshole. In fact, on the eve of their wedding, his sister called Anne and counseled her to call it off.

When she told Billy she wanted out, he was distraught. He promised to stop drinking and treat her better. But she held firm. Surprisingly, he respected her decision. He moved out, paid child support, visited the kids and was very civil to her. He began going to Alcoholics Anonymous and really seemed to turn himself around. He "made amends" to her for all he had done to destroy their relationship. He opened up and shared his feelings with her. She even saw him cry for the first time.

Within a month, she took him back. Within three more, she discovered she was pregnant. Within a year, it was worse than it had ever been. When the youngest child turned two, she told him again she wanted out. He responded quite differently. He refused to go. He became more verbally abusive with her and the two older

children. He routinely threatened her with physical violence and hit
her on several occasions, including in front of the children. At its
worst point, he pulled a gun on her when she was packing to leave.

Anne finally got out, after another year, lots of abuse and a
restraining order against him that he usually obeyed (he went to jail
twice when he didn't). She wound up with no money, no house
and certainly no one with whom to share parenting duties.

While this is an extreme case, it is not an unusual one. When a
guy decides to make it hell for you to leave, he can. Anne was
lucky enough to get away smoothly the first time. Her luck ran out
the second time. More often, it is hell both times.

Aside from the suggestions already made (stick to your guns,
use family and friends for support, expect to be uncomfortable for
a while, do it the easy way), there are two additional pieces of
advice to avoid being pulled back in, only to have to get out
again:

Cut off as much contact as possible. If he were a nice guy, perhaps you could remain friendly. But you have already established
that he is *not* a nice guy. You have probably never really been
friends, because you wouldn't freely choose as a friend someone
with the qualities he's shown you. Any contact with him keeps you
connected. Even if you are cussing him out and reminding him of
what a dog he is, you are connecting with him and experiencing
some kind of emotion. This is dangerous in two ways: (1) he can
interpret even your most negative statements as evidence there is
still hope (and keep pestering you), and (2) you are continuing to
relate to him instead of putting him out of your life and moving on.

If there are no children, we unequivocally recommend a policy
of no contact whatsoever. If he calls, hang up. If he comes over, tell
him (through a closed door) to leave. If he doesn't go or returns a
second time, call the police. This may sound extreme, but he needs

to get a clear message: "I'm done with you. Really."

It is trickier if you have children. By all means be civil, don't bad-mouth him to them, and talk about issues related to their well-being, financial matters, and the logistics of visitation. Do not rehash relationship issues, chat about your personal lives or allow conversations about topics other than those just listed.

Any contact makes you vulnerable. Many women say that they have trouble being "mean" and doing what is suggested here. You are not being mean; you are being firm and clear. He won't understand anything else and will certainly misconstrue your being nice as his still having a chance.

If you really think he's changed, give it a lot of time before you reconcile. If the change is real, it will last, as will your feelings for each other. A year is reasonable, and six months is probably too little. While that time is passing, get on with your life and have as little contact with him as you can manage. He will argue that you won't know if he's changed if you don't spend time with him. Perhaps that's true, but even if it is, going back is a risky decision. Staying away from him is no great loss to you. If there are children involved, there is a loss to them, but you will see changes he makes through how he deals with them (time devoted to them, financial support, how he interacts with them). If he can demonstrate, consistently, for a year or more that he's very different with them, you can then spend some time with him to see if he can be different with you.

Having as little contact as possible and making him prove himself several times over are two good ways to avoid going through this whole process twice. That is an experience well worth avoiding.

Coping with (and Maybe Changing) Them

11

The Direct Approach (and Why It Usually Fails)

*The more things change, the more
they remain the same.*

—French proverb

Prepare yourself now to embark on the unenviable task of coping with a toxic man. The next several chapters will operate from two assumptions: (1) you have determined that the guy you're with meets our criteria for men to avoid, and (2) you have decided to stay anyway. Many women make the latter choice, and we by no means wish to imply it's a bad one. As un-Hollywood as it sounds, there is a lot more to real-life relationships than love, or even getting along well.

Further, there is a huge difference between being hopelessly *trapped* in a dead-end relationship with a toxic man and *choosing* to stay in the relationship after a careful consideration of your situation. You

can always choose to leave if new information becomes available. Making the decision to stay can itself be empowering. You can now move on and focus your energies on yourself, improving your own sense of well-being in the relationship and diminishing the distress you feel because of your partner's manipulations.

As you read the chapters to follow, please keep in mind the first assumption. We are not discussing how to deal with reasonable, mature, straightforward guys. We are suggesting ways to deal with unreasonable, immature and deceptive men. Indirect, manipulative, surreptitious methods are not the preferred choices for dealing with intimate partners. But those are what it often takes to hold your own with an asshole.

Still, direct and reasonable approaches are not necessarily doomed to failure with these guys, particularly if you haven't tried them already or haven't done them well. Assertiveness, negotiation and limit setting are three ways to approach difficult partners. In two of those three, assertiveness and limit setting, you don't need his cooperation or participation to try them out. And even difficult men will negotiate if they feel they have something to gain (or lose). Look on these approaches as experiments. If they work, great. If not, on to other strategies.

Assertiveness

For many years now, women have been learning they need to be more assertive. And they are. Standing up for yourself and speaking your mind frankly beats being wimpy and submissive. However, when dealing with the men described in this book, it doesn't always work as advertised.

Assertiveness comes in three forms: asking for what you want, saying no to what you don't and letting him know how it makes

you feel when he does certain things. All three are basically ways to say, "Here's what makes me happy and comfortable, or unhappy and uncomfortable." It by no means assures he will do what you wish, but it gives him the opportunity to by letting him know clearly where you stand. If he doesn't respond positively, it means either that it is very important to him to do things his way, and/or you and the relationship are not priorities. Regardless, by being direct in this way, at least you find out where you stand.

Asking for what you want. This aspect of assertiveness is as simple as it sounds. Whether it is as basic as what you want for dinner or where you want to go on vacation, or as meaningful as what you need emotionally in a relationship, you assert yourself by clearly stating it. No beating around the bush. No trying to spare his feelings. No playing it safe so you don't get hurt by rejection.

Keep it simple and don't overelaborate. As we'll discuss later, the more you explain yourself, the more power you give him (by sounding apologetic for having needs or as if you have to have a good reason to have feelings). Examples that would be appropriate in some of the situations we have previously described would be:

"I want you to consult me more about decisions."

"I want you to get a full-time job rather than trying to start another business."

"I want you to be home with me and the kids more, and out with your friends less."

Those statements almost sound stupid, they are so obvious. Yet they often go unsaid. Maybe you don't want to admit it's as bad as it is, or don't want to hear him say no or make lame excuses.

There's not much else to say about this. If you haven't told him what you want, for whatever reasons, it's certainly worth a try. Do it clearly, succinctly and without a lot of explanation. The worst

that can happen is that your fears will be confirmed (that he doesn't care what you want, can't or won't change, or will agree with what you say and do what he wants anyway).

Saying no. This, too, is ridiculously simple—in concept at least.

Him: "I want to quit my job, cash in our retirement accounts and buy a bar."

You: "No."

Him: "I'll handle all the money and decide how to budget it."

You: "No."

Him: "You don't know what the hell you're talking about. We'll do it my way."

You: "No."

Don't explain. Don't justify. Don't capitulate in the name of marital peace. Don't think you're only "allowed" to say no when you have good reasons to (or ones he can accept). You are just plain allowed.

Remember, he may well not respect your words or your wishes. You can say no, and he's free to do whatever he wants regardless. But at least you and he will both be clear as to where you stand on the issue. You won't have regrets later about not sticking up for yourself, and he can't make the excuse that he thought you wanted what he did, too.

Speaking up when you like or dislike something. Some women believe being in love means reading each other's minds. Others are afraid to hurt their partner's feelings by being honest about their own. Whatever your personal excuse is for not expressing your feelings, you can't afford it when you are involved with someone who takes advantage of you or isn't sensitive to your feelings.

The key to this type of assertiveness is taking responsibility for how you feel. It's not, "You shouldn't be out with your friends every night. It's not right" or even, "You really piss me off when you go

out every night after work." Being assertive and taking responsibility means saying, "When you're out every night, I feel hurt and angry because it says to me that I'm not important to you."

That might sound wimpy, but it isn't. You're letting him know how you feel and why. You're not debating whether what he's doing is right or wrong, you're just making it crystal clear to him how you feel when he does it. He can argue with your opinions ("You shouldn't do that. It's not right.") or your perceptions ("You don't care anymore."), but not your feelings. If you hurt, or you're angry or sad, you are the one who knows; you are the expert. He might not care, but if you clearly let him know, you give him the opportunity to discontinue doing what hurts you. If he's an asshole, he'll likely not take advantage of that opportunity, but at least you will know it was deliberate and not inadvertent.

Negotiating

When couples come in for marital counseling, unless there is an immediate crisis (like an affair) or serious problems with one of the individuals (habitual lying, alcoholism), a lot of what they learn is how to negotiate with one another. Negotiating is a skill all couples should have but most don't. It does take two to negotiate effectively, so if he won't, it won't work. Just because a guy is an asshole doesn't mean he's incapable of trying in good faith to work things out. It's not really likely, but it's possible.

Negotiation is a process couples go through to resolve differences in a way that allows both partners to walk away feeling satisfied with the outcome. This means it is not a win/lose situation in which one person convinces the other his or her position is correct. Negotiating is a process that involves going through a series of steps to reach your desired outcome. Here are those steps:

1. **Acknowledge there is a problem and define it.** Much like the decision-making process discussed earlier, negotiation has to begin with a clarification of what is being negotiated. Usually, one of you has a problem and that person needs to articulate it. For example, you might have a problem with your husband's using physical discipline with the children. Telling him that is the first step.

2. **State your positions on the problem.** You might say, "I think you hit the kids too often and too hard, and they are becoming afraid of you." He might reply, "There needs to be consequences when they act up. You're too easy on them. Talking doesn't bother them. A good smack every once in a while gets their attention."

Sometimes, the negotiation ends here. If one of you doesn't feel strongly about the subject or just didn't know how the other felt, this is the last step necessary. For instance, the man in our example could have responded, "I didn't know you felt that way. Physical punishment is all my parents ever used, and I turned out okay. But I'm willing to try other methods." This is more likely to happen on less significant issues, but it does happen.

Another scenario in which this can be the last step needed is when your positions are not too far apart. If the wife in our ex-ample is willing to accept some corporal punishment of the chil-dren and the husband is amenable to backing off some, that would be all it takes.

3. **Think about what steps each of you is willing to take toward the other's position.** If the problem isn't resolved at step two, be sure you understand the other person's position, and think about what movement toward his position you are willing to take (without feeling you're doing something you don't want to). He, of course, needs to do the same. Open up a dialogue along these lines, and see what you come up with. In our example, the wife could offer, "I would be willing to be more strict and enforce more

consequences if you will back off on physical punishment."

Don't get defensive if your partner doesn't like or accept your offer. You are both just trying out ideas on each other. If one doesn't sit well with the other person, move on. Try another. If this step works well, there is a gradual give-and-take that winds up with a mutually satisfactory solution.

Something that often happens to sabotage this process at both steps two and three is that one person holds fast to his or her position and tries to badger the other into caving in to it. State your position clearly and briefly, don't keep defending it or restating it, and look for ways to move closer to his that you can live with (and expect the same from him).

4. **Brainstorm.** If you haven't reached a resolution by this time, turn to brainstorming. Brainstorming is a process during which you both try to think of all the possible ways to resolve your disagreement. The rules are: quantity not quality (don't censor yourself—even "stupid" ideas could lead to workable ones), no discussion or judgment of individual ideas during the process (this stifles creativity and leads to arguments) and be as creative as possible.

After the ideas are on the table, begin to sift through them by each picking out the ones you think have promise (or combinations of two or more ideas), and see if your lists overlap. Again, don't wed yourself to the ideas you came up with. Keep your mind open.

5. **Quid pro quo.** *Quid pro quo* means "this for that" (more or less). If the first four steps haven't brought you to a solution, consider this alternative. One of you might be prepared to "give in," willingly, on the issue in question in return for getting something in another area. For instance, in our example, the husband might be willing to cut way back on physical punishment if the wife would get baby-sitters more often so the two of them could go out. The two issues involved need not be related in any way, as long as no one is feeling cheated or "beaten."

6. **Try it out, and monitor how it works.** If any of the preceding steps yields a workable solution, you still have to decide when you'll start doing it. As obvious as this seems, misunderstandings regarding whether the new program starts right away and all at once or is phased in over a few weeks can undermine the whole process. Much less obvious is the need to sit down at a predetermined time and discuss how the new plan is working out. One of you might think everything is now hunky-dory, while the other is teeming with frustration. The new plan is an experiment; make sure it is seen as a successful one by both of you.

Of course, this process won't always work. Areas in which there are strong and legitimate differences in values and priorities can be tough nuts to crack. More often, the process fails because it isn't done well (a therapist could help here) or one person isn't really trying (guess who?).

Setting Limits (and Sticking to Them)

Limit setting is very different from assertiveness. When you assert yourself, you let the other person know how you feel and think. You give him the opportunity to change what he's doing to make you happier or more comfortable. But you are not aggressively attempting to control his behavior.

You are when you set limits. You are saying, "You need to do A or else I will do B." This is the way you would deal with a teenager, or even a child. By resorting to limit setting, you are admitting to yourself that you cannot effectively deal with him on an adult-to-adult basis. Either he is incapable of rational discussion and negotiation, or he cannot be trusted to keep his end of a bargain (unless he faces consequences if he doesn't). It is sad to have to admit this to yourself about a partner. However, it is

counterproductive to ignore the obvious and pretend you're dealing with a reasonable, caring, mature person if you're not.

You need to pick your battles carefully when setting limits. If you try to control too many things, you end up diluting your influence and controlling none. Think of one or two behaviors or habits of his that are intolerable for you, and leave the rest alone. The issues need to be both important and specific (so you both know if he's changing or not)—physical or verbal abuse of you or the kids, intimate contact with other women, the amount of time he spends away from home, how he spends money. The list of possible subjects is endless, but you get the idea.

As far as actually setting the limits, approach him when you are both fairly calm and rational. Don't give him an ultimatum during the course of a fight or when you've just caught him doing something. Wait until you are relatively less upset. Then lay it out for him very directly. "If you (call me names in front of the children, get caught in another lie about where you are or what you are doing, come home late and drunk), I will . . ." The tricky part is what you will do in response. Don't threaten to end the relationship unless you are absolutely prepared to. Other consequences, however, are not as strong or meaningful, so you need to choose them carefully. Make sure you pick one that matters to him (separating the finances, not going out with him socially). If what you choose should matter to him but doesn't, your limit setting will obviously be ineffective. We generally don't recommend withholding sex or conversation as consequences. On the other hand, not wanting to have sex, conversation or much contact with him is natural when he is acting badly.

Why Direct Approaches Don't Work: They Don't Play by the Rules

Most of what you read about in self-help books are direct, straightforward ways to handle relationships, much like the few we just covered briefly. A wide variety of direct methods are tried and true—as long as the other person is, to some degree at least, open, direct and motivated, and cares about your experience of the relationship. Not the profiles of the men described in this book.

Using a direct approach with someone who cares about you and the relationship gives him a blueprint for how to make you happy and satisfied. Using it with a guy who is looking to control you, get away with things or just meet his own needs involves giving him a blueprint for how to upset, manipulate and control you.

With a reasonable guy, letting him know how you feel and what matters to you is like letting a bridge partner know what cards you hold. You are on the same team, and that knowledge can only help you both. With toxic men, being open and direct is like showing your cards to an opponent in a poker game before you bet. You are adversaries, and the information can help him but hurt you. So be careful in trying direct strategies like assertiveness with these men. Not only could it not help, but it could also make things considerably worse for you.

To reiterate conditions under which direct strategies do have a chance of working:

- If he is afraid of losing you and values (or at least needs) the relationship.
- If what you are doing is truly different from what you have been trying all along.
- If you are consistent in applying the strategies and following through on any consequences.
- If you are as calm and unperturbed as possible when you

deliver them (an emotional response is seen as a temporary state of mind or a ploy to win an argument).

Even with all these conditions in place, direct strategies are likely to fail or only to work for a short while (fear of losing you wears off, and his old habits are strong). Still, you have little to lose by trying them as long as you see them as experiments, not panaceas, and are prepared for the possibility they will backfire on you. When we talk about "experiments" and being "prepared," we assume that you realize other, less direct methods are available, and are willing and able to use them. Let's briefly look at the rationale for some of those less direct methods now.

12 Making Your Own Rules

If you want good service, serve yourself.

—Spanish proverb

ear Abby, John Gray, therapists and other personal-advice gurus prescribe the guidelines discussed in the previous chapter all the time: Be open and honest. Play by the rules of "good" communication. Try to work things out together. But if your partner is unreasonable and refuses to listen or won't even acknowledge there is a problem, playing by the rules gets you nowhere. Or under water. Consider the following Japanese folktale:

> A farmer working in the rice fields high above a coastal village saw a tidal wave rapidly approaching. The villagers could not have heard her had she yelled to them, nor did she have time to run to the village to warn them. All the sensible, reasonable options would not work. What could she do? She

set the rice on fire. When the villagers rushed to save the vital crop, they were spared certain death from the tidal wave.

By questioning her own rules and assumptions about appropriate things to do, by breaking free of traditional thinking, the farmer saved the villagers. Questioning rules and defying conventional wisdom are often what it takes to save yourself from a problematic man. Consider these rather strange strategies:

- If he is a Mr. Know-It-All and constantly criticizes your cooking, don't run out and enroll in chef's school. Deliberately burn the toast and undercook the pasta, then agree with the criticism, apologize and question whether you should cook given your impaired abilities.
- If he is a Chameleon or Fence Sitter and chronically whines, don't be a Pollyanna striving in vain to get him to see the brighter side of life or the relationship. Encourage him to complain even more and add some gloom and doom of your own.
- If he is a Boss and insanely jealous, don't get angry, defensive or secretive. Provide a ridiculously detailed diary every day and cheerfully offer to fill in blanks or answer any questions.

Using the seminal ideas of John Weakland and others at the famed Mental Research Institute, as well as those of Steve de Shazer and his colleagues, the next several chapters will explore how these seemingly illogical and ridiculous tactics can help you live more comfortably with a difficult man and even promote possibilities for change.

Breaking the Rules

Experience tells us that should we encounter a large, fast-moving gray-hued animal with thick, pounding legs, big floppy

ears, a long trunk, tusks, and emitting a loud trumpeting sound, we'd best move aside and let it pass. It is probably an elephant. Here, experience has high predictive value.

However, what if our experience tells us that when we encounter *this* type of guy, with *this* problem, we apply *this* strategy? The results by no means may be as certain. Unfortunately, it is frequently true that despite the best intentions, experience leads us to hold on to a method even though the result is an intimate relationship with a brick wall. Experience, then, is a two-edged sword. What one gains in conviction may be at the price of flexibility.

One surefire way to get bogged down in dealing with a difficult guy is by thinking you are trying a variety of solutions when you are really just doing slight variations on the same theme. Usually the theme is one of patience, understanding or honest communication.

Consider the puzzle depicted in figure 12.1. Connect the nine dots in figure 12.1, using only four straight lines and without taking your pencil off the paper. If you have not seen this puzzle, please take a few minutes to try to solve it.

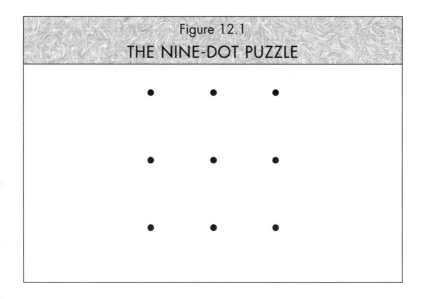

Figure 12.1
THE NINE-DOT PUZZLE

Now look at figure 12.2, which shows the solution. Few people think of extending the straight lines beyond the dots, even though nothing in the instructions prohibits it. Most people, in effect, superimpose an imaginary square on the dots, which precludes resolution. By acting on the erroneous assumption that the lines cannot extend beyond the dots, you guarantee two things: frustration and failure. Those are the identical outcomes women face when they are stuck in relationships with difficult men. By acting on the erroneous assumption that making him aware of your discomfort, or your understanding and patience, will encourage him to change, you will face only further distress.

After just one try, you probably felt that the solution to the puzzle was impossible. Even so, you likely continued to apply the same solution over and over again, just as you do when approaching problems with an unreasonable partner. But your solutions based in the restrictions of the imaginary square were doomed to failure. Being freed from the constraints of the imaginary square shifts our view of the nine-dot puzzle and makes it immediately obvious to solve. New solutions occur as we discard the blinders of current rules.

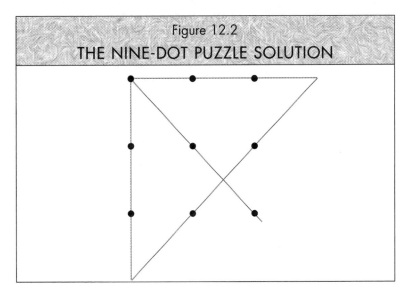

Figure 12.2
THE NINE-DOT PUZZLE SOLUTION

A fresh perspective is needed to break the rules that our culture and your partner have established for you to follow in resolving problems. Because of his personality, he requires a different mindset, and perhaps even extraordinary measures that sometimes look like guerrilla tactics.

Here is an example of the old pattern:

Problem (jerk)—Rules (honesty, patience, understanding, self-blame)—Limited, restricted solutions—Worse problem (bigger jerk, and you feel worse)

The new pattern will be:

Problem (jerk)—Flexibility of options—New, effective solutions—Problem resolved (he may or may not change, but you feel great)

Before we fully describe these fresh new solutions in the chapters that follow, we will first give you a crash course in what systems thinking means. This will help explain how you can make real changes, even without his active cooperation. We also will discuss why direct communication is not always best.

Systems Thinking: It Only Takes You

In 1334, history tells us, the Duchess of Tyrol encircled the castle of a neighboring province. She knew that the fortress, situated on a steep rock, was impregnable to direct attack and would only yield to a long siege. In time, the situation of the defenders became critical: They were down to their last ox and bag of barley. The duchess's situation was also pressing: Her troops were getting unruly, there seemed no end to the siege in sight and she had urgent military business elsewhere. At this point, the commandant of the castle had the last ox slaughtered, filled its carcass with the remaining barley and ordered it thrown down the steep cliff in

front of the enemy camp. Upon receiving the scornful message, the discouraged duchess abandoned the siege.

This example illustrates the type of strategies that are most appropriate when dealing with toxic men. These methods seem crazy at first pass, but on further reflection, make total sense and are very effective. The ensuing chapters will examine how common sense and logical behavior often fail, while actions as illogical and unreasonable as those taken by the defenders of the castle succeed. When you switch the rules, things can change. Welcome to the surprising world of systems thinking.

Systems thinking represents a radical departure from many of the prevailing ways of describing people, problems and change. It offers a refreshing way to observe human behavior—shifting the focus from what goes on inside a person to what takes place between people, the study of relationships. Systems thinking emphasizes what people do and say to each other, their interaction, and how that interaction, in turn, influences each individual's well-being.

When two individuals come together in a relationship, something is created that is different from, larger and more complex than those two individuals apart—a system. The most important feature of such a relationship is communication. Relationships are established, maintained and changed by communication. As relationships endure, communication falls into patterns over time. As you well know, sometimes those patterns begin creating difficulties, and new patterns are needed.

Communication occurs at different levels, even though most of us focus our attention on only one—the content, or the literal meaning of the words. More important, but less obvious, is the *demand level*. It indicates how the sender of the message is attempting to influence the receiver. "My back itches" may mean "Scratch my back." "I had a rough day" may mean "Leave me alone," "I need

your support" or "Fix me a drink." Even "I love you" can be an implicit demand. It may mean "Tell me that you love me." Kurt Vonnegut captures the subtle demand of "I love you" in this passage from his novel *Slapstick*.

> "Eliza . . ." I said, "*so many of the books I've read to you said that love was the most important thing of all. Maybe I should tell you that I love you now.*"
>
> "*Go ahead,*" she said.
>
> "*I love you, Eliza,*" I said.
>
> *She thought about it. "No," she said at last, "I don't like it."*
>
> "*Why not?*" I said.
>
> "*It's as though you were pointing a gun at my head,*" she said. . . ."*What else can I say, or anybody say, but 'I love you, too'?*"

The implicit demand in communication suggests that when we talk to people, we are trying to influence them, indirectly, to do what we want them to do. This sounds like manipulation because it is, at least to some degree. But it's okay. Influence is unavoidable in communication; it is natural to how we talk. When we communicate, one item on our agendas is to get our needs met or our points across. Both direct and subtle ways occur routinely.

Subtle attempts to influence are largely automatic and occur outside of awareness. As a result, we often address the most important parts of our lives, our relationships, in an extremely haphazard fashion. By becoming aware of the influence implicit in communication, we can deliberately use it to improve our relationships. Many of the strategies we suggest use the demand level in a conscious, planned (but still subtle) manner to cope with a Prince of Darkness.

In a system, all members are *mutually dependent*. What one

person does depends on what the other person does. As discussed in chapter 1, a widely held belief is that in order for a relationship to change, both individuals have to actively participate in changing it. We disagree. In a relationship system, a noticeable change by one person can set in motion a change in the whole system—that is, the couple. A couple is like a mobile: When one piece of the mobile ripples, it affects the entire mobile.

Once you recognize your partner's dependence upon you, you can change your behavior, and influence him and the relationship in a self-enhancing manner. The good news is that regardless of how he became an asshole or how long he's been one, if you change your behavior noticeably and consistently, his reactions will change. His active cooperation is not required. Viewing behavior itself as a powerful means of communication increases your options when verbal methods are not working. If you have tried to fix your relationship by talking ad nauseam, then behavioral options may provide a more effective solution.

A systems view enables us to offer very explicit suggestions to women who want to work on coping with problematic men, and perhaps on changing their relationships—especially their experience of distress and self-blame. A lot of women feel hopeless and powerless because their partners don't want to come in for help. The idea that one person can initiate meaningful change in a relationship, which comes from systems thinking, helps them to feel stronger and more hopeful. Many times a small adjustment, strategically employed, is all that is needed for some much-needed relief and a more emotionally endurable situation.

Systems thinking highlights your ability to influence patterns that are destructive to you. It should not be interpreted to mean that you have equal power over, or are responsible for, his problems. The point of this book is that you are not equally responsible if you are involved with a jerk. Likewise, if you are

in a relationship with a guy who abuses you or drinks heavily, you do have influence, but you do not have responsibility for the drinking or violence. There is a distinction between influence and responsibility, and also between actually doing the serious problem behavior (e.g., alcoholism, violence) and engaging in the problem pattern. The ultimate responsibility for behavior lies with the individual. This is an important qualification because women sometimes infer that they are to blame for a spouse's alcoholism, battering or other seriously problematic behavior. They are not.

Two central implications emerge from systems thinking:

- You, as one motivated person using effective strategies, can turn your experience of the relationship around, even without the active participation of the other person.
- You can use both direct and subtle methods of influence, as well as verbal and nonverbal means, for changing your experience of distressing situations, and perhaps the situation itself.

The Self-Abuser

The notion that one person can produce meaningful change in a relationship is not part of conventional wisdom. Nor is the implication that change can happen without the knowledge or cooperation of one member of the couple. To pull together these unconventional ideas, let's look at the simple example of a woman trying to get her health-ignoring man to stop smoking. While this example is obviously not as complex or emotionally distressing as others we describe, it does offer a good illustration of the ideas presented in this chapter.

Jean was very worried about her husband, Mark, who had just been advised by his doctor to stop smoking. After tiring of Mark's

all-talk-and-no-action approach, Jean began an intense antismoking campaign. She regularly spoke about the benefits of stopping and the health consequences for everyone in the house. She left brochures from smoke-ending programs around as well as articles addressing the dangers of smoking.

Of course, Mark already knew about the health hazards of smoking; awareness was not the problem. Jean, however, didn't give up, and took every opportunity to press the issue. She stopped buying cigarettes at the store for him. Her persistent barrage began to get on Mark's nerves. They began fighting regularly, and Mark got more and more defensive about his smoking. Unfortunately, Mark was smoking even more than before.

Hopefully, the nine-dot puzzle aspects of Jean's solutions are obvious. Jean's solutions of direct confrontation, reasoning and education only made it more likely for Mark not to quit smoking. As she intensified her efforts, it escalated the smoking issue into the realm of a power struggle. Smoking became a symbol of his independence, a badge of his integrity. This struggle will prevent even nice guys from changing. The macho stuff kicks into overdrive and has a life of its own.

Jean needed to change her approach and break out of the imaginary square surrounding her ineffective methods. She required something far less direct and seemingly illogical. Jean found what she needed in a tactic we call **invite what you dread**. Jean began by apologizing for harassing Mark, telling him both verbally and nonverbally that quitting was entirely up to him, and that it was okay with her if he didn't.

Here's where it gets a little wacky: Jean then actually encouraged Mark's smoking and in effect, invited what she dreaded. She picked up a pack of cigarettes even when he didn't ask, picked up two packs when he asked for one, brought an ashtray or his

cigarettes into the room when he left them in another room, asked for smoking sections at restaurants without waiting for Mark to ask and so on. Jean made it easier for Mark to smoke, not harder. She became the farmer setting the rice fields on fire, the commandant throwing the last ox over the castle wall.

Nothing much happened for a while, except that they were no longer arguing about Mark's smoking and consequently started getting along better. Several weeks later, after Jean had purchased another extra pack of cigarettes for Mark, he thanked her but asked her not to buy any more cigarettes because he was thinking about quitting. Jean resisted the temptation to become a cheerleader. A few weeks later, to Jean's utter delight, Mark enrolled in a smoking-cessation class at a local hospital and successfully stopped smoking.

A noticeable and consistent change in Jean's behavior paved the road for a change in Mark's smoking. Jean exited the freeway to failure built by her direct, "reasonable" approaches and instead took the on-ramp to avenues that encouraged the very behavior she wanted to stop. Through indirect and behavioral methods, Jean undercut the power and control aspects of the smoking problem and created the conditions for Mark to stop ignoring his smoking.

While this example sounds too good to be true, it is, in fact, an accurate account of countless successes that women have described to us after breaking old patterns and initiating new ones.

Common Relationship Myths

Earlier we discussed how rules keep women stuck in old patterns and stifle their creativity in solving problems. Some of the most difficult assumptions to recognize and change are those based on societal myths. A myth can be defined as "a notion based more

on tradition or convenience than fact." Even though myths are non-factual "half-truths," people continue to believe in them. Those beliefs guide behavior and perpetuate old, ineffective habits and patterns. Since relationships—particularly committed, romantic relationships—are key threads in the fabric of society, many myths have been woven around relationships and how they function. Many of these myths oppress women by promoting subservient and self-blaming roles for them. These myths sabotage change in the same way the imaginary square hinders solution of the nine-dot problem. Myths have a particularly strong influence for two reasons: (1) they have been around for so long that we are not even aware of them or how they affect us; and (2) even if we do recognize them, they are so well supported by our society (dominant social discourse) that it doesn't occur to us to challenge them. Each of the chapters containing tactics for dealing with impossible men will debunk a myth that we have found to be counterproductive to coping with them.

Table 12.3 COMMON RELATIONSHIP MYTHS	
Myth 1	Women can and should understand why their men do what they do.
Myth 2	Being completely honest is critical if the relationship is to work.
Myth 3	What men say has a big impact on what they do.
Myth 4	If you give unselfishly to a man, he will eventually come around.
Myth 5	Being direct, open and honest are good. Manipulation is bad.

Guidelines for Change: A Preview

As a preview, here are some very practical guidelines for creating change that you will notice throughout the chapters that follow.

- *Stay off the defensive.* If you spend all your time justifying what you're doing, you become reactive and lose track of what you are trying to accomplish. Most people are too busy trying to defend themselves to see other ways of approaching a problem.
- *Create confusion.* Change the rules. Be unpredictable. That encourages your partner to find new ways to react.
- *Don't be completely honest and open at all times.* If your partner tends to manipulate or use power plays, openness just tips your hand and makes you more vulnerable.
- *"Lose" an argument by telling him that you agree that he is "right," but continue to do what you think is best.* Allow yourself to give up power verbally so that you can gain control emotionally and behaviorally.
- *Recognize that words and behaviors are not consistent.* People often say one thing and do another. Believe what he does, not what he says.
- *Do things that are truly different, not just variations on a theme.* Change 180 degrees in how you approach a problem. That alteration can loosen things up and produce real change in your partner's response.
- *Go with the flow whenever possible.* If your partner openly resists change, don't push. Finding a different, less confrontational path of change is much more effective and far less frustrating.
- *Look at what is going well in your life, instead of what is going wrong with your relationship.* Shift the focus from him to making your life enjoyable.

We hope that you are intrigued by these ideas and are ready to move on to specific strategies for managing life with particular types of troubling men. Keep your mind open. These suggestions will be quite different from what you have traditionally heard about how to handle problems, and we all tend to be a little reluctant at first to consider truly different ideas.

Moreover, these tactics are clearly not for everyone. They may not fit your situation, your personal style or your view of how change should occur in a relationship. That's okay. Think of our suggestions as food for thought, a menu of possibilities from which you can select based on your preference.

13 Refusing to Be Controlled

My husband, Richard, is a tyrant.
All he does is run his business and act
like the "king." I call him 'King Dick.'
He expects everyone to bow and
genuflect because he pays the bills.
Most people do. He can't understand why
I am so unhappy, and he has no
tolerance for it. He works sixteen hours
a day and does nothing else for the kids
or me. He constantly puts me down.
Sometimes he threatens me with,
"Plenty of young girls would love to be
in your shoes." I say go for it. He thinks
I need to get a boob job and that will
fix everything. He just doesn't get it.

—Veronica, twenty-five-year-old homemaker and mother of two

B y far the most common type of problematic man is the controller. At the root of nearly everything he does lies his
desire to be in charge. The reason these guys freak out over seemingly insignificant issues is that even the smallest one symbolizes
who is in control and who is being controlled. Everything, then, is
the object of a win-lose, competitive battle. Competition is at the
core of the controller.

The strategies explained in this chapter allow you to redirect his
attempts at control to your self-enhancing ends. Our suggestions
are analogous to a judo maneuver in which the force and energy of
the opponent are used to redirect or throw him to the ground. Each
case will highlight specific strategies for reversing the control
game. However, all of the tactics presented in this chapter may be
helpful for dealing with any type of controller. Let's first explore a
common myth that impedes implementation of the suggested
strategies.

Myth #1: Women Can and Should Understand Why Their Men Do What They Do

This myth holds that understanding the reason "why" your man
is an asshole is crucial to solving a problem. From the perspective
of this myth, any attempt to deal with a problem in terms of how
it currently exists is only scratching the surface. There are two
major shortcomings to this view. One is that searching for "why"
produces only possible explanations. Behavior is the result of a
tremendous number of interacting influences (biological, psychological, interpersonal, situational). For every explanation we arrive
at, another, more deep-seated one, can be speculated.

We never get answers to "why" questions, only plausible-
sounding guesses. Sometimes mental health professionals

masquerade as scientists, pretending to know the answers when they say impressive things like "chemical imbalance" or "dysfunctional family." But when you scrutinize official-sounding "answers" to real science, the sad story is that some mental health professionals are promoting their own self-interests and don't know with any certainty what causes even the simplest behavior.

A second and more important reason to abandon the need to know "why" is that knowing "why" seldom produces a solution. Identifying the reason for a behavior and solving it are often two completely different phenomena.

Mental health professionals have done more than their part to perpetuate the myth of "why." Freudian theory and its still influential derivatives hold that insight is critical to change. Therapy is like an archeological expedition that gradually and painfully uncovers layer after layer of the subconscious mind to find the deeply hidden explanations. Thankfully, many other theories now exist that look to current behaviors and ways to change them as key elements. Still, the influence of Freudian thought on our culture is significant. Most people still believe looking for "why" is important, if not critical, for change to occur.

This is not to suggest, however, that looking for explanations of problems is always an impediment to change. What we are arguing against are the excesses or extremes of such explorations into the "why" of any problem. We are especially railing against using the need to know why to: (1) excuse your partner's behavior; or (2) keep you stuck in an endless struggle that sinks you deeper and deeper into the quicksand of his manipulation and control.

Firing the Boss

This section describes how to cope with the most common type of controller—the Boss. By controlling virtually every aspect of the

relationship (money, decision making, social life, conversation topics), the boss sets up a relationship that looks more like parent-child than adult-adult.

When you are treated as less capable than you genuinely are, and when someone else calls all the shots, it can have dramatic effects. Common ones are decreased self-esteem, lack of confidence and depression. In addition, when you are treated like a child, you feel inferior, helpless and trapped. As you feel less able and confident, you find yourself less willing to try new things.

Consequently, the disparity in power grows, and the controller gets worse. As you are called upon to do less, you become less able to do things. A vicious cycle ensues in which you become virtually powerless, and any attempt to speak out sounds like the helpless protestations of a child.

Tony and Gina: The Case of David and Goliath

Recall Tony and Gina. Tony is a forty-year-old professional, well respected and successful. Gina was working as a model when she met Tony but ultimately gave up several jobs and almost everything else because of Tony's jealous tantrums and other methods of control.

Gina's story

> My husband treats me like a child—he doesn't let me do anything without passing judgment. At first, I liked Tony's take-charge style. He makes a good living and gives me a comfortable lifestyle. He is great at running our life and takes care of all the details. But he's always disappointed in me. He has so many expectations of me that I can't ever live up to—and he knows about everything and how to do everything. I just don't operate the way he does. I can't have dinner at a certain time every day.

I can't constantly clean the house. And no way can I read all the stuff he gives me about how to raise our son. All he does is lecture me about what I should be doing different. He won't discuss things because his way is the right way, and believe me, he can always list twenty-five reasons why he is far more qualified to make a decision about something than me.

It's like I never have anything of value to say. He shows me no respect. When we are with friends, he puts me down and patronizes me. He flirts with other women while watching me like a hawk to make sure I'm not looking at anyone. He openly gawks at other women and rates them on the basis of their breast size and ass tightness. If I complain, he says I can't take a joke. Every once in a while I "rebel" and don't cook dinner, or go out with a friend. He yells and gives me the third degree, implying that I was seeing someone else. Or worse, he gets quiet, and I wind up feeling so guilty that the rebellion is never worth it.

I can't do anything right, and I don't know what to do. I know I'm letting myself go. It's stupid, but I'm drinking more heavily, and doing less and less around the house. I haven't worked in weeks because I am so tired of Tony's accusations and jealous tirades. He tells me I don't know men like he does. I think he really means that I don't know men like him like he does. Tony just took the checkbook away from me. I get so mad, but I wind up feeling so stupid. It's useless to talk to him because the focus always goes back to me and the one hundred ways I've been screwing up.

What Doesn't Work

One important reason that women get stuck in dealing with the Boss is that they look at the content instead of the control. The content is the specific issue under discussion (what time to be home from work, how well the house gets cleaned). The real issue

is the control, or game, that takes place over and over, regardless of the subject matter. By no accident, the Boss is in a no-lose situation. If the woman acquiesces to his rules, he wins. If the woman struggles, it is in reaction to the Boss; the struggle is a defensive one, and she is subsequently punished one way or another.

Let's look at the strategies that Gina and others use to reduce their discomfort. First, controlled women usually try to do a better job of following the "rules." If those rules are broken, they are scolded like disobedient children. Trying to do a better job of following the rules rarely works. Even if you are obeying the rules, you are just further buying into the submissive, childlike role.

The next solution often tried is to assert yourself and not "give in." This is worth trying, but, as mentioned earlier, it seldom works. For one thing, the controlled woman usually has little practice in standing up for herself. Compounding the lack of experience is the fact that it is a scary proposition to challenge the Boss since he has been calling the shots for so long. The Boss has a lot of power and wants to keep it that way. He will pull out all the stops to put down a rebellion. The Boss usually argues better and with a frightening passion, uses past examples of your "bad" decisions or even subtly threatens you. Making an out-of-character attempt to be assertive seldom works because it is treated like a child's attempt to overrule a parent: amusing, but futile.

A less conscious attempt to deal with the Boss involves the woman actually becoming more childlike as she gets consistently treated that way. She might miss work, spend money irresponsibly, drink more, take worse care of the house, miss appointments, forget things. In short, the person being treated like a child begins to act like one. Thus, self-esteem drops even lower, and the control becomes more exaggerated. Women who don't feel powerful enough to stand up to the Boss often resort to childlike behavior to irritate and get back at him. The woman is usually unaware of

the purpose of the behavior, not realizing it is an expression of anger. Unfortunately, these passive-aggressive actions usually result in more control by the Boss.

What Works

The first strategy involves doing what you want to do. Then, if you are criticized, *verbally* agree that you were wrong. Agree in words, not in deeds. If the same situation arises, feel free to do the same thing again even though you agreed with him it was a bad idea previously.

This sounds confusing, but the key is that the Boss is using your *words* to control your *behavior*. If you can allow yourself to be inconsistent—to do one thing and say another—you break free of that control. But that is easier said than done, especially if you are used to "obeying" a Boss. It is hard to disobey and not feel guilty. But it is possible, and here is how.

Women with Bosses usually have mixed feelings about doing what they want to do. On one hand, they feel they have the right to make their own decisions. On the other hand, they think they should comply with the Boss's demands (since it's always been that way, they feel insecure, and they pay a big price when they don't). By defending yourself, you verbalize one side of the mixed feeling ("I'm allowed to do what I want"), but the other side ("Maybe I shouldn't have") stays in your mind. If you can say out loud, "You're right I should have done it your way," what stays in your mind is "That's not true. I can do what I want." You therefore feel more sure of yourself and less guilty.

To summarize, you do what you want to do and then, if you are criticized, you *verbally* agree you were misguided, but *behaviorally* continue to do what you believe is best. You gain control in three important ways. First, you are doing what you want. Second, you

are not getting defensive or guilty, both of which weaken your resolve and make you backslide and "atone" for your independence. Finally, by changing your behavior, you disrupt the control of the boss.

A second strategy for the Boss is called **just desserts**. This method can be especially useful, in combination with the one just described, when the Boss is coercive, verbally abusive or relentlessly critical. It involves doing something (being late, stupid, inefficient) that bothers him but that looks unintentional. For example: A man complains daily about how his wife cooks dinner. She deliberately over- or undercooks the food for the next week and apologizes profusely for her ineptitude.

The just desserts need not have anything to do with the specific situation (as in the example above). The Boss can criticize his wife for spending too much time with her friends, and she can pay him back by "accidentally" blocking his car in with hers when she knows he's in a hurry or "forget" to pick up his dry cleaning just before he leaves on a trip.

Yes, this may sound childish. As noted earlier, it is generally ineffective if done outside of awareness because then you don't have control over when and how you do it. But if done in a planned way, it offers several advantages:

It blows off anger without confrontation since you never admit you're doing it on purpose. It's like a safety valve that permits you to discharge the frustration that accumulates from the Boss's control.

It shows the Boss that unacceptable behavior will meet with unpleasant consequences. What goes around comes around.

It's fun and can loosen up an otherwise "heavy" situation. Harmless revenge can be enormously entertaining. By doing silly and "immature" things like this, you give yourself the message that the situation is not life-or-death. Look for mildly irritating but

noticeable ways to put across your message. The sillier and less consequential, the better. You are not making mistakes, forgetting things, or performing poorly in a nasty, vengeful or powerful way, but in a forgetful, clumsy or powerless way. It should not come across as a challenge.

Just desserts confuses the Boss and allows him to view his behavior in a different light. Confusion is often a necessary precursor to behavior change. "Why is my spouse acting so weird? I need to attend more to her and find out."

It is probably obvious that payback can be very frustrating to the person receiving it. With most people that frustration is uncomfortable, but not dangerous. In fact, it can motivate positive changes. *However, if your partner has been violent or seems easily provoked to violence, do not try this strategy. The benefits will not outweigh the risks.*

If you use these tactics, things will change. At first, that change may not be pleasant. The Boss will see himself losing control and will not go down without kicking and screaming. The Boss may get louder and more critical or try to be even more controlling. That's normal.

Stick to your guns. A person who escalates is confused and threatened. That confusion can act as a catalyst for change since people who are confused get uncomfortable and look for new ways to behave to lessen that discomfort. If his escalation doesn't work, the pattern will be broken, and a new, more equitable one can be established.

Gina's success

I feel like a new person—this has been so much fun. First, I did "agree in words, not in deeds." My son and I spent more time out of the house and I went out more with friends. And I didn't cook

dinner every night. When Tony told me how irresponsible and self-ish I was, I honestly told him how badly I felt about neglecting him. Nevertheless, I continued doing what I wanted. First he got more critical and tried to set up more "rules." If he got particularly unpleasant, I kicked in "just desserts." Ha—it was great! I did laundry but misplaced his socks. I cooked his favorite meals but left out key ingredients. I couldn't do anything right, but it was all on purpose; so when he got upset, it didn't bother me. I responded with such pitiful apologies and whiny criticisms of myself, he just stared at me with the weirdest look on his face. I've never seen him confused. He's always the master of all situations. "Just desserts" made me feel like David slinging the payback "stone" at my Goliath husband.

The best part is that within a few weeks, Tony seemed to get the message that controlling me and treating me like a kid would not work anymore. He's less demanding, discusses things with me more and actually asks my opinion occasionally. He is not a different person, but this makes him easier to live with. It especially feels good to put one over on him for a change!

In this section, we looked at the Boss. We suggested two ways to demote him and feel better about yourself in the process:

1. Agree in words, not in deeds. Do what you want to do and agree you were "wrong" to do it if criticized—but continue to do it.

2. Just desserts. Respond to the Boss's overcontrol with "inadvertent" mistakes that make the Boss's life a little more difficult and your life a little more entertaining.

Let Mr. Helpful Help *You*

Mr. Helpful maintains control through his annoying energy and desire to please. Doing and pleasing are the ways he has learned to take control. He manipulates with guilt and makes his partner feel whiny and spoiled if she argues or complains. The result is often depression, confusion and an underlying misunderstood anger.

Leslie and Herb: The Case of Making Helplessness a Science

Recall Leslie and Herb. Herb was a dream come true that turned into a nightmare. His control game appears less harmful than the Boss's but is actually the same iron-fisted control, only covered up by velvet gloves. Leslie felt depressed but didn't know why. Everything seemed like it should be right, but it wasn't.

Leslie's story

I just can't cope anymore, and I don't know why. Sometimes I'm depressed for days for no apparent reason. It just comes on out of the blue. My kids are great—just the normal problems, and my husband is a dream come true—not like other men—very helpful and considerate of me. In fact, he says I have it too good and that's my problem. Herb really encouraged me to get help. He thinks that I was spoiled as a child and my previous relationships have predisposed me to be unhappy regardless of how good things are. Sometimes I feel so angry at him, but I can't figure out why. He really does do everything; he has an unending supply of energy. There's no way I can keep up with him. He really does do a lot more around the house than I do and manages almost everything in our lives. Sounds perfect, doesn't it? There must be something wrong with me. Maybe I have some kind of chemical imbalance or something. I guess the only thing that bothers me about Herb is

that he always seems to manage to get things his own way—but I guess he deserves it since he does everything. But sometimes I would like to do things on my own without his help or advice, and every now and then I would like to decide what we are going to do on the weekends without feeling guilty for even opening my mouth. It's like because of all that he does, I have somehow given up the right to have an opinion—at least that's how I feel. Why do I feel so guilty if I want it my way once in a while? Is that normal? Why am I so angry?

What Doesn't Work

The Mr. Helpfuls' control mechanisms are so subtle and insidious that their partners ultimately think they are crazy for feeling unhappy. They question their own sanity because having intense feelings of anger in the face of an avalanche of thoughtfulness is very unsettling. Their mindset is "It can't be him—he's so considerate!"

Leslie and others dealing with Mr. Helpfuls tend to verbalize their desires and attempt to get their way directly. These efforts are met with smoke and mirrors—confusing guilt inductions and other conversational maneuvers designed to modify your request to fit Mr. Helpful's opinion. He is a master of subtle manipulation, at getting his way without directly ordering it. Conversations are like tangled knots with only one outcome certain: You feel angry and confused.

Another often tried but unsuccessful solution is to shoulder more responsibility around the house. Mr. Helpful really kicks into action then because his method of subtle control is undermined. He will complete tasks once started, suggesting that he is better equipped to handle them. He will supervise entire operations, making sure they are done to his specifications. He will redo tasks because they weren't done correctly. Mr. Helpful will take on more

burdens, all the while insisting he doesn't mind and enjoys doing them anyway. Each time he does something, however, he puts a tally up on a scoreboard so he can ensure he gets well compensated for every act of consideration he performs. It's no wonder that women tell us they can't understand why they would like to chop such helpful partners into little pieces.

What Works

There are two strategies for dealing with Mr. Helpful. The first is to **make helping hurt**. Instead of thinking you have to do more to counter his energetic overcontrol, *do less*. Make his helping an ordeal, even for him. Get more "depressed" and incapable of doing things for yourself, and make more mistakes when you do anything. Make him lists of things to do, and ask for his advice and input on the most simple of tasks. "Honey, I'm having trouble changing the toilet paper roll—can you come in and help me?"

Test the limits of his energy and desire to control. Even he has limits and will begin to back out of the duties he doesn't like. He will finally complain about the workload, perhaps leading to a more egalitarian distribution that you can feel better about.

The second tactic is to **deal from the bottom of the deck** and think about the controlling maneuvers of Mr. Helpful as a game. This strategy applies in those situations where he gets his own way by manipulating what you have suggested with his conversational sleights of hand. You either give in because you don't want to argue about trivial things, or you don't want to feel guilty because of all the things he does for you.

This technique requires you to decide what you want to do in advance. For example, you want to eat Chinese at 7:30. When he asks you what you want, you simply give him a bogus answer—say,

Mexican at 9:00. He counters with Thai at 8:00, and you respond with Italian at 8:30.

The idea is twofold. One is that you don't make his subtle manipulations easy for him. Make him work for it by playing it stupid, making him become more direct with his attempts to control. He doesn't like to be direct, so it will make him uncomfortable. Second, this strategy can become a game for you to thwart his control by seeing how close you can come to what you really wanted to do in the first place. He may think he has manipulated the situation, but in reality you have done more closely what you wanted in the first place. For example, he might say Chinese at 7:45. Dealing from the bottom of the deck enables you to fix the game in your favor.

Leslie's success

I haven't felt depressed in weeks. I finally realized that I felt whiny and spoiled because I was not in charge of my own life. Herb ran the whole show. I just followed him around allowing myself to be manipulated because I didn't see what a control freak he is and how bad I felt as a result of it. The more "depressed and helpless" I pretended to be, the better I felt. I don't know if it was seeing Herb stretched beyond his limits or feeling like I was in control of him for a change. Anyway, I started driving him nuts with questions about the silliest things. I even had him laying out my clothes! I made helplessness a science. Herb finally said he had had enough and complained how I wasn't doing my share. His "input" into everything I did decreased significantly. If he did start to take over a task, I instantly quit and was totally "helpless" the rest of the day. Herb quickly backed off thereafter. Since Herb was no longer doing everything, I felt better about insisting on doing things my way from time to time. Several times, though, I dealt from the bottom of the deck and made it difficult for Herb to modify our plans after he pretended

to ask me what I wanted to do. I told him I really wanted to do things, when actually I wanted to do something else. He seemed confused, and we finally ended up doing what I wanted to do more often. The best thing is, I don't feel so angry at him without knowing why. If I get mad, I know now that he is controlling too much, and I kick in the ways I can feel back in control.

In this section, we covered two ways to reverse Mr. Helpful's subtle maneuvers for control:

1. Make helping hurt. Become more helpless, thereby overloading the most energetic Mr. Helpful until he complains and backs off.
2. Deal from the bottom of the deck. Make a game of concealing your real desires, making his control manipulations difficult for him (and fun for you as you see how close you can come to getting your way).

Outsmarting Mr. Know-It-All

Mr. Know-It-All seizes control by forcing his opinions on others and relentlessly arguing his way until his partner is pummeled into submission. He will win an argument at any expense, and at an especially high cost for his partner. Mr. Know-It-All ultimately uses his verbal and controlling skills to demean and criticize his partner, keeping her off balance and unsure of herself.

Carol and Neil: The Case of the Robot

Recall Carol and Neil. She was in her early thirties, had been married seven years and had three children—four-year-old twins

and a two-year-old. Neil was an up-and-coming executive who availed himself of every opportunity to control his wife with heavy-handed personal condemnations.

Carol's story

I'm trying to understand what Neil is so upset about so I can work on saving our marriage—but I don't know what to do. I do know that I don't seem to do anything right. Every time I turn around, Neil points out to me another chance I missed to be supportive. But maybe he is right; maybe it is my fault because I get so overwhelmed with all I have to do just taking care of three kids. He wants me to handle the kids all day, do my job—I do telephone soliciting for an online service—and then be waiting for him with a candlelight dinner and a rose in my teeth. And somehow I'm supposed to figure out if he is in a good mood or not. I try so hard, but it is never enough.

Sometimes I get mad at him and blow up, but he's so convincing. Then I just feel guilty for not figuring out what he wants. Maybe he is right. Maybe I'm not capable of real emotion because of my upbringing. I try to talk to Neil, but when I do, he tells me what I am saying is trivial or that I'm talking on the surface and not really discussing my deep feelings. If I don't say anything, then he criticizes me about that. He calls me an emotionless robot and says I'm too caught up in practical things. Sometimes he walks around yelling, "Danger! Danger! Danger!" like that robot from Lost in Space, *just to make fun of me. He puts me down about other things, too. When I argue back, he just criticizes me more. Neil is a great arguer. I always lose; he is always in control. I've tried explaining my reasons for whatever it is I did or didn't do, but he never accepts my reasons, only criticizes them. It's very frustrating. I wind up getting real defensive, which he never fails to*

point out. I can't think that fast, and before I know it, I've got that
same old crummy feeling that he got me again.

What Doesn't Work

Let's take a look at how Carol and others being controlled by
Mr. Know-It-Alls tend to react. The first attempt usually made in
the face of criticism is to try to do better or to try harder. Along
with this, the Carols of the world defend themselves. They explain
their reasons for doing things, hoping that they can reason their
way out of the argument. Naturally, none of this works because the
real issue is control, not the particular activities (housework,
money management, etc.) being debated.

No explanation is adequate, and no performance is acceptable.
Defending only gives Mr. Know-It-All more fuel for the fire and
will lead him to pull out the trump card: heartless personal attacks
that cause you to cry or blow up in anger, allowing him to perceive
himself the undisputed winner.

What Works

To deal with Mr. Know-It-All, it is important to get away from
the specific argument and address the struggle for control. For him,
the hidden agenda is always, "I'll prove I'm right and make you
give in." Mr. Know-It-All criticizes, and by defending yourself, you
inadvertently go one down by buying into the assumption that "I
owe an explanation." You only *owe* an explanation to a superior
(boss, God). When you overexplain, you take the inferior role and
are putty in the hands of Mr. Know-It-All.

A first strategy is one applicable to almost every situation
involving a struggle for control. It is simply, **don't defend or
explain yourself**. Criticism only works if you take it seriously and
defend against it. By responding to criticism, you give it credibility

and get yourself more worked up. Instead, you can be silent or walk away. When you respond to criticism, you play his game by his rules.

Some people have a hard time not arguing or defending themselves. That's based on the ridiculous notion that in every situation, someone is "right," and you have to prove that person is you. In an argument, the person who is "right" doesn't necessarily win. Either the best arguer wins, or both people lose since they wind up more angry at each other and less able to see the other's point of view. You "win" when you do what you want and feel all right about doing it.

The second tactic is to agree with the criticisms and even expand or exaggerate them. "Yes, I'm a terrible driver, and I can't believe you're brave enough to ride with me." "Not only am I a lousy cook, but I'm generally a rotten wife. I'm amazed you continue to put up with me." You are only agreeing with words; you are not in any way changing your behavior. It is critical that you not sound sarcastic, as that just creates hostility.

Agree and exaggerate takes you from a "no-win" to a "no-lose" situation. If you agree and Mr. Know-It-All accepts it, you still do whatever you want, the argument's over, and you didn't get angry and defensive. So, you win. If he disagrees with you (remember, you are now accepting criticism), that means he is absolving you of blame. So you still win. You win when you break the old pattern and when *you* decide what the new pattern will be. You win when you—and not your partner—are in control of your emotions.

Women who try this strategy are often amazed at the results. Mr. Know-It-Alls, for once in their lives, usually have no idea what to say. Women also feel a lot better. It feels very good not to be defensive and not to argue.

Carol's success

The "agree and exaggerate" was great. One time, right after he came home from work, the kids were screaming, the house was a mess, and dinner wasn't even started. Neil said, "I can't believe that you don't have dinner started. You're so disorganized." I said back, "Not only am I disorganized, I can't even control these kids. I'm a terrible mother and wife." Neil looked surprised—and then just simply changed the subject. He didn't say another word about it; he just started helping with dinner. But the best one was last Friday night. Neil had a terribly bad day at work. He lost a major account because of someone else's screwup, and he was very angry. He came home and was kind of quiet, but I really didn't notice because I was feeding the baby and trying to fix dinner at the same time. Just as we were sitting down to eat, he jumps down my throat and tells me how insensitive I am for not picking up how upset he was. It really bothered me. But I calmed myself, and when he was done, I said, "You're right. I am like that robot, and I'll probably always be that way. I guess I wonder how long you're going to put up with me." As I said it, I got up from the table and walked away to get something from the counter. Neil came over and put his arms around me and reminded me that things were getting better and that he was probably overreacting and should have brought it up himself that he was having a bad day. It was great not to feel crummy about his criticisms. Friday evening turned out great after that. He still can be an asshole, but it's nice to know I can influence where our conversations wind up.

> We made two suggestions to outsmart Mr. Know-It-All:
>
> 1. Don't defend or explain yourself. Ignore the bait and avoid a no-win argument.
> 2. Agree and exaggerate. When criticized, agree with him and exaggerate the criticism far beyond his intended meaning. Leave him speechless.

Silencing the Critic

In any relationship, there is a division of labor. Deciding who gets what task is based on a number of things, including skills, interests, societal gender roles and availability of time. However, in a relationship with a Critic, he depends on the woman to the point where there is a tremendous disparity in responsibilities. In some instances, the Critic may have a physical disability, which renders him incapable of doing things independently. More often, social deficits or lack of skills in everyday living create the dependency. Regardless of the cause, there results an imbalance in responsibility.

By being tirelessly critical, the Critic keeps his partner on the defensive and off balance. He is like a movie critic. He has never acted in or made a movie, but he has plenty of opinions about how they should be made. Thus, the Critic takes control ("Do things for me and do them my way"), and the responsible woman feels obligated, trapped ("I have to do these things") and resentful because her efforts are not appreciated. She also is riddled with self-doubt, weakened by countless criticisms and observed shortcomings.

Lynn and Josh: The Case of "I Really Screwed Up Today"

Recall Lynn and Josh. Josh worked part-time as a maintenance person for a building management company, while Lynn was the

assistant director of marketing at a computer software company. Josh did a Monday morning quarterback analysis of everything Lynn did; Lynn never threw a touchdown or scored any points with Josh.

Lynn's story

My husband is driving me nuts! He is always on my case. He watches everything I do and takes every opportunity to criticize me. I can hardly get through the door without him nailing me about something. Josh is so sarcastic. I do my best. I work long hours, and then I come home and take care of the kids and do whatever else I need to do. But I never do anything right. I get so angry at him, but that never helps. I try to do things the way he wants them done, but it never is right. Here I have this responsible job in which forty people report to me, and I have a budget of several million dollars; and I come home to criticisms about how I care for the kids and how I manage our money. But then look at him. He can do no wrong— although he hardly does anything. I think he resents my success and has to put me down to compensate for it. I don't know. But I feel like I'm on a treadmill, and no matter how fast I go, it's never fast enough. He says he is not threatened by my job, and often makes fun of it and says it's a Mickey Mouse job in a company run by a bunch of PMS women on Prozac. He puts everything and everyone associated with my work down.

What Doesn't Work

Let's take a look at how Lynn and other responsible-but-criticized women tend to react. The first attempt usually made in the face of criticism is to try to do better or to try harder. This results in an endless spiral of working harder for appreciation that never materializes. Not much fun.

When the first line of defense doesn't work, the responsible woman usually turns to anger, arguing and confrontation. "I do everything for you, and all you do is complain. If you don't like the way I do it, do it yourself." Not only doesn't this work, it also leads to guilt and depression.

The responsible woman is used to handling the load, so she goes ahead and completes her duties, then feels guilty for having picked a fight. Remember, these women are likely to want to please, and they'll feel guilty when someone is upset with them. They have usually been able to succeed in pleasing people with their achievements and take-charge abilities. However, these same abilities cut no ice with the Critic.

What Works

The first strategy to deal with the Critic is one mentioned earlier: **Don't defend or explain yourself.** You will only incite more criticism and feel worse when the argument is over. Allow yourself some space to contemplate better tactics by removing yourself from a futile verbal struggle for control. Give up verbal control to gain emotional and behavioral control.

Helping in obvious ways or taking responsibility is not always helpful. Picking up the pieces for alcoholics often just allows them to continue drinking, because they are shielded from the consequences of their behavior. Parents always want to protect their children, but effective parents know that learning from mistakes is a critical part of development. With the Critic, doing things for him that he neither graciously accepts nor appreciates may be keeping you under critical fire.

You may be giving the Critic what he demands, but what also makes him feel powerless and threatened. So while your perspective might be that you are doing what he wants by carrying the load, the

Critic's might well be (subconsciously) that you are robbing (emasculating) him of self-respect, that you are secretly putting him down. After all, even with all his bluster and bull, he recognizes that he is a loser and hates it—or you. If that belief exists, resentment will occur and fuel criticism. Remember, the Critic is basically insecure and miserable. He cannot be pleased because, in his own mind, he would have to accept what a loser he really is. Sadly, he feels good about himself only when he puts you down. So the key is to begin removing the things he criticizes you about.

This tactic is called **creative interpretation**, a method that entails interpreting or spinning his critical message the way you want to—a way that allows you to do what you want without guilt. For example, when he criticizes you every time you cook for him, you could make the interpretation: "Since you always dislike how I cook, I guess you're trying to tell me you don't want me to do it anymore, but you're too polite to tell me directly. I get the message. I won't cook for you, in spite of how much I would like to." If he argues, you can always fall back on, "You're just trying to spare my feelings. I know you don't want me to cook." In place of "cook," fill in any activity for which you are criticized.

By doing this you are saying, indirectly, "From now on, when you criticize me, it means you want to do it yourself." And you are saying it in a way that does not cause confrontation since the only argument the Critic can make is to say you are really doing it well enough already. It is very important, when using this strategy, to clearly maintain a "one-down" position, which does not convey confrontation or an "I'll-show-you" attitude. You do not want to come across as "Okay, you've been treating me badly, and now you'll get yours." Rather, you want to sound (not feel) defeated. The message should be: "I tried my best and failed, so I won't inflict myself on you in that way anymore."

Finally, another way to influence the Critic's incessant

criticisms and insecurity is to **beat him to the punch**. This entails sharing your insecurities and little failures, and openly asking him for advice in his areas of competence. This puts him in a one-up role without having to criticize you. The Critic may find that he likes taking care of you once in a while. That would be great. We are not suggesting that you share all of your inner secrets or mistakes, but rather, choose the ones you feel comfortable about and share those *before* he starts on something else that *he* chooses.

Sometimes, beating him to the punch by admitting your vulnerabilities, pointing out your foibles, and asking for advice allows the Critic to experience himself differently, and he doesn't need to put you down to feel better about himself. Validating his competencies may allow him to appreciate yours. Maybe.

Lynn's success

The more I did, the more I couldn't do anything right. Josh constantly yelled at and criticized me. So I decided that I wouldn't try as hard to please since it never worked anyway. I also started interpreting Josh's criticism in a way that allowed me to do what I wanted. I said, "Josh, you say you need me and want me around, but every time I am around, you yell at me and criticize me. So I guess I really get on your nerves, but you're too polite to tell me directly. From now on, when you yell at me, I'll know I'm getting on your nerves, and I'll leave if I can." Josh protested that that wasn't what he meant, but I replied, "You're just sparing my feelings. I know I get on your nerves." And I stuck to it. When he got abusive, I left and saw my friends or took the kids out to dinner. It was terrific. Josh's criticism decreased markedly. Not only could he not get my goat by criticizing, since I just agreed with him, but if he criticized me too long or loudly, I would leave. As he stopped criticizing as much, I found I wanted to be home more. Evidently, there were some things Josh really didn't want me to do

because he began doing them instead of criticizing me. I did much less, and he did much more.

I also began asking Josh for his input about what cars I should buy for my company's sales force. Josh is a car buff and was on top of the latest data on dependability and cost effectiveness. I also requested his help in other areas in which he was knowledgeable. Josh seemed delighted, and he responded by giving less advice and offering input into fewer of my affairs.

I occasionally shared some of my fears about my job and some other things I believed I had messed up. One night I came home and said, "I really screwed up today." I told him about a big fight I had had with my boss. Surprisingly, he was very understanding at times, even sweet. He made me dinner and did not make one woman-bashing joke about my company. Josh also shared that perhaps he was frightened a bit about my job success. He is not perfect now or anything, but now I know I can handle him.

We made three suggestions to silence the Critic:

1. Don't defend or explain. Step back and look at ways to not engage in the Critic's struggle for control.
2. Creative interpretation. Respond to the criticism in a way that allows you to stop doing the criticized behavior for his own good (which, basically, involves saying that the criticism means the Critic does not want your help, so you'll stop).
3. Beat him to the punch. Share your own self-criticisms and vulnerabilities. Ask the Critic for his opinion in his areas of expertise, enabling him to feel competent and therefore less likely to seize control by challenging *your* competence.

14

Turning the Tables on Liars and Cheaters

> When I first started seeing him,
> he was married, so I guess I should have known
> better. We worked in the same department, and
> I knew his wife was really a bitch—at least,
> that's what I thought. His wife
> finally caught us, and I was relieved to be
> with him without hiding and sneaking around.
> I went over to his apartment one night,
> about a year later, let myself in with my key and
> found him in bed with a twenty-year-old temporary
> from work. Then he got furious at me for bursting in
> on him! At that moment I knew it was over, but it
> took me another six months to break up.
> He still calls me.
>
> —Erica, twenty-six-year-old computer programmer

This is perhaps the most difficult chapter to write because these men have so few

redeeming qualities. However, some of you have good reasons to stick with them, or you may be evaluating your decision to leave or stay. The suggestions in this chapter help you to make living with the Lying, Cheating Asshole more manageable, and to further examine the costs and benefits of staying in the relationship.

There is a joke that men say to each other to justify lying to women. It is like a secret asshole society rule of conduct: "*It doesn't count as a lie if you tell it to a woman.*" In other words, lying is totally acceptable as long as it's just to a woman. Never lie to your buds, but to a chick—ha! It's especially not lying if it is to manipulate a woman into bed. It's also totally understandable to lie to get out of trouble with a woman. Of course, if you say this to your man, he will deny it, even if tortured. He has to—rule number two of the secret asshole society is to deny everything.

Lying to women to get them into bed has a long and undistinguished history. Way beyond the all-too-common "I love you" as a means to the bedroom, men consider it an incredible coup if women are seduced into sex under false pretenses. Remember what you are dealing with: A recent survey in *Mademoiselle* as cited in a 1996 *Newsweek* article, "Bad Boys," found that 100 percent of male respondents said they'd have sex with a woman even if they weren't interested in a relationship. Nothing is sacred to this mentality. Everything, including malicious deception, is fair in love and war.

The quintessential movie example of this behavior is found in *Animal House,* when the Delta House president, played by Tim Matheson, presents himself to a sorority house to pick up a young woman for a date. The young woman, he knows from a newspaper article, was killed in an auto accident the night before. Pretending that he is deeply in love with the deceased woman and finding out the tragic news for the first time, Matheson's character feigns grief and cons a gullible young woman to accompany him to bed to ease his pain.

This is funny because it's so outrageous, and as we all know, boys will be boys, and frat rats will be rats. However, it taps into a vein of truth concerning men and their views of honesty with women. Screwing women under false pretenses is a status symbol among men. That scene depicts, for men, the ultimate in deceptive power over women and the attitude that women who are dumb enough to believe them get what they deserve. Women have just not been armed with the facts about how unscrupulous guys can be. It is generally unfathomable to women to use deceit in such a calculating fashion.

This chapter presents some guerrilla tactics for coping with these guys and perhaps jarring them enough to at least come clean with you. But first, let's look at what gets in the way of managing these men.

Myth #2: Being Completely Honest Is Critical If the Relationship Is to Work

Of all the myths, this one will probably provoke the strongest emotional response. It may seem paradoxical to discuss honesty and its limitations in the context of dealing with a dishonest partner. However, honesty, when it is not reciprocal, can put you at an extreme disadvantage.

We will take "honesty" to mean telling the truth—that is, not lying or deceiving, or holding back any of the truth. A person who is being honest tells the truth, the whole truth, and nothing but. One obvious problem is that it is impossible for anyone to be totally honest. You can only be honest about things of which you are aware. In order for you to be totally honest, you would need to be aware of not only all internal needs, desires and beliefs, but also all external factors influencing you. In addition, you would have to be motivated to share all those experiences. No one has ever met such a mythical creature.

But for the sake of discussion, let's assume that one can be totally honest in a relationship. Even given that assumption, honesty of expression is not *always* the best policy. Being open with someone who uses what you tell him to manipulate you or lie more effectively is like playing chess and discussing your next move with the other player. But it's worse with a lying, cheating guy. It's more like revealing your entire strategy to someone whom you've already caught cheating in the game. We, of course, advocate honesty. It can enhance closeness and trust, and make both people feel better about the relationship and themselves. We also advocate that honesty be tried first and continued until it is clear that it is not reciprocated and is, in fact, making things worse. We are saying only that honesty is not the only way, and in some situations, certainly not the best way. If you persist in honestly trying to work things out with a liar or a cheater, you will most certainly wind up in the confines of the imaginary square of the nine-dot puzzle. With the kind of men discussed in this chapter, honesty is not the best policy.

Unmasking the Great Pretender

Women who live with the Great Pretender believe they have finally found the man of their dreams. In due time, however, as the bizarre inconsistencies mount, women begin to feel dazed and as if they're in a dream. They question what is real and what is not. They know something is wrong but feel crazy and confused. *Can this be happening to me?* The theme of the *Twilight Zone* fills the background. Unfortunately, Rod Serling will not appear and explain these situations away with an ironic twist.

Consider Air Force Lieutenant Kelley Flinn, the first woman to fly a B-52 Bomber. It is appalling to think that this very intelligent

young woman, acclaimed as "the most distinguished student" at flight training school, and destined for a brilliant career, could be hoodwinked by a Great Pretender to such a degree that she faced a court-martial on charges of adultery and disobeying an order.

Her real crime was falling in love with and believing in Mark Zigo. He convinced Ms. Flinn that she was the love of his life, spoke of marriage and gave her an Irish promise ring. The whole charade came to a head when Zigo, after agreeing to deny his affair with Flinn, told air force investigators everything, including incredibly personal details about their sex life. Now, here is a guy that sticks with you when the chips are down.

This Great Pretender lied about almost everything, including his birthplace, age, marital status and probation for wife abuse. The ring he gave Flinn was the same one he had given his wife. Zigo even invented a soccer career. Flinn's story is one of millions that involve an intelligent woman falling for the Great Pretender's lies.

Sharon and Dennis: The Case of Losing Her Mind

Recall Sharon and Dennis. Dennis started out as Prince Charming, but he turned into the Prince of Darkness as his lies sucked the lifeblood from Sharon and her hopes of a trusting relationship.

Sharon's story

I must be going out of my mind, or I am just plain stupid—I don't know which. My other relationships were so abusive and such nightmares that Dennis seemed like a saint. He was so kind and considerate, and so worldly. But things just started not adding up. I kept finding out things about him that were different from how he described them. He said he had money when I met him and was very generous before we got married. He said he cashed in

stock options—ha! It turns out he's broke and has always been that way. He seems to be involved in one new business after another, but he never makes any money. In fact, he has no credit and filed bankruptcy just before we met. He had money from getting advances on his credit cards just before he filed. I'm really worried—what kind of person am I with? The final blow, I hope, was when I found out that he had a girlfriend and a family overseas. He said that he had never been in a serious relationship. He was too busy in his career. What is going on here? He denied it for weeks until I finally received copies of their birth certificates and pictures of them in the mail. When I showed him, he finally confessed and apologized. He then goes on and on about how he's not good enough for me and maybe I should leave him. I get so tangled up. I don't really want to leave. I wind up trying to convince him that our relationship is worth saving. After all, we do really love each other. But how can I believe him about anything? I'm ready for the loony bin.

What Doesn't Work

The main thing that Sharon and other women do is continue to believe the Great Pretender in the face of mounting evidence. They believe and hope for the best. All the while, their worlds crumble around them. They often believe the lies are isolated events and not examples of a bigger picture. That, of course, is a losing strategy.

They also confront the Great Pretender with his lies, hoping to talk it out and understand what it's all about. After all, there must be some explanation for this situation besides his being as big of a lying asshole as he appears. This is big mistake number two.

Talking and lying to women are what these guys do best; they are downright artists at it. Case in point: Dennis employed a favorite

strategy of Great Pretenders. He apologized sincerely (yeah, right) and gave Sharon the "I'm not good enough for you" routine. Sometimes this song and dance includes a pitiful story of childhood abuse or other heart-rending fable designed to help you understand why he is such an asshole. Then you can make excuses for him. Being honest themselves, the Sharons of the world can't quite believe that anyone could actually fabricate such a story. They don't see how he uses his charm and ability to lie to flimflam his way through even when he is discovered—to the point that Sharon and the others question their own grip on reality.

He will also deny incontrovertible evidence until he is blue in the face. He adopts a strategy similar to the husband's (Phil Silvers) in the movie *Guide for a Married Man* when he is caught in the act of having an affair. It's his wife who catches him, in their own home. Phil Silvers's character quickly ushers the other woman out of the house while saying, "What woman?" The scene ends with Silvers sitting comfortably, reading the paper while his wife just stands and looks perplexed, and finally says, "Oh, never mind." The Great Pretender denies and denies until you question your own grasp of reality. Then he tells you another lie designed to explain the other one, and on and on.

What Works

Before discussing the kind of tactics that will help you deal with this guy, first let's look at some pragmatic tips. **Protect yourself!** Cover your assets, so to speak, so you cannot be further taken advantage of financially. Separate, as much as legally possible, your credit from his. It's okay that you still love him and want to stay with him, but that does not mean you must keep yourself in jeopardy. You can always reunite your assets if he establishes a more trustworthy track record. If he stays, you'll know that more than

your money motivates him to be with you.

Next, **make the worm squirm** and put pressure on him to come clean. Let him know that you are on to him and have ironclad evidence of something he has lied about. But don't tell him what it is. Wait until you do actually have some evidence, so that your confidence in your position is unshakable. Don't tip your hand. Make him squirm, and he may ultimately tell you more, perhaps more than you really want to know. However, the more you know, the better equipped you are to take better care of yourself, and the more likely you are to take action to protect yourself.

A woman we know found a picture in her husband's briefcase of a naked woman. Without showing him the picture, she told him she had it, along with other undeniable evidence of an affair. He confessed—to an affair with a different woman! Now she knew there were at least two.

Another woman found a receipt for the purchase of a tent and sleeping bag bought in a certain city when her husband was supposedly away on business in another state. She gave him the "I have evidence but won't tell you what it is" routine. She told him to come clean or the marriage was over. Not knowing for sure what she knew, he admitted to a two-year affair with a customer.

Finally, put your feelings of going crazy to work for you. We call this simply **acting crazy**. Most people are quite predictable in the ways they act and react. Their predictability allows other people to anticipate and prepare responses for actions that are likely to occur. Predictability allows the Great Pretender to plan his next lie. Unpredictability and other methods that create confusion set the stage for change. When people get confused, they become uncomfortable. This motivates them to find ways to reduce their discomfort.

When a person has been predictable, confusion is easily created by doing something very different from the predictable pattern. Acting crazy is particularly effective when you, a person who has

been reasonable, begin to do and say things that don't make sense. Time and time again, men who have been engaging in outrageous and senseless behaviors have been stopped in their tracks when their partners "got weird" on them.

Like "just desserts," acting crazy can be fun. Probably one of the most significant effects of this strategy is that it interjects looseness into situations that have become tense and desperate. In fact, many women tell us that they feel a lot better just thinking about these strategies, without even trying them.

There is another benefit to acting crazy. It allows you to channel your anger into doing things back to him, in a way that achieves a specific purpose. It is all right, and even natural, to get a little secret enjoyment out of acting crazy, and it can prevent the buildup of anger.

Sharon's success

I don't know how much is really different, but I do know that I feel a lot better about things. Mainly I think that the tension has reduced a lot, and Dennis and I have enjoyed one another's company again. So much has happened. A credit card company called, and I found out that Dennis had opened another card and had maxxed it out already. I didn't tip my hand, but instead made the worm squirm and told him I found out something and wasn't going to tell him what it was. After denying for days, he wound up telling me many things I didn't know about. Of course he then started the "maybe we should split up because he is a jerk and not the caliber of man I deserve" routine. I then simply agreed with him as a means of telling him I was separating our accounts. I said, "You may be right about that. After all, look at all the deceitful things you have done. But I love you too much to leave, so I'm just going to open separate accounts until I can trust you." I am going to use every lie I find out about as an opportunity to agree with his "I'm

an asshole" strategy and protect myself from his escapades.

But the most fun thing was acting crazy. I feel I really expressed what was going on inside me. When I found myself questioning my own sanity and tied in knots from his lies, I started doing some really bizarre stuff. When we started to argue, I laughed and told him, "Dennis, you really crack me up." I did a bunch of crazy things. Trying to describe all the different methods I used to act crazy cannot do justice to how downright weird I got.

I did this so well that Dennis became genuinely concerned about my mental health. He seemed to be walking on eggshells, where he used to do whatever he pleased. I overheard him talking to his business partner on the phone, saying, "I'm worried about Sharon. I really think she's losing her mind." I took advantage of this opportunity to act even stranger. That night Dennis went to the refrigerator for his bedtime snack and found my running shoes. I explained to him that my feet really got hot when I ran. I can't describe the pleasure I got from the look on his face.

I don't know how long this will last, but Dennis is more cautious and considerably more respectful of my feelings. He also seems to have toned down his lies somewhat. For me, I am relieved to be doing something that had some positive effect, if only for me.

We offered three suggestions to unmask the Great Pretender:

1. Protect yourself and your wallet. Eliminate your financial vulnerabilities.
2. Make the worm squirm. Don't tip your hand and divulge all you know. Use the information you have to pressure him to come clean.
3. Act crazy. Express in action-oriented ways how he makes you feel. Point out the emotional consequences of his behavior without directly confronting him.

Exposing the Chameleon's True Colors

The Chameleon is a curious kind of guy. His intentions are not generally malicious, but the results of his deception are just as destructive as those of other liars and cheaters. He is like the guy who runs over you with his car, but he didn't mean to do it. You are just as dead—but his intentions were good, and he feels terribly guilty. Just like Mr. Helpful's efforts at control are insidious, the Chameleon's misrepresentations are subtle yet dangerous.

The Chameleon is like Woody Allen's character of *Zelig*, taking on the characteristics of those he is around, accommodating to his surroundings perfectly. But like Woody Allen, he is only playing a part in a movie. When the movie is over, or when the Chameleon abruptly decides he is not happy with his new role, the problems begin. The artistry of the Chameleon is that he does the same hurtful things that other lying, cheating guys do, but you think that it is your fault and feel sorry for him.

Mary and Darryl: The Case of "Who Am I Today?"

Recall Mary and Darryl. Darryl started out as Mr. Perfect but turned into Mr. Perfect Asshole as he became disenchanted with the role he was playing in the drama of Mary's life.

Mary's story

I am so confused. I thought everything was going so well between Darryl and me—but then his complaints started. He is so unlike other men I've known. He is so sensitive. The kids love him. Boy, did he chase me! He called and sent flowers. Darryl is such a romantic guy. I thought he was okay with me making decisions and running things—you know, the little details of life—but lately I can't do anything right. I am on an emotional roller-coaster. I don't know what I've done. I'm no different than

before, but he doesn't seem happy with me. Maybe it is me and I can't see it. Maybe I am too controlling. Is it that I sabotage a good man when I get one? I don't know. I try to discuss what I can do to get things back to the way things were before, but he just shrugs and says that maybe it's too late. He looks like he is in terrible pain about all this. When he is with me, he complains about missing the single lifestyle. When he is not with me, he tells me he misses me. Exasperating!

What Doesn't Work

The Marys of the world typically bend over backwards trying to figure out what's wrong so they can fix it. They are patient and understanding, and work hard at finding an explanation. They read books by supposed "experts", and learn all the reasons why men can't commit and have trouble with intimate relationships. They ultimately blame themselves and take the responsibility for the Chameleon's U-turn.

However, the problem isn't the Marys of the world, nor is it anything particular about the relationship. So trying to discuss what he is unhappy about and how that can be addressed is futile and frustrating. It doesn't work because the Chameleon is a spineless amoeba. He will not give you a straight answer because he is so conflicted about being liked vs. pleasing himself. He doesn't want to hurt you, so he won't be direct. But he will let you know how miserable he is so you will let him off the emotional hook.

This kicks in another oft-used strategy of women's in dealing with Chameleons—they nurture and comfort them. Let's look at this situation. He rides into your life straight out of a romance novel. He courts you big time and wins you over, going to any means to ensure your interest in him. Then he backs out of the relationship, changes everything, and turns your life upside down

and inside out. And you're the one providing sympathy and regular sex to help him through his guilt-ridden process of dumping you. Hmm.

Ultimately, the Chameleon will say he needs some time to sort things out and will propose having less contact in the hopes of letting you down gently so you won't hate him. He won't end the relationship because he doesn't have the courage to do it directly. Rather, he will leave you no other choice but to end it yourself.

What Works

First, **give him what he wants—and more**. When the Chameleon complains about the relationship not meeting his needs and suggests spending less time together, don't try to talk him out of it. Instead, say, "That's a good idea. I know you are struggling, and need some space to evaluate what you want to do and how our relationship is not meeting your needs. I have been having second thoughts, too. How about we see each other every two weeks instead of once a week."

This gives him *more space than he wants*. The idea here is that whatever contact schedule he suggests, you lengthen it. This effectively puts you in charge without saying so, makes him uncomfortable and reverses the rules he usually applies at this point in a relationship. The Chameleon typically plays his gut-wrenching "this is going to hurt me a lot more than it's going to hurt you" card until the woman finally folds in frustration, tired of playing a losing hand. Your new stance doesn't fight his pulling away, but rather, encourages it. It puts the Chameleon on the spot without confronting him. If done effectively and genuinely, this strategy makes it clear that the direct pressure is off, but an implicit pressure squeezes him to figure out what he wants. It makes the Chameleon's life far more difficult because perhaps for the first

time, he may have to make a decision himself, rather than force the woman to do it. This often represents new territory for the Chameleon. It may be entertaining to watch him struggle through it.

Another tactic that shines a light on his indecision is to **mess with his mind**. Because his modus operandi is to figure out what pleases you so he can accommodate you, "mess with his mind" invites you to play a different role every time you see him. It requires that you figure out who you want to be—a living, dead or imaginary character—and then act out that part with the Chameleon. You dress differently, you act differently, you like and dislike different things. You demonstrate your complexity, not your stability, because he uses your stability to form his own identity.

This makes life unsettling for the Chameleon. You are essentially breaking the mold he has constructed for you and making it impossible for him to anticipate your needs and desires. This strategy flushes out the Chameleon by making it difficult for him to know how to react to you. It encourages him to say what he really wants from a relationship, maybe for the first time in his life.

Another goal accomplished by this strategy is to change the "feeling tone" of the situation. The Chameleon strives for the perception that his decision to back off has painfully thrust him into a heroic struggle of epic proportions. This encourages you to see his guilt, overlook your hurt feelings, and give him patience and understanding. Messing with his mind, as well as tactics in its class (see chapter 17), has a goal of lowering the emotional intensity surrounding the problem and putting it in a different, less crucial perspective. By playing a different role and getting ridiculous, your behavior is also saying, "This is kind of silly, and I'm not going to let it become a life-and-death issue." Once the situation becomes less grave, it becomes more workable.

Finally, it is important to have a mental timetable regarding how long you will wait for things to improve and/or evolve into a

long-term relationship. **Know when to say when.** How long you decide upon is not important. The fact that you decide and put a time limit on it is crucial. Knowing when enough is enough and how much is too much gives you, not him, control of your life.

Mary's success

I don't know if we are going to stay together, but things have certainly lightened up between us. It was very hard for me because I wanted to convince him how good our relationship could be, but instead I supported his idea to cut back on contact. I encouraged even less contact and suggested it would give him more time to figure out what he really needed from me and a relationship. Well, he didn't like that, but he didn't say anything. Darryl can never go the whole two weeks without at least calling me, and he seems to be whining less about how much of a struggle he is having with what to do.

The other thing I tried (not every time, but a few times) was to "mess with his mind" by acting out different roles with him. The first time, I took on a Marilyn Monroe persona, which is about as far from me as I can get. I wore lots of makeup and a very tight short dress. I expected to be catered to: I waited for Darryl to open car doors and stuff like that. It was great fun and it was interesting how people reacted to me. Women hated me, men loved me. Shows the male mentality. Darryl didn't know what was going on and seemed very disturbed at first. He finally asked me about it, and I told him I was experimenting with different lifestyles. Ultimately, he kind of got into it, and we had a good time. Another time I adopted a Katharine Hepburn role and had very sophisticated tastes. Usually I am an order-a-pizza-and-rent-a-movie kind of gal, but this time I got us dinner reservations at an exclusive French restaurant and opera tickets. Darryl had a puzzled look on his face all night and wasn't sure how to react to

me. He told me what he really liked about me was my stability and asked me to go back to the way I was before. I didn't tell him that he wasn't happy with me before, but rather, told him that I was keeping my options open. We have resumed regular and frequent contact, and I am hopeful that it evolves into marriage; but I am keeping my eyes open and continuing to evaluate what I want from this relationship. If he begins to whine and back off, I know things I can do to make myself feel better. I have a timetable in my head that if things don't work out by then, I will ultimately end the relationship.

We offered three suggestions to cope with life with the Chameleon:

1. Give him what he wants—and more. Lean toward the Chameleon's desire to back off, give him more space than he wants, and encourage his struggle to determine what he wants. He'll hate it.
2. Mess with his mind. Assume a pretend identity and break the mold of you that he has, making it difficult to accommodate you and pressuring him to come clean with what he wants from you.
3. Know when to say when. Have a mental timetable in mind with the Chameleon to enhance your feeling of being in control.

Rendering Don Juan Impotent

Of all the men discussed in this book, Don Juan is the most loved and missed. The curious thing about Don Juan is that men also like him—unless, of course, he is after their women. They envy his success with women and admire, even idolize, his abilities

to mesmerize women into the bedroom. To Don Juan, women are truly objects, toys to be appreciated for their beauty or functionality, but for nothing else. Underneath his smarmy interpersonal arsenal is a general disrespect for women and a secret fear of his inadequacy. Don Juans are often married.

Danielle and Pete: The Case of the Wild Thing

Recall Danielle and Pete. Pete was every woman's fantasy. And in many ways, Pete delivered on Danielle's fantasies. He was great fun and seemed to breathe life into everything he did. Pete made Danielle feel very special, as if she were the most desirable woman on earth. Pete was like the character Michael Smith in Robert A. Heinlein's *Stranger in a Strange Land*. Danielle was like the character Anne, who describes a kiss in the following passage.

> *"I've been kissed by men who did a very good job. But they don't give kissing their whole attention. They can't. No matter how hard they try, parts of their minds are on something else. Missing the last bus—or their chances for making the gal—or their own techniques in kissing—or maybe worry about their jobs, or money, or will husband or papa or the neighbors catch on. . . . but when Mike kisses you he isn't doing anything else. You're his whole universe. . . and the moment is eternal because he doesn't have any plans and isn't going anywhere. Just kissing you." She shivered. "It's overwhelming."*

These guys generally don't misrepresent themselves regarding sensual pleasures and excitement. They give you what you are looking for. However, there is a price to be paid for feeling so special.

Danielle's story

I don't know if I can go on. I feel so depressed and betrayed. I just moved out of my boyfriend's house because I found out he was

seeing other women. He doesn't want to stop seeing them and doesn't understand why I am upset. Sometimes I don't understand why I am upset either. Pete says it's just sex, that it doesn't mean anything and that he loves me, and that should be enough. But that doesn't really give me what I want in a relationship. I know I should just move on, but our relationship can be so good. Pete treats me like a queen, and I feel incredibly alive when we are together. He is exciting, and I've never had such good sex. Sex was always just okay before. It was fun, but nothing I really looked forward to or daydreamed about. Pete has such an appetite, and sometimes I literally tremble at the thought of sex. I fantasize about him and feel like—I know this sounds stupid—like a sexual goddess. Ha! I see myself doing things I would have never done without Pete. And not just in the bedroom. He is in such command and has taken me places I would have never gone. But sex and excitement are not what long-term relationships are about. I know that—I just can't bring myself to let him go. I know I should.

What Doesn't Work

There are two general strategies that women try when choosing to stay with Don Juan. One is that they confront him and get Don Juan to say he'll *try* to do better, which they interpret as meaning he *will* stop seeing other women. Of course he won't, because trying means that he can't really do it. Trying implies failure is forthcoming. "I told you I would try, but you know what an appetite I have." This just sets up a revolving door situation in which your hopes are built up, only to be obliterated each time you find that he has fallen off the wagon—and onto some other very willing woman. This becomes an emotional roller-coaster ride that can last for a long time—even many years.

The other thing women do is try to understand why he cheats.

They talk to him about his past, read self-help books about men who cheat and come to believe that he can't help himself or that he is a sex addict. This may be an accurate way of looking at it, but do not take an explanation of his behavior and allow it to exonerate him. He can choose to change if his behavior is distressing to him. The problem is that it is rarely distressing to him. Your feelings of misery are usually insufficient grounds to encourage Don Juan to change.

What Works

Although the outlook is often dismal, it is not necessarily and completely hopeless. Some Don Juans do settle down. However, expecting that he will, and basing your life and happiness on that expectation, is surely a losing strategy. The trick is to, as the song goes, hang on loosely but don't let go, and continue to evaluate whether change is possible.

First, a pragmatic tip for dealing with a Don Juan. **Protect yourself from HIV!** Don't take chances with unprotected sex. Obviously, Don Juan's promiscuous lifestyle puts him at much higher risk for exposure to HIV. And of course he will lie about whether he used condoms. Remember, he is an uncontested master in his ability to tell you what you want to hear in the most sincere way imaginable. These guys give Academy Award-winning performances every day of their lives. Don't think for a minute you can figure out whether he is lying. Assume that he is. He often believes his own lies. We know that no one likes to think about AIDS or death, but you should if you are sexual with a Don Juan. We won't share the tragedies we have observed in these situations, so please take our word for it and use condoms.

Dealing with Don Juan requires a three-pronged approach. First, **give him what he wants—and more**. *Temporarily* accept his

lifestyle. You do not have to like it. Your message to him is simply that you do not like him seeing other women, but you know you can't change him. Consequently, you will go along with his lifestyle because the benefits outweigh the costs for you. Remember from our discussion of the Chameleon that this strategy also requires that you give him even more space than he wants. This simply means that you make yourself less available to him, but without an attitude about it.

In Don Juan's case, more space obviously enables him to seek out other women. So *this strategy is not for everyone*. If temporarily staying with him is too difficult and you find yourself getting depressed or devaluing yourself in any way, *don't do it*. These ideas are for women who want to try to work it out, or at least desire to allow things to unfold a bit more to see if change is possible. This situation likely creates new ground for the Don Juan to walk on because women usually bail out when the unfaithfulness surfaces. Another option that may be more palatable to you is to stay in touch with him, but only remain friends. Do not date him or have sex. Let him know that he has your blessing to live his life as he sees fit but that it is not for you. Don Juan then will have to decide about the relationship based on how he feels about you, rather than his usual experience of women leaving him and severing all ties with him.

To employ this wait-and-see coping strategy, you need to **know when to say when.** Establish a mental timetable, a predetermined period of time to accept the situation as it is and evaluate the possibilities for change. The amount of time is not important. You have to do some soul-searching to establish what is right for you. It may be three months or a year, or whatever. Your own comfort level is your best measure of what a reasonable stretch of time is for you. During this set time period, you are a behavioral scientist, an observer of asshole behavior. Your job is to experiment with the

strategies we are suggesting and evaluate if any hope exists for change. At the end of the designated mental timetable, you tally up your findings and react accordingly. A mental timetable allows you to justify to yourself why you are staying and gives the relationship the shot you obviously feel it deserves. It also permits you to stop putting up with the situation when the time runs out. You, therefore, are in control of your destiny.

Finally, the third tactic is the **life is good** strategy. It involves perceiving a problem circumstance, the very situation that you would like to see changed, as *beneficial* for you. Sounds nuts, doesn't it? Maybe so, but it can be very effective. You must think of the advantages of the situation for you and then verbalize those advantages to your partner. If you cannot think of any legitimate advantages of remaining in the relationship, then this tactic is not for you.

Interpreting negative situations in positive ways may sound bizarre, but it isn't as difficult as you may suspect. Problems are not all bad, and everything will not be all good when the problem is gone. Take, for example, a promotion on your job. A promotion may mean a better salary, more prestige and another career goal accomplished. It may also mean more hours, more responsibility, and less time spent with family and friends. Problems and events in relationships can similarly be described in terms of their advantages and disadvantages. Even the most negative of circumstances can be analyzed and determined to contain some benefit. Living with assholes is never all bad; there are always advantages.

"Life is good" can set the stage for several positive outcomes. It allows you to see the advantages of the situation the way it is, thereby giving you a different perspective that may open other avenues for solution. At the very least, acceptance of the situation is promoted, which can be quite helpful in and of itself. If any power issues are involved, they are undercut because now you are

not pushing for change. Instead, you are accepting and even liking that things will stay the same.

With the pressure removed, the asshole now has the freedom to change by his own choice and determination. If he freely changes, it will reflect a change that will likely be enduring and not just a response to coercion. Once Don Juan is made aware that you understand there is benefit to the situation the way it is, then he can begin to see the disadvantages for himself and truly evaluate what he wants. Once you allow yourself to see the advantages, you may feel a little better if it doesn't change.

So back to Danielle and Don Juan. Danielle's task is to find the advantages for her in staying in the relationship with Pete despite his screwing other women. Sounds impossible, right? Not really. Remember that if you have any chance for this situation to work out, you have to slow things down and enable Don Juan to consider his lifestyle.

Danielle's success

This was so hard. But I am really glad I gave the relationship a chance. When I decided to move out, I was really miserable because I felt that the relationship was over since Pete was unable to change his fooling around with other women. It was good knowing that I could choose to stay with the situation awhile because I was really not ready to give him up—yet. I could actually stay in the relationship on my terms, which gave me a sense of control. So I gave him what he wanted and accepted I couldn't make him stop, which I shared with him. Pete was delighted to continue our relationship. I also stopped having unprotected sex and had an HIV test, which was negative, thank God. Pete didn't like that much and complained about the lack of spontaneity, but I stayed firm. After a lot of thinking, I decided that I could put up with this for

six months. I thought that that should be enough time to see if this leopard could change his spots. I got a lot of relief just knowing that whatever was happening was time limited. I knew I could endure anything for that long. It also allowed me to relax and enjoy the good times we had.

Whenever I got an opportunity, I told Pete about the advantages about our relationship for me. First, I said the really obvious ones, like it was great fun and I liked the adventurous things we did together. I also shared how I liked the way he treated me and made me feel like a real woman. He really liked that. I also told him other things that he didn't like so much, but that were all true at least to some extent. I said that I liked how he brought out the wild side of me and how I had suppressed that side all my life. I told him he was allowing me to really be able to express myself with other men. Our relationship, I told him, had unleashed the "wild thing," which I was very grateful for.

Although he didn't say it directly, I believe it bothered him that I was thinking about other men and life after Pete. I also shared with him the benefits of being in a noncommitted relationship: no hassles, no pressures and no bullshit about the future. I actually believed most of what I said, and it lightened me up significantly. It was especially gratifying to see Pete look bothered. He told me a woman never said those things to him before and would often question me about other men. Sometimes he would talk about our future together. But he didn't commit, and I reached the end of my timetable. It was still hard, but I was able to more objectively evaluate the possibilities with Pete. I felt in charge, and I followed through with it. He was shocked and called me for some time, but I started seeing someone else fairly soon. I still fantasize about Pete, but I like the guy I'm with a lot better. It's nice to not worry about where his—you know—has been when he comes over.

We suggested four tactics to cope with a Don Juan:

1. Protect yourself from HIV. Don't let his acting abilities convince you not to worry about AIDS.
2. Give him what he wants—and more. Accept his lifestyle and allow an observation period.
3. Know when to say when. Determine a mental timetable.
4. Life is good. Think of the benefits of the relationship and verbalize the advantages to the Don Juan.

15 Peter Pan No More

Workshops we would like to see
for immature men:

- *Understanding the Female Response
  to Coming in Drunk at 4:00 A.M.*
- *Parenting: It Doesn't End with Conception*
- *"The Weekend" and "Sports" Are
  Not Synonymous*
- *Romanticism: Ideas Other Than Sex*
- *Male Bonding: Leaving Your Friends at Home*
- *Introductory Foreplay: The Drive Home Does
  Not Count*

Immature assholes grow tiresome after a while. Most women, sooner or later, see the writing on the wall and dump these guys. Nevertheless, if you decide to stick with them, hoping they will eventually grow up, this chapter provides methods of

managing life with those boys who never became men. Before we begin our discussion we present another myth that often hinders successful coping with immature guys.

Myth #3: What Men Say Has a Big Impact on What They Do

Our behavior sends powerful messages about our true feelings for our relationships. Of particular interest are situations in which words and behavior give conflicting messages. Consider the Don Juan from the last chapter who says "I love you" but has continual affairs. Which message is real? Which indicates his true opinion of the relationship?

Many women stay in destructive relationships because they believe (or pay attention to) their partner's words, not the behaviors, when the two send opposing messages. This is not surprising in a society that places such emphasis and value on words. "A man is only as good as his word." "Say what you mean and mean what you say." Those ideas may be countered with "Actions speak louder than words," but the truth is that most of us don't have much training or experience in "listening" to behavior. In spite of the fact that we are all aware that people can say one thing but do another, many of us still hold the belief that people will act in accordance with their words.

To avoid this pitfall, you must make a conscious effort to attend to what he does, not what he says. Behavior tends to be a far more tangible and meaningful expression of beliefs and values than words. This is, of course, easier said than done. If we hear a politician lead the family value bandwagon, but then see him involved in a sex scandal, we know what to believe and are not confused. However, in relationships in which we participate and not just observe, and that involve our needs and feelings, the picture is not nearly so clear.

Unfortunately, many women listen to a guy's words when it's the behavior that is much more indicative of their commitment and the value they place on the relationship. Women unwittingly become victims of their belief that what these men say has a big impact on what they do. Once you accept that words fall short of accurately depicting his intentions, it becomes obvious that what you must count on is behavior. Behavior is what gives evidence of his true intentions.

Disowning the Mama's Boy

Mama's Boys are caricatures of male ineptitude. They are the kind of men that if you leave town, you compose a twenty-five-page instruction letter that appears written for an Alzheimer's patient, or you give up altogether and get someone else to watch the kids and take care of household business. They are 1950s-style men who never evolved with the rest of the planet. They believe in men's and women's work, usually defined very narrowly, and with 95 percent of the responsibility on women. Their domestic ineptitude allows them to be taken care of by women who are natural caretakers, who are unwilling to risk entrusting things to the Mama's Boy.

Joan and Donnie: The Case of Getting a Life

Recall Joan and Donnie. Donnie's chronic irresponsibility, persistent mismanagement of his affairs, and self-centered dependence made Joan question herself and bear an inordinate burden in the day-to-day running of life.

Joan's story
I grew up my whole life wanting to get married, have kids and be a nurse. I didn't know that having a husband and having kids

would be the same thing. My husband defies all reasoning. He's not really a bad guy or anything. He's just a big blob—no initiative, ambition or realistic sense of the world. He never thinks about the future or worries about anything. The only thing that gets to him is me. He thinks I am queen bitch of the universe. I guess I am sometimes. I hover over him like an overbearing mom. I walk around picking up his stuff more than the kids'—I should say, the other kids'! He just doesn't get it.

Anything that gets done, I do or have to ask him to do. There is no partnership here. I need a man, not another kid. I want someone to share the responsibilities of life with me, not someone else to take care of.

What Doesn't Work

There are two general strategies that women employ with Mama's Boys. First, they directly bring the Mama's Boy's inadequacies to his attention. They are sick and tired of his childish and irresponsible behavior, and they let him know about it. But how does he respond? Just exactly the way you would expect an overgrown eleven-year-old to act. He sulks and broods, throws temper tantrums about your mean nagging, and/or passive-aggressively defies you by not doing what you would like him to do.

A subset of the strategy of directly letting him know is permitting him to see the effects of the overwork on you. A woman with a Mama's Boy repeatedly points out her tiredness and illnesses, hoping he will get the idea to pitch in and help out. He won't. It's hopeless because he believes *it is your job to suffer and sacrifice for him.* After all, his mom did, and it didn't kill her.

Second, Joan and women like her ultimately accept that the Mama's Boy is a child and treat him accordingly. They resign themselves to doing more and more. What else can they do? They are unhappy and resentful but continue nevertheless to take care

of the kids, house, finances, etc. They give up, often thinking that things could be worse. For example, at least he doesn't fool around, beat me, pick his nose or (you fill in the blank). Women sometimes blame themselves and come to believe that it is them, that they just need to get more efficient at their duties. Unfortunately, this type of thinking makes these women vulnerable to depression and exhaustion. It also makes them prime prey to Don Juans, who give them temporary relief and look, on the outside, to be far more independent and responsible.

What Works

Managing life with Mama's Boys can be accomplished with three strategies. First is **shifting the focus**. This requires you to dethrone him as the king of your happiness universe and elevate yourself to royalty for a change. We mean "for a change" in two ways. One is that it likely is something that you rarely, if ever, do. Second, placing yourself on center stage will permit changes to occur in the relationship as well. Recall the mobile metaphor of mutual dependence.

Shifting the focus to yourself can accomplish several positive outcomes. First, tension is reduced because you aren't pointing out his inadequacies to him anymore. Undercutting tension allows people to draw upon their own inherent capacities for making changes. Focusing on your existing strengths and areas of control tends to increase confidence and self-esteem. Feeling in control and good about ourselves enhances our ability to consider different solutions.

More specifically, shifting the focus involves consciously removing attention from the Mama's Boy and his problems, and redirecting that attention toward yourself and your interests. Your sense of responsibility for the relationship has probably taken an expensive toll on your pursuit of your own passions.

Although it sounds very simple—and it is, in concept—shifting the focus is very difficult to actually implement. It requires you to let go of direct attempts at change and instead focus on your own personal growth. For example, you might return to school, take up a hobby, join a civic group or pursue a political activity. It doesn't matter what you do, only that you do it for yourself. It will then behaviorally convey to the Mama's Boy (and to you) that you are worth the time and attention you are devoting to yourself.

This shifting-the-focus strategy sets the stage for part two of coping with the Mama's Boy. This component requires you to "let go" and allow him to muddle through without you while you are gone taking care of yourself. Essentially, you are going to provide him with something he never got at home—training to be an adult. Now, this can be very scary for you because you are going to have to live with his foul-ups. But the only way for him to grow up is to subject him to **trial by fire**.

You are just going to be too busy to do what you used to do. He will have to do more around the house if you do not do it. You are not on strike or doing it out of resentment; you are simply too involved in taking care of yourself to manage everything. He is not going to like it because, for the first time away from work, he will be expected to act like a grown up—a tall order, to be sure.

Thinking of it in another way, the Mama's Boy should really be pitied. Because of his upbringing, he has been denied the opportunity for mature adult life. So you are doing him an incredible service. For example, by being busy a couple nights a week, you give him the privilege of helping with the kids' homework, bathing them and preparing them for bed—actually parenting them. In many ways this strategy of trial by fire means that you are truly accepting the Mama's Boy for what he is—a child—and taking action, indirectly, to set up developmental experiences for him to mature into adulthood. It allows you to "mother" him without all

the associated burdens and could enable the Mama's Boy to take independent action.

Finally, the last tactic is one you are now familiar with: just desserts (see "Firing the Boss" in chapter 13). In this instance, it can help you cope with your resentment in a useful way. This strategy also requires you to stop trying to persuade the Mama's Boy to change (for example, to pick up after himself). You merely request his compliance in a harmless way ("I would appreciate it if you would please pick up your clothes"). Then, employ just desserts when he does not comply with your requests (for example, wash his clothes, but "forget" to put them in the dryer).

Joan's success

> If nothing else happens, at least I finally got out of the house and tried to "get a life." I enrolled in a computer class and am having a lot of fun with that. I'm finding a lot of great medical stuff on the Net that is really helping divert my attention from trying to change Donnie. That has really reduced the tension around the house. Except for when Donnie gets miffed about my leaving to go to class, or staying on the Net so long, we are getting along a lot better. His lack of concern about the future and zero ambition have not changed, but he seems to be more involved with the kids as a parent. I think maybe I was hindering his "development" by doing too much of the parenting because he gladly deferred to me. Now that I'm gone two nights a week, he has had to take over. He said he wouldn't "baby-sit" at first, but I told him if he wanted to arrange for someone else to do it, that was up to him. At first he took them to his mom's house, but that got to be too much hassle at bedtime. So he started actually doing it himself, and I think he's kind of proud of himself. He, of course, thinks he deserves a medal for what I have to do as a regular course of my day. But hey, I'll take the help however I can get it.

I tried "just desserts" whenever he really pushed my buttons. I can't stand it when he leaves his dishes on the counter, when all he has to do is rinse them and put them in the dishwasher. We have a problem with ants, which I hate, and I've practically begged him to not leave dirty dishes out. I completely backed off and didn't mention it at all, except to kindly ask him to do it. Then, I nailed him for it every time. One time I ate crackers on his side of the bed, and another time I disconnected the cable before his Sunday football ritual. I felt so good about it I almost felt guilty. Almost. Like I heard in the movie Dolores Claiborne, sometimes all a woman has to hold on to to survive is being a bitch. Ha!

I know this didn't solve all my problems, but it helped me to cope with them better and to figure out in the long run whether Donnie and I are going to work out. We are still worlds apart on lots of things, and I know he will be slow to "develop" into an adult; but I think I am on the right track.

To cope with a Mama's Boy, we suggested three strategies:

1. Shift the focus. Remove the Mama's Boy from the center of your universe and pursue your own passions and growth.
2. Trial by fire. Set up situations that, by your absence, give the Mama's Boy the painful opportunities to mature into an adult.
3. Just desserts. Nail the Mama's Boy for the things that *really* get to you.

Grounding the Eternal Teenager

While the Mama's Boy acts like a child and seems to be stuck at a developmental age of about eleven, the Eternal Teenager is firmly planted in a far more offensive and dangerous developmental stage. His bumper stickers illustrate his view of the world and women: "Shit happens" and "If I tell you you have a great body, will you hold it against me?" In other words, if you want to hang out with him, don't complain; accept him as he is, and view yourself as a decorative pleasure toy for his amusement.

Tammy and Chad: The Case of "I Just Love Your Friends"

After a while, life with an Eternal Teenager comes to resemble the events in the movie *Animal House* more and more. Recall Tammy and Chad. Chad talked a good game but always seemed to maneuver the relationship onto the back burner.

Tammy's story

Why is it that just when things are going the way I want them to, the roof falls in? Things were going great with Chad—not perfect, but not anything I couldn't live with. He partied too much, but I don't think he is an alcoholic. It's his lifestyle. I like a lot of it, but sometimes you gotta just get on with your life. It's time to move on. Chad doesn't know when to stop. He spends three or four nights a week with his friends. He has a blast when he is with them, and sometimes I do, too. But I want something more. I want a home and family. These are not priorities to Chad. He says he has plenty of time to think of those things. Now he just wants to enjoy life. He always comes back with that silly commercial, "Life is a sport. Drink it up!"

I don't want to break up—at least not yet. I love Chad and really believe that down deep, below his "party on, dude" attitude,

he loves me, too. But it's hard being so low on the totem pole of priorities. And his friends drive me nuts, but God forbid I ever say anything negative about any of them. That is truly sacred ground. He is like two different people. He is a vulgar, sexist pig when he is with his friends; but when he is alone with me, he is very nice. The problem is that we are never alone except when we are having sex. We also never talk about anything meaningful, and certainly never about our relationship. One of his friends is married and his wife is unbelievably tolerant. But she is also a party animal. I'm just not like that. I don't know what to do. I have tried talking to him until I'm so frustrated. It's always the same. He winds up telling me exactly what I don't want to hear—that he's not ready to settle down and have his wings clipped yet, but when he does, he would like it to be with me. I really would just like to spend some couple time with him so I can really see if there is something salvageable here.

What Doesn't Work

Like many of the other women in this book, Tammy tried to bring her concerns about the relationship to Chad's attention. She unfortunately believed that if she directly addressed her concerns, he would attempt to change to accommodate her. Instead, Tammy found out where she really stood on the hierarchy of Chad's priorities: well below his friends and activities, somewhere just ahead of his WaveRunner, but below his car.

Another often used but seldom successful solution is to start knocking his friends and pointing out their weaknesses. This is a big mistake. These are his buds, man. His drinking bros. They cannot do any wrong because the things you criticize them for are the very things he idolizes them for! She says, "Bob drinks too much." He says, "Bob can really hold his liquor." She says, "Frank is vulgar

and comes on to me." He says, "Frank is a riot, and you are too sensitive." Get the idea where you stand here? The Eternal Teenager will always make excuses for his friends at your expense. You are the expendable commodity here; they are not. After all, no woman can come between him and chest-pounding buds.

Another strategy that women like Tammy use is to show their misery over the situation. They think, either consciously or otherwise, that if he sees how much it hurts, guilt will induce him to change and pay more attention to their needs. Bad idea. First of all, guilt is not an emotion that Eternal Teenagers have an abundance of. How many teenagers do you know who readily complied with parental wishes when made aware of their parents' hurt feelings about what they were doing? Remember, you are dealing with the teenage mind here. Second, even if he does care about your feelings when he is with you, that will quickly dissipate as soon as he joins his friends and his mind is absorbed in the collective Neanderthal mentality.

What Works

First, you have to allow a time of reevaluation to occur that permits the possibility of change. This calls for a dose of **give him what he wants—and more** (see "Exposing the Chameleon's True Colors" in chapter 14). In this case, it means leaning toward his view of the relationship temporarily to see if there is any hope of his growing up or taking the relationship more seriously.

Next, **invite what you dread**. This requires a total reversal, an acceptance and even encouragement of the Eternal Teenager spending time with his friends. It also involves you finding good things to say about his friends at every opportunity. Specifically, you must comment on the positive qualities that the Eternal Teenager's friends possess. Verbalizing your approval of them

prevents any knee-jerk reaction on his part to spend time with them because you don't want him to.

Second, similar to the woman involved with a Mama's Boy, it is time to **shift the focus** from your partner to your own growth. Pursue interests that allow you to decline his company from time to time when it involves his friends. This obviously reduces the amount of contact and begins to offer the Eternal Teenager some choices in how he spends his time. You must, however, be completely okay with whatever he chooses so that you don't pressure him in any way. If he feels pressure, he will do what any other teenager does—exactly the opposite of what you want.

Providing schedule choices to the Eternal Teenager *without* harassing him about his friends will likely be a first for him. Usually women get tired of his sophomoric lifestyle and leave him, or he meets someone else when he grows weary of complaints about his time with his fellow Neanderthals. These strategies permit the Eternal Teenager to make up his own mind for a change. He can now evaluate the relationship based on how he feels about you, rather than how he resents you for coming between him and his friends. This is a big difference for him because it gives him a passing acquaintance with being an adult.

The Eternal Teenager also requires you to **know when to say when** and have a mental timetable, as previously discussed. If the Eternal Teenager does not meet your minimal acceptable standards regarding time together and commitment when your timetable elapses, then it is time to cut your losses and move on. You can also add the dimension of dating other men, but not spitefully, toward the end of your timetable to see if that affords both you and the Eternal Teenager any additional information upon which to base a decision.

Tammy's success

I'm still evaluating my relationship with Chad, but I'm not miserable anymore. I started by completely stopping my complaining about our lack of private time together and his time with his friends. I also stopped ragging on them and pointing out all the stupid things they did. Instead, I made a real effort to say nice things about them and get along with them. I started telling Chad that I just loved his friends. He seemed a little jealous. It was funny to hear Chad then criticize one of his buds and tell him to back off of saying crude things to me. It was the first time I had seen a protective side to him.

I also started going to the gym a lot and went back to visiting my parents more, like before I met Chad. This way I could be busy sometimes when Chad asked me to do things. Sometimes I just turned down doing things I didn't like doing very much, like bowling or WaveRunning. I was careful not to act mad or disappointed. Chad had a curious reaction. Not every time, but sometimes he changed his plans to spend the time with me rather than his friends. We have had more time alone together since I backed off trying to "make" him be the way I want him to be. He actually chooses to be with me sometimes. Of course, his friends ride him and call him a wimp, but that's kind of what they do anyway. I have been more relaxed about everything.

He hasn't proposed to me or anything like that, and he still is not sure what he wants. But I'm not pressing him about it. I mentioned to him that I wanted to start dating other people and encouraged him to do the same. He was very angry at first, then he got real hurt and even cried. I was very surprised when he asked me to hold off on that for a while. I agreed for a couple of months, but I followed my timetable and started seeing other guys. He accepted it but still doesn't like it. I haven't found anybody any better yet,

and I'm still seeing Chad. He treats me pretty well, and I don't do things with his friends that I don't want to do. I think Chad has grown up some, but not enough. I'm okay with that until I find someone more like what I'm looking for.

We suggested four things to deal with the Eternal Teenager:

1. Give him what he wants—and more. Go with his definition of the relationship so that you can evaluate its potential.
2. Invite what you dread. Encourage his time with his friends and back off criticizing them. Compliment his friends.
3. Shift the focus. Spend more time pursuing your interests. Allow the Eternal Teenager conflicts and choices (without pressure), so that he can evaluate what he wants rather than having his usual knee-jerk reactions.
4. Know when to say when. Have a mental timetable to allow yourself to be in control of the situation.

Dethroning the Fence Sitter

Fence Sitters may be the most frustrating of all men to deal with because they set women up with great expectations, only to pulverize them when they withdraw into ambivalence. TV and movie characterizations of the Fence Sitter are far too sympathetic. He is portrayed as having cold feet or just afraid of all the responsibilities of commitment and marriage. But that's no excuse. They leave in their wake women who waste their lives waiting for Fence Sitters to grow up and make up their minds.

April and Dan: The Case of He Loves Me, He Loves Me Not

Recall April and Dan. Dan, who pursued her obsessively until he caught her, swept April off her feet. Then his meticulous inspection of the relationship found fault after fault that he just couldn't take anymore. So he broke it off but found that he still loved April and pursued the relationship again. And so on. Sometimes Fence Sitters are married, but of course unhappily, and are ambivalent about ending their marriages. They seem constantly on the lookout for someone else who will make them happy.

April's story

Dan is such a jerk! I don't know why I put up with him, but things can be so good when he's not going through these things he goes through. It can be terrific and terrible from one moment to the next. Like the other night: I was over at his apartment, and we were just watching a movie, and he started in on me, out of the blue, about some guy I work with and whether I was seeing him. I was dumbstruck and didn't know what to say (as usual). The situation escalated to him throwing me out of his place and packing up all my stuff that's over there and sending it to me. It's like he manufactures something to go wrong, berates me and ends the relationship. He can be really cruel. When things get tense at all, he diminishes the relationship and says how it just can't be one that will ever go anywhere.

He knows I really want things to work out, and I believe he uses that against me. He also knows that our separations drive me crazy, yet he won't put me at ease and tell me how long it will be or what needs to be different. Instead, after a period of time he will call and want to get together. If I don't act as if it will be perfectly

okay, he gives me a hard time and hangs up. He wants to go on, and have sex, like nothing has happened. He watches my every move, and if he sees any sign of distress, he attacks me, and the whole thing starts over. He especially goes off around holidays because he knows how important they are to me.

Funny thing, though: When we aren't in these times, we have a good time and share a lot of the same values. It's like when we get too close—I think he is afraid of intimacy and commitment. I try to understand and talk to him about it, but he's never much into talking about the relationship and never reads any of the books I suggest. It's like I'm the only one trying to make things better.

What Doesn't Work

As in all the situations described in this book, maintaining the status quo is a surefire prescription for a hopeless relationship and a demoralized you. The woman in April's position tries to deal with things in a reasonable, straightforward way. She talks to the Fence Sitter, making him aware of what she wants from the relationship and how his all-or-nothing approach is very painful. The Fence Sitter, however, does not take responsibility for his behavior, and gets defensive and accusatory. If she didn't (fill in the blank), then he wouldn't break off the relationship. Your pain is of no consequence to him. His perceptions are not only central, but are the *only* valid ones.

Another common strategy of a woman with a Fence Sitter is to try to be perfect in every respect. This usually includes totally revolving her life around his whims, desires and expectations. Trying to be perfect creates a lot of tension and is an impossible standard to live up to. Working harder, dancing faster and walking on eggshells are incredibly exhausting strategies that ultimately backfire. One woman pressured herself to leave original love

messages on her Fence Sitter's answering machine every day. If she didn't, he took it as a sign of her obviously wavering commitment to the relationship.

You can never do enough for these guys. Every day is a test of your love, a test that you will inevitably fail. You either wear out or wind up hating the Fence Sitter's guts. He believes, in many ways, that if you were that good, you wouldn't be with him. It becomes his job to find out all your imperfections to justify his withdrawal into ambivalence. His scrutiny of you also allows him to squeeze every last drop of relationship-saving effort you can muster.

You may not even mind revolving your life around his. However, such a choice is rarely productive. It gives several dangerous messages to the Fence Sitter that he has no trouble believing: that your life is insignificant next to his, that your needs don't matter compared with his, that you will endure anything to be with him and that you are desperate to be in a relationship with him. These are just the kinds of messages that enable the Fence Sitter to destroy your life.

A final losing strategy is one discussed before—trying to understand his motives. This is particularly self-defeating because there are a million books about this problem. April read them all. She was truly informed about her situation. However, like almost everyone else we've talked to over the years, she could not convince the Fence Sitter to read any of the books, let alone accept their interpretations of him.

What Works

First, as we've described, pay attention to his behavior, not his words. He says the relationship is over, but it never really is. This guy can't break off the relationship for good. You are going to have to use a crowbar to pry him out of your life. He's the kind of guy

who would harass you for months if you broke it off. Use that information to your advantage. As you begin to appreciate his dependence on you and *his* desperation for the relationship, you can pull out the stops and get more creative in your approach.

Next, **gloom and doom** can be helpful. It involves leaning toward his negativity about the relationship. Don't be a cheerleader by attempting to counter all his sour comments with upbeat retorts. This rescues him and places sole responsibility for the relationship in your lap. You are always in the position of convincing him about the good parts of the relationship, which inevitably keeps the pressure on you to dance faster and please him more. When he says, "This relationship will never make it," instead of saying, "Oh honey, you know I love you and we have a strong relationship," say, "You may be right; we have had our share of troubles, and it looks very bleak. But I hope we make it." Don't let him off the hook. Accept his view and reflect it back to him.

Similarly, **don't explain or defend yourself** with him. Don't forget that he is the one with the problem. When he makes outlandish accusations or picks a fight, don't take the bait. You haven't done anything wrong. No explanation is required.

Give him what he wants—and more is also applicable, similar to its use for the Chameleon. When he throws you out or breaks off the relationship, don't try to talk him out of it. Instead, give him more space than he wants. This is a very hard strategy to implement. When he eventually gets around to wanting you back, resist the urge to rush back into business as usual. When he calls, don't go over to his house and allow him to act as if nothing has happened. Instead, when he calls, make a date for dinner or whatever, but not for the same day of his call. Make him wait longer than he anticipated. Put yourself in charge of the length of separation. Increase your desirability by not being at his beck and call. Permit him to feel the discomfort of separation, rather than

avoiding it by immediate gratification.

It is easier to accomplish this if you also **shift the focus**, as dis-cussed earlier. It is very important for you to develop a life separate from him. If you don't have a life, the Fence Sitter will terrorize you for putting all of your eggs in one basket. More important, shifting the focus gives both you and him the message that you are of value apart from him.

Finally, the prime strategy for Fence Sitters is called **the dangers of change**. This method entails thinking of the disadvantages of the relationship for the Fence Sitter and verbalizing those dis-advantages to him. You don't have to lie or make up wild stories; just look at the situation and brainstorm plausible drawbacks for him to stay in the relationship. In other words, *you* are telling *him* what is wrong with the relationship. Not only is this likely to stop him in his tracks, but it also involves your saying things you need to hear. Otherwise, you become so committed to convincing him how good things could be that you lose sight of the fact that they really aren't so hot now (and haven't been).

"Dangers of change" directly addresses the ambivalence that the Fence Sitter has about the relationship. By aligning with the side of not being in the relationship, you undercut any power issues if there are any. You are no longer saying, "You must change," but rather, "I understand why you are not changing." By accepting the inherent difficulty of the situation for the Fence Sitter, you allow him the opportunity to move beyond his ambivalence.

In addition, "dangers of change" further removes you from the cheerleader role and slows things down a bit. In many ways, this tactic encourages you to be the one to put the skids on the rela-tionship. Part of the issue with the Fence Sitter is that he senses your desire for the relationship, fears a loss of control, and there-fore resists and withdraws. When you slow things down to an uncomfortable pace for him, he will likely resist that as well. But

when he does, you have to stick with the "go slow" strategy. You have to be the conservative one about the relationship.

Think of this "dangers of change" strategy as analogous to how racehorses are trained to run. Trainers don't just whip them and exhort them to run. Instead, they lightly restrain them from running by pulling back on the bit. The horse then resists the restraining pressure and runs faster in the process. Get the idea? By verbalizing the disadvantages and encouraging a slow pace, you are pulling back lightly on the reins. Of course, horses are not people, but assholes are not much smarter and are about as stubborn.

Finally, as with other impossible men, you need to **know when to say when** and have a mental timetable to guide your experimentation and observation process. If you prefer, with the Fence Sitter you can also predetermine a number of times that he withdraws or breaks up with you. Again, it doesn't matter if it is fifteen or three times; what matters is that you are in control and will stop contact when the preset time or number of occurrences becomes a reality.

April's success

Things are better. Not perfect, but I'm holding my own better with him. I don't feel so manipulated by him all the time, and it seems like we are getting a degree of stability. I'm using his predictability against him. To start with, I'm just not getting into it with him anymore. When he criticizes or accuses me, I simply don't argue with him or defend myself because I didn't do anything wrong in the first place. When he dumps on the relationship, I agree with him. It's great. Most times he just looks at me puzzled and shuts up. A couple of times, he told me he knew we would work things out. That's a switch.

It was inevitable that he got incredibly pissed at me for some stupid event—I didn't call him at exactly the time I usually do—

and he told me to leave his apartment and that he didn't want to see me again. Of course, it was two weeks before my birthday. My birthday came and went, and he called me about a week later and very sweetly asked me over to his apartment. I told him I was busy. I had started taking tennis lessons, and I asked him if we could meet for dinner the next night. He was furious and hung up. He called one week later and asked me over, and I was too tired and suggested dinner the following night. He was irritated but agreed this time.

At dinner he was taken aback by my taking tennis lessons. He was even more surprised when I told him I was going to a movie with a friend. I told him I had been neglecting my own personal growth lately and so I decided to change a few things. When we got back to his apartment, I dropped the bomb on him. Before he started being romantic, I apologized to him for being so pushy about the relationship and too dependent on him. I told him that I now understood, after some extensive soul searching, that it was my fault that he broke it off with me a few weeks ago. I just hadn't come to grips with all the disadvantages for him in the relationship. After all, the relationship and I had faults: I was needy and demanded a lot of his time; the relationship prevented him from shopping around and finding someone more suitable for him. I probably was going to continue to expect the relationship to progress to something long-term and committed, put a lot of pressure on him, and, frankly, long-term relationships and the thought of marriage were very scary. I told him that I now recognized how frightening things can be for him and that he had legitimate cause for concern. He didn't know what to say.

So from now on, when I notice him getting nasty or critical, I am going to interpret that as his way to get some much-needed space. I will respect his need. I also told him that I thought we needed to slow down to give me a chance to not be so dependent on him. He immediately retorted that he liked our level of contact and my dependence because that made him think I really loved

him. But I persisted. I thanked him for sparing my feelings but said I knew I had to work on it.

It was really hard, but I went home the next morning instead of staying the weekend. He called me right away and asked me over again. I put him off again, and he got mad and accused me of having another man with me. I ignored his comment and apologized again for putting so much pressure on him. I don't know where this is going, but I am doing a lot better with it. He is after me all the time to see him more. Sometimes I do, but sometimes I don't. I am trying to make new friends and develop more interests. I think the key with me was seeing his predictability and how he was never going to dump me. He's really a lot more insecure and needy than I am. It's a nice feeling to know I am in control.

We made the following suggestions to cope with the Fence Sitter:

1. Gloom and doom. Lean toward the Fence Sitter's negative comments about the relationship and reflect them back to him. Stop being the relationship cheerleader.
2. Give him what he wants—and more. When he breaks up, make him wait longer than he wants to wait. Increase your desirability by increasing his discomfort. He is far more needy and insecure than you know.
3. Shift the focus. You must stop revolving your life around his because he interprets it as your desperation and ability to endure anything from him.
4. Dangers of change. Align yourself with that side of him that is afraid of the relationship, and verbalize the disadvantages for him of being in the relationship. Slow down the relationship and pull back on the reins.
5. Know when to say when. Have a mental timetable.

16 Dealing with Emotionally Retarded Men

When I first met him, I thought he was a real man.
He was always cool, calm and collected—like a
rock. He was just the stability I thought I needed.
Over time, however, his "cool" became cold
and unfeeling, his "calm" became distant
and withholding, and his "collected"
became restricted and insensitive.
I was dying of emotional starvation.

—Anita, forty-six-year-old executive

I f immature men are often caricatures of male childishness and underdevelopment, emotionally retarded men are stereotypes of extreme masculinity and aversion to emotional experience. They see feelings and their expression as being the domain of women, annoyances to be endured or avoided.

Myth #4: If You Give Unselfishly to a Man, He Will Eventually Come Around

Most women have a great deal of ambivalence when it comes to this myth. They know they need to take care of themselves, but the idea of giving unselfishly sounds so nice and idealistic. Giving is an important part of any relationship. It just needs to be kept in perspective.

More germane to dealing with assholes, unselfish giving is a prerequisite for failure. The *Stand by Your Man* mentality is a great idea for a country-western song but an incredibly bad credo for dealing with the guys described in this book. These men will not come around through your kindness or love. Instead, they will immediately accommodate your selfless giving and will expect no less from you for the rest of your life. Unselfish giving to these guys will lead to continued unselfish giving until there is no more of you to give.

Weakening the Strong, Silent Type

The fact that living cardboard cutouts of John Wayne and Clint Eastwood exist should not be surprising, given what we learn growing up in American culture. Women are encouraged from an early age to express their feelings and be sensitive to others. Men, on the other hand, learn it's not "manly" to do so. Sociologists, psychologists and journalists may tell you that's changing, and we hope it is. However, we still see men who have difficulty with feelings and who use that difficulty to manipulate, punish and control; and women who feel naturally uncomfortable with that state of affairs.

Georgia and Byron: The Case of Silence Is Golden

Byron was in middle management in a large corporation, where he had worked since college. Georgia was a housewife who had

given up a career in business to raise a family. Both were in their early thirties, and they had three school-age children.

Georgia's story

I don't think Byron loves me or anything else for that matter. He never talks to me. When he comes home from work, I am busy with dinner and the children, so conversation is difficult. But later in the evening, when the children are in bed, I make sure I am available to talk. Byron seems to prefer to read business publications, watch television or drift off to sleep in his easy chair. It is an emotional vacuum in our house.

At first, I initiated more conversation. I tried to keep up with Byron's projects at work and asked specific questions about them. He generally didn't want to talk about work. So I would tell him about my day or about the children. Occasionally he would grunt in recognition but tended to keep his eyes glued to the magazine or television set.

Since these attempts to get him to open up didn't work, I tried harder. Some evenings, I got a baby-sitter for a couple of hours so we could go for a walk or a drive by ourselves. I asked him to spend some time with me each night just to talk, without reading or watching television. He agreed but had little to say either during those times or on our walks and drives alone.

Then I only felt worse. We had time together, but he still had nothing to say. What was even more frustrating was that Byron seemed to have no trouble talking to anyone else. I began to get depressed and to believe that there was something wrong with me. What is it about me that makes it so difficult for him to talk to me? I don't understand how it could be so difficult for him. I'm not looking for Alan Alda, just a little attention and conversation.

What Doesn't Work

Let's consider some of the "sensible" and "reasonable" ways women try to cope with the Strong, Silent Type. Probably the most common is to encourage him to talk, usually by asking him questions: "How was your day today?" "What's the matter?" "Why don't you ever talk to me anymore?" If he doesn't want to talk, he probably sees the questions as intrusions or irritations. They most likely make him more reluctant to speak because now he knows it bothers you.

Another common solution is to attempt to schedule time to talk. Women will get the kids to a baby-sitter, turn the television off early or plan a quiet dinner for two. Unfortunately, lack of time isn't the problem, and sitting there with no distractions and still having nothing to say can be doubly frustrating.

What Works

There are two general points that we hope will leave an indelible impression on your problem-solving style. First, it's important to do something that signifies a noticeable change from your previous strategies. Most women get locked into an idea ("I'll make it easier for him to talk"), and try small variations on the same theme over and over. Break out of the rut. Do something that is really different.

Second, focus on a noticeable change in *your* behavior, not his. By placing too much emphasis on his behavior as a source of your happiness, you allow him to take advantage of and manipulate you. When the Strong, Silent Type figures out how bothered you are by his silence, he will make you pay every time he is dissatisfied about something. Instead, set the stage for him to change by doing something noticeably different.

The Strong, Silent Type has two good reasons not to change.

One, he knows silence is a good weapon, and he likes getting under your skin. And two, he may feel pressured by you to talk. The perceived pressure raises his masculinity hackles, and he will resist change at all costs.

One thing to try is a version of "give him what he wants—and more" called **silence is golden**. It entails making yourself less available for conversation, stopping the initiation of conversation and cutting it short when it does start. "Silence is golden" requires you to accept his position and give him more of it than he wants. This accomplishes many things. One is that it not only removes, but also reverses, all pressure on the Strong, Silent Type. Also, it gives you more control. You're not trying to make him talk, so you're not failing. If he talks, you decide when the conversation is over. The entire pattern is changed, and the power shifts. "Silence is golden" removes silence as a power weapon. You are no longer invested in his talking more and no longer emotionally held hostage.

The second specific strategy is another version of **creative interpretation**. It involves reinterpreting (for you and him) the meaning of the silence. Women with the Strong, Silent Type assume that he should talk more and that his silence connotes lack of caring. He then learns, perhaps in a less than conscious way, that his silence gives him power. If you can begin to interpret, out loud, the silence as being a positive thing, it will change its meaning for both of you.

For instance, say things to him like "I really respect you for being able to keep your problems to yourself" or "I feel good when you're quiet because I know that means everything is all right between us." By doing this, you learn (by hearing your own voice saying it) that there are other ways to look at the situation that are less gloomy. If he disagrees with how you are interpreting it, he has to speak up and tell you (and you succeed because he's started

talking). His continued silence implies agreement, so you still come out ahead.

A final strategy involves **shifting the focus** from the Strong, Silent Type to your making positive changes that are not directly related to the relationship. These would include getting involved in exercise programs, educational endeavors, hobbies, clubs or closer friendships. The idea is to take more responsibility for making yourself happy and place less emphasis (and pressure) on your partner to do it for you.

An important change can occur when you do more for yourself. Not only does your partner see you treating yourself as more important (by devoting more time and energy to your interests), but you see yourself doing that as well. We all have a part of us that watches and judges what we do, and that part has a lot to say about our self-esteem. When you treat yourself better, you observe that, and your self-esteem grows ("I must be okay if I'm treating myself as worthwhile"). When you feel better about yourself, you generally need less from others in the way of attention and assurance.

Georgia's success

I was able to completely stop asking questions to get Byron to talk. Instead, my conversation consisted of statements about things I wanted to bring up or found interesting, many of which required no response at all from Byron. I also interspersed creative interpretations of his silence. One time after a particularly long spell of not talking, I looked at him and said, "Silence is golden." I couldn't believe his response—he said it was as long as it wasn't too much. I just about bit my lip off holding back the laughter. I felt so smug!

I did very well at abruptly ending conversations once they had started. I would remember something I had to put on my shopping list and leave the room to do it. I kept a magazine in my lap and

went back to reading it at the first lull in the conversation. And, more subtly, I just didn't try too hard to keep the dialogue going. Not being as available for conversation became easier as I pursued other interests. I went out with friends more and talked to them on the phone after the kids went to bed. I took a course at college and often had homework to do at night. Byron's changes were dramatic, if not rapid. For the first few weeks he seemed to enjoy being left alone and was happy to let me go my own way. After about a month, he began to get more curious about some of the things I was doing and started to ask me questions (to which I responded very briefly, of course). Finally, he appeared to get a little jealous of the time I was spending doing other things, and he asked if we could find a way to spend more time together! That was certainly new for him.

I think that as soon as he saw his main weapon was now a dud, he let it go. You know, I felt better even before he started talking more, and I believe I would be okay either way. By focusing less on him and how much he talked, and more on what I wanted to do, I put myself first for a change and didn't revolve my happiness around him. He's still a macho asshole, but silence is no longer an issue, and I am figuring out how to get my needs taken care of without him.

In summary, we presented three ways to approach the problem of the Strong, Silent Type differently:

1. Give him what he wants—and more. Silence is golden. Become less available for conversation and try less hard to initiate and maintain it.
2. Creative interpretation. Interpret the silence to him in a positive way in order to negate any power the Strong, Silent Type is expressing through silence ("I'll show you that you can't make me talk").
3. Shift the focus. Take him out of the center of your universe because he abuses that privilege. Instead, pursue your own growth and passions.

Melting the Ice Man

While the Strong, Silent Type can drive you nuts in his attempts to harness power by silence, the Ice Man pummels you into insanity with his relentless pursuit of rationality and intolerance of people. The Ice Man prides himself on his intellect, yet his social and interpersonal IQ is too low to measure. These guys were not socialized to be sensitive to interpersonal cues. They are oblivious of their effect on others and wouldn't even care too much if they found out.

Monica and Walter: The Case of Mr. Spock

Recall Monica and Walter. Monica was ready to settle down with a stable man, and build a life and family together. However, one small problem surfaced, or rather, landed. Instead of Mr. Right, she got Mr. Spock. Her man wasn't from Mars; he was from a different galaxy altogether, from a planet called Vulcan.

Monica's story

Walter is such an asshole! He just doesn't have a clue about what my needs are in the relationship. He thinks I'm so "high maintenance" because I actually want someone to talk to me, and maybe even hold me once in a while. He doesn't recognize any emotional needs at all. In fact, he makes fun of anything emotional in that dry, sarcastic way of his. He says I have a talk-show mentality and should grow up and recognize the good things I have in life. In some ways he is right. I have everything I want: kids, family, career when I want it, beautiful home—everything except a husband, a real human being to share my life with. Walter just doesn't get that part. He is so cold sometimes. He embarrasses me around our friends. You haven't seen politically incorrect until you have seen Walter in action. He's so smug about his ideas. When we are out, he makes snide comments about service people and treats them rudely. He has such a superior attitude about almost everything you can mention.

He is a sexist pig and puts down women. When the conversation turns toward relationships and self-help books, he puts them all down. He said last Saturday night that the book he is looking forward to is Women Who Bitch Too Much *because we were talking about* Women Who Love Too Much. *Real cute. Of course, all the men laughed. The women didn't. When we are not with our friends, he criticizes them, too. I don't think Walter truly likes anyone or has ever had a friend. He calls my friends losers and recommends that we stop seeing this couple or that couple because the guy doesn't work the right job or the woman is too liberal. He's got a reason to dislike everyone. It's only when he can see a direct benefit to the "friendship" that he wants to socialize. He has a lot of good qualities—just none of them are personal ones or have to do with me.*

What Doesn't Work

Most women, when confronted with the Ice Man, will extol the virtues of emotional experience and counter his judgmental criticisms of people with optimism. Women like Monica often spend much of their time trying to persuade their Ice Men that they are missing out on the pleasures of life. Women become emotional cheerleaders for the Ice Man.

The problem with the cheerleading strategy is that it doesn't work, despite the enthusiasm of the cheerleader. The Ice Man interprets the cheerleading as a lack of understanding of the way things really are. He then will pull out lecture 101 about the facts of life. He takes your efforts at defending humanity as a challenge, and proceeds to prove beyond a reasonable doubt how misguided and childishly naïve your perspective is. You can't win a debate with these guys about anything. They will criticize your arguments as illogical, ill founded and based in emotion.

Another losing strategy with the Ice Man is to let him know what your needs are. Since he does not recognize the value of emotional intimacy, it's a sure bet that he won't comply with your requests. Since he has no emotional needs, he believes you shouldn't, either. He sees your needs as weaknesses and therefore refuses to fulfill them. He demeans your requests as unreasonable and overemotional. One scintilla of any emotion is overemotional to the Ice Man.

What Works

This guy is *really* challenging because he so steadfastly believes his own reasoning. However, that same blockheaded rigidity about his own opinions also makes him vulnerable. First, regarding his criticisms, cynicism or general negativity, a variation of **gloom and doom** can be helpful. It involves taking his position about

whatever topic is under consideration and validating it. You validate the position by agreeing with him and recognizing the inherent truth in his complaints. Rather than cheerleading and perhaps throwing down the gauntlet to him to enlighten you, convey a message of understanding and support. Let him know his point of view is valid and that he has every right to his opinion.

Sometimes, if you encourage expression of his judgmental opinions, it also allows him the space to express other, more positive ideas. "Yes, you're right. Scott and Karen do leave a lot to be desired. Maybe we should look for other friends." The best message to convey accepts, validates and slightly exaggerates the issue under discussion.

If you can, it also can be helpful to initiate conversation on a more negative, cynical or pessimistic tone than even he does. If you know that it is inevitable for the Ice Man to bring up a topic, then "gloom and doom" before he does. This can free him up to make different choices about what he expresses. Rather than opening the gates of negativism, "gloom and doom" has the capability of bumping him to a more positive position without imploring him to do so.

Beat him at his own game can also be useful. It means talking his language and using his blind obeisance to facts against him. Essentially, you are going to outlogic Mr. Spock. This requires you to let go of your efforts to persuade him of the emotional benefits to anything. Rather, you allow the facts to speak for themselves. Ice Men are at times open to facts when presented in their language.

There are many different ways to do this. There is a wide body of literature to support the value of almost any of your concerns. You have to do your homework, but it can be effective. You just have to pick your battles—the things that are truly important to you.

For example, imagine that you and your Ice Man have different views about children and television violence. You say, "Honey, I'd

like to talk to you about our kids and television violence." He says, "What talk show did you watch today that warned you against damaging their little psyches? Our kids will be fine if you stop trying to psychobabble everything." You say, "You're right about that part, but I wanted to show you this pamphlet I got from the American Psychological Association on children and TV violence. It cites decades of scientific research that virtually proves that observed violence increases children's aggressive behavior." He says, "Really? Let me see that."

Often, using the kids as a rationale to make your points is a good place to start because if there is a prayer for a soft spot in him, it might be with the kids. Again, your arguments have to be logical ones, based in proven facts from reputable sources.

When you do ask for what you want, do it in a way that not only cites the evidence, but also gently restrains him from doing what you request. Recall our discussion about racehorses. For example, she says, "I would like you to show me more affection because studies show that children who observe affection in the home are less likely to divorce. I know that this will be very hard for you and perhaps you may not even be able to do it, given your own views on affection. But I would appreciate your consideration." The idea is to make the request in a way that doesn't challenge his viewpoint directly.

The final strategy with the Ice Man is to simply nail him when he really gets under your skin. You could use **just desserts**, or any of the techniques that increase his discomfort while simultaneously helping you manage your own anger. Since the Ice Man is so freaked out by emotion, sometimes just **acting crazy** or emotional can be sufficient payback, if done in a planned and purposeful way.

Monica's success

*I like this stuff. I am getting to him rather than vice versa. It
really drove me nuts to hear him harshly criticize our friends and
me. I gloomed and doomed along with him. Once he commented
about how financial success had gone to Steven and Gigi's head. I
was ready and retorted that they were lame-brained social climbers
whose success in their own business could never elevate them
above their hillbilly background. He said to me, "Don't you think
that's a little harsh? After all, Steven and Gigi have worked very
hard in their business and deserve some credit for that." I knew I
was on to something. I just stopped being Jane Curtin to his Dan
Aykroyd—I stopped defending everything and everybody. He can
no longer say, "Jane, you ignorant slut."*

*I also stopped railing about "feelings" and tried my best to take
a scientific attitude about the really important stuff to me. The rest
I just blew off. Instead of begging him to understand my feelings
and be intimate with me, I suggested we try to be better friends to
one another. He at first got annoyed, thinking that I was going to
get into another emotional tirade about him not meeting my emotional needs. I quickly countered with the facts I had been reading
about successful long-term marriages and how research was
demonstrating that good marriages are ones where partners see
each other as friends. He then really blew me away by taking the
book I was reading and starting to cite it to me! Walter thinks I am
coming around to his way of thinking, but really, I'm using his language to beat him at his own game. I'm getting a lot more productive interaction out of him, and I have some hope that he will
soften. When he really pisses me off and says something really stupid, I intentionally cry and don't stop until he really gets uncomfortable. He hates it so bad when I cry—not because he feels sorry
for me; he just doesn't see the point in it. But I do, especially now.*

We suggested three ways to melt the Ice Man:

1. Gloom and doom. Accept, validate and exaggerate the Ice Man's negativity about life. Don't be an emotional cheerleader.
2. Beat him at his own game. Use the Ice Man's logic against him. Pick the important areas, cite the evidence and restrain him from following it.
3. Just desserts or acting crazy. Make him uncomfortable for a change.

17 Female Survival Guide: General Coping Strategies

> The foolish reject what they see,
> not what they think; the wise reject what
> they think, not what they see.
>
> —Huang Po

This chapter describes in detail the five core strategies for dealing with problematic men that were the basis for the suggestions made in the past several chapters. By giving you a good feel for these tactics, you can cope with Mr. Wrong should he come your way. This chapter also presents the final myth about relationships and discusses the thorny issue of manipulation.

Don't Be Defensive— *You* Are Not the Problem

How many times have you found yourself explaining, in great detail, your reasons for doing

something, only to wonder later on, *Why did I feel I had to justify what I did?* Usually the explanation comes in response to extensive questioning by an unreasonable partner. Other times, you are so used to doing it that you do it without thinking.

When you defend yourself, you describe motives for and reasoning behind certain actions. Explaining involves pointing out the reasons that a course of action was the correct or proper one. Defending is justification that occurs when an attack or hostile questioning is perceived. There is, of course, nothing wrong with any of these activities, done in proper measure and in appropriate circumstances. However, in relationships with the men described in this book, you do the bulk of explaining, defending, etc. The explanations and justifications become overly long, and the defensiveness is present in the absence of attack or accusation.

In such situations, the person not on the defensive—the guy— usually spends a great deal of time on the offensive. It can take the form of relentless questioning, frequent accusations, criticism of a wide range of behaviors or universal advice on how to do just about everything. The effects on the woman who routinely takes the defensive role are predictable. First of all, she gives up a great deal of power, and becomes vulnerable to manipulation and a decrease in self-esteem. In addition, this pattern keeps the focus on her, the person who is doing the defending or explaining. Her behavior is subject to constant, detailed scrutiny, while the asshole's is not. The best defense is a good offense.

To counteract his offensive tactics, there is the class of strategies called **don't be defensive**. Basically, all the tactics that fall under this category are offshoots of not allowing him to set the agenda and put you on the defensive. The basic tenet of this general strategy is very simple and involves not explaining, not defending, and not justifying what you do or why you do it. We offered three forms of this strategy: (1) *don't explain or defend;*

(2) *agree in words, but not in deeds*; and (3) *agree and exaggerate*. The general idea is that as you stop pouring energy into trying to explain your position, behavior or motives, you can get a clearer perspective on what's happening and establish equal footing (rather than an inferior position). You use this tactic so that you can pick your battles wisely: the ones that are most important to you.

These strategies are often used prior to the implementation of the other change strategies to be described since they serve to break old rules and allow you to "gather" yourself before employing more active changes in behavior. In other words, this class of strategies helps you to stop, observe and think before pressing ahead in more productive ways. These tactics are also change inducing in and of themselves. Without offering counterpoint to the asshole's comments or accusations, the "buzz" he gets from the argument is eliminated. If he does not get a rise out of you, he often will give up and move on to more productive territory.

Go with the Flow

Direct attempts at changing some men is analogous to swimming upstream. You probably will not reach your destination, and your efforts will be rewarded with fatigue, frustration, and wear and tear. When dealing with these guys, going along with their point of view or behavior can be far more conducive to problem resolution.

We call this strategy **going with the flow**. This entails listening to and accepting his statements, recognizing the values and beliefs that he holds, and avoiding taking a position that opposes his beliefs and actions. Successful implementation of "go with the flow" requires you to overcome the temptation to confront, reason or argue with him. After recognizing his point of view, the focus of "go with the flow" is to actually encourage or promote that point

of view and the actions that come from it.

"Go with the flow" is a perfect strategy because these men respond to change with defensiveness. If you bring anything up to them, they feel forced, pressured and threatened. They respond to the perceived pressure and the threatened loss of independence by clinging to their points of view so intensely that they often deliberately do the opposite of what is requested. Since these jerks can make any situation into a competitive struggle for power, they most often respond with an escalating move and give the message "I'll show you I can't be pushed around." Remember, competition and control, especially with women, are core behaviors of these Neanderthals.

Another way to look at it suggests that when these guys feel pressured, they tend to take an even more extreme position. The pressure prevents them from considering the alternatives and possibly changing the problem of their own volition. They feel backed into a corner. "Go with the flow" requires you to do a reversal and to say in words and in action, "You don't have to change; it's okay with me the way things are. I'll even help you stay the same." This tactic makes it clear that the direct pressure is off, and frees him to evaluate the situation and explore his options.

If there are any stubborn tendencies left once the pressure is removed, the only way they can now be expressed is by doing what you initially wanted. By reversing your request or encouraging things to stay the same, you can utilize his contrariness to your advantage. "Go with the flow" can take as many different forms as there are situations. By virtue of encouraging things to stay the same, the context in which the problem behavior occurs is dramatically changed. Many examples presented in part 4 represented variations of "go with the flow": (1) *make helping hurt;* (2) *beat him to the punch;* (3) *give him what he wants—and more;* (4) *invite what you dread;* (5) *gloom and doom;* (6) *beat him at his own*

game. Each strategy reflects an attempt to accept things and even encourage more of the very behavior you don't like and want to change. Such a position sets the context for change to occur.

The Spin Doctor's Prescriptions

We've all heard the saying that an optimist is a person who says a bottle is half full, while a pessimist complains it's half empty. The difference, of course, lies in their different views of the same reality; neither view is more correct than the other. Both descriptions accurately account for the "facts" of the situation: a container of liquid holding 50 percent of its capacity.

Whether the bottle is seen as half full or half empty has nothing to do with the facts, but with the interpretation, or "spin," placed on those facts. The interpretation of, or spin on, the facts speaks not only to things like the bottle, but also to real-life situations. This is the idea that gave rise to the political spin doctors, who take political lemons and turn them into lemonade. They take the same facts and spin them in such a way as to make their bosses or candidates look good.

When you are stuck in a problem, you pick a particular way of viewing the problem and get locked into whatever solutions fit that view. That spin, or meaning you attribute to the problem situation, may not only prevent problem resolution, it may also actually help create your distress. A given view provides just one way (not "the way") of describing a situation and limits problem solving to that specific description.

If we can redefine the meaning attributed to a problem behavior, this itself may have a powerful effect on attitudes, responses and the relationship itself. If the meaning attributed to the troubling situation is altered, then the consequences of the

situation will change as well. That is the exact purpose of a general category of strategies called **spin doctor's prescriptions**.

"Spin doctor's prescriptions" attempt to change your partner's experience of his problem in such a way that his original motivations and beliefs now lead toward quite different behavior. This strategy emphasizes that "reality" is not set in concrete. Our spin on an issue affects how we behave in a given circumstance. Different spins allow for alternative and, perhaps, more useful or self-enhancing solutions.

"Spin doctor's prescriptions" generally entail perceiving a problem in an entirely different light and verbalizing your new perceptions to the asshole. We offered three versions of this category: (1) *creative interpretation*; (2) *life is good*; and (3) *dangers of change*.

Push His Buttons (for a Change)

The kind of situation appropriate for **pushing his buttons for a change** is one in which he is doing something that has a direct, negative impact on you. Direct attempts such as assertiveness to address the issue have not been effective. The clear implication is that he is deriving enough benefit from the noxious behavior that your pain is not a sufficient reason for him to stop.

"Pushing his buttons for a change" involves finding ways to make it more difficult for him to do what bothers you, but without being direct or obvious about it. It sometimes involves simply making his life a bit uncomfortable, thereby giving him an opportunity to mature or change his behavior. There are several ways to implement this strategy: (1) *just desserts*; (2) *deal from the bottom of the deck*; (3) *make the worm squirm*; (4) *act crazy*; (5) *mess with his mind*; and (6) *trial by fire*.

"Pushing his buttons for a change" is based on sound behavioral

principles. Punishment, like reward, can be effective even if it is not fully explained to or understood by the recipient. This concept is particularly important with problematic men, for whom not being "controlled" may make any punishment worth enduring. In other words, if a man hears, "If you swear at me, I will leave," he may swear as a way of saying, "You can't tell me what to do." In that case, the punishment is less important than feeling in charge. The strategies in this class make the reason for the "punishment" less obvious and look less like an attempt to control. It works, but provokes less resistance.

There is another benefit to these tactics, beyond the ability to more effectively influence his behavior. In the situations for which this strategy is recommended, anger is usually present and growing. The guy's behavior is irritating, or worse, and it will not stop. These strategies allow you to channel that anger into doing irritating things back to him, but in a planned way designed to achieve a specific purpose. Feeling entertained by your efforts is completely acceptable and even encouraged. The more these tactics allow you to lighten up, the more likely you will take a different vantage point and lessen your feelings of distress.

Take Care of Yourself—He Won't

We are taught throughout our lives to solve problems by tackling them directly and staying with them until we've worked them out. Tenacity and persistence are sacredly held Western values. Sometimes, just figuring out ways to break the intense attention paid to the problem and redirecting it elsewhere can be helpful. The strategies of **take care of yourself—he won't** entail withdrawing your efforts from changing your partner and instead becoming more aware of what else is happening, or could be happening, in your life.

All tactics in this class have certain qualities in common—each helps you experience your life separate from his, emphasizes your existing strengths and highlights the areas over which you have more control: (1) *protect yourself;* (2) *know when to say when;* and (3) *shift the focus.*

Focusing on yourself instead of him communicates very clearly that you hold yourself to be important. Once that is communicated, you can begin to be seen—by yourself and your partner—as an equal in the relationship. Focusing on your existing strengths and areas of control will increase your confidence and feeling of competence. Finally, by leaving the problem alone and relaxing your problem-solving attempts, it can recede to its proper (diminished) perspective in the overall context of the rest of your life. Once that occurs, you take responsibility for your happiness away from your partner, as well as his methods of control and manipulation.

Myth #5: Being Direct, Open and Honest Are Good. Manipulation Is Bad.

This myth, like the other ones discussed, is to some extent true. Because the strategies we suggest do not involve being direct and completely honest, we fully expect to be criticized by some for promoting manipulation. And we are. We advocate manipulation only when more direct methods have been tried and failed. Many of the men discussed in this book warrant the use of commando tactics.

We readily agree that we have advocated conscious, planned attempts to influence difficult men without their knowledge or active participation. We have suggested ways you could influence changes in your partner while simultaneously blocking his manipulation. In all cases, either unplanned (e.g., the Mama's Boy's dependence overburdening the woman) or planned (e.g., the Boss's tight-fisted grip on control) manipulation was already occurring, or else honest, open attempts to deal with the problem

Table 17.1
FIVE CORE STRATEGIES FOR DEALING WITH DIFFICULT MEN

Don't Be Defensive	Spin Doctor's Prescriptions
Agree and exaggerate	Life is good
Don't explain or defend	Dangers of change
Agree in words, but not in deeds	Creative interpretation

Take Care of Yourself—He Won't
Protect yourself
Shift the focus
Know when to say when

Push His Buttons	Go with the Flow
Just desserts	Gloom and doom
Act crazy	Make helping hurt
Trial by fire	Beat him to the punch
Mess with his mind	Invite what you dread
Make the worm squirm	Beat him at his own game
Deal from the bottom of the deck	Give him what he wants —and more

had already failed (as with every situation described). As systems thinking teaches, each of us tries, consciously or subconsciously, to influence people with whom we communicate. Those attempts are every bit as manipulative as anything we have suggested, and they occur constantly. So the kinds of things we are suggesting happen

all the time. All we advocate is that you do it consciously and effectively—either in the best interests of the relationship, or to prevent manipulation, pain or control inflicted on you by someone who doesn't have your best interests at heart.

If you still see these suggestions as sneaky and dishonest, it is certainly your prerogative not to try these ideas. At times it may boil down to a choice between being "sneaky" and effective, or "open and honest" and frustrated. We are not saying our way is right. We just want you to know you have a choice. There are many different ways to approach relationship problems.

Think back to the metaphors we used in chapter 12. Was the farmer manipulative when she set fire to the rice fields? Absolutely. She could have tried sensible, straightforward methods, and her family and friends would have all died. Was the commandant manipulative when he pitched the ox over the castle wall? Of course. He could have continued the holding-out strategy and everyone would have starved to death. Doing reasonable things that you know won't work will have equally devastating results for you.

Part 4 described four other myths about men and relationships that get in the way of change. Should you choose to hang on to those myths, you won't implement our suggestions. We downplay what these men say, emphasize what they do, and sometimes encourage women to be inconsistent in word and deed. We explicitly tell women not to explain themselves in many instances. We discourage total honesty when it will be used against you. We instruct women to be more selfish.

It is not that we wouldn't like to believe these myths. On the contrary—they are ideals. But ideals rarely exist in the real world. If you act based on what life "should" be like instead of how it is, you will often find yourself stymied and frustrated. The bottom line is that solving problems in ways consistent with these myths

can, especially with impossible men, lead to repetitive failures and personal demoralization. Our assumptions may not always sound as noble as the myths, but we believe they are more realistic and can lead to more effective solutions.

We've tried to put to rest the issue of manipulation being bad, on several grounds: (1) people automatically and inadvertently use manipulation every day, we just suggest using it deliberately toward a positive goal; (2) toxic men require guerrilla tactics because of their own manipulative practices; and (3) it is the only thing that is effective many times, especially when more "direct" and "honest" methods have failed. Of course, you have to be your own judge. These strategies are clearly not for everyone.

18 Writing Your Next Chapter

*Until lions have their own historians,
tales of hunting will always glorify the hunter.*

—African proverb

This proverb speaks to our intention for this book. Men have traditionally been glorified in relationships and somehow exonerated from taking responsibility—especially the ones we have described in this book. These guys hunt unsuspecting women who fall prey to their arsenal of manipulation and deceit. This book has identified that arsenal and provided women with tactics that disarm the hunter or make him shoot blanks. More importantly, this book has documented the lion's story of the hunt. In this tale, women demonstrate their power, courage, cunning and compassion in overcoming all the obstacles placed before them. We have attempted to be historians for the women

we have seen in therapy for the past eighteen years. We hopefully have done justice to their tales of the hunt—their views of the hunter, their stories of resilience and reclamation of their own lives, and their triumphs over despair and powerlessness. Moreover, we hope by sharing those stories, you will begin writing the next chapter of your life in a way that privileges your fulfillment and expresses the lion in your heart. Throughout the book, you've read a lot of information on how to categorize, recognize, avoid, leave and deal with difficult men. The objective now is to distill that information into a sort of pocket guidebook or quick reference.

Use the guidelines as ideas for developing your own action and maintenance plans for dealing with the difficult men in your life.

Acknowledge You Are Powerless to Change Him

Before you can effectively cope, you have to realize you are powerless to change the other person. In other words, you can't *make* him *not* be a jerk. You can interact with him in different ways to allow him the opportunity to act better. You can be hurt less by his actions. But you can't *make* him change.

It is easy to get sucked into the "potential" of a guy or a relationship. "He *could* be such a great guy." "If only things were a little different, we *could* have a great relationship." Those hopes can hang in front of you like a carrot on a stick and pull you, donkeylike, further and further into a hopeless situation. A lot of things in our culture and our psyches encourage us to dream and to see the future the way we want it to be. When you are dealing with assholes and are vulnerable to them, you cannot allow yourself to lapse into that type of thinking. Focus on what is, not what could be.

Another factor that can make it hard to realize you can't

change him is that it is easy for boundaries to become blurred in relationships. The romantic myth is that when people fall in love, they "become as one." You are he, and he is you. If you let yourself start believing that, it's even easier to delude yourself that you can change him. After all, he's part of you now. It will be like changing part of yourself.

Please don't buy that drivel. In the *best* relationships, people share an emotional and spiritual bond, and a deep, intuitive understanding of each other. But they remain two distinct individuals. Relationships without boundaries are far from ideal. With toxic men, relationships without boundaries are downright dangerous. You lose yourself in his reality, and his reality is a distorted, self-centered one.

Keep in mind that you are two separate, distinct people. He's responsible for his behavior, as you are for yours. It is his job to change himself, to recognize he needs to change and to summon the motivation to do so.

Don't Let Hurt Alone Keep You or Draw You Back

Once you are in a relationship, it can be very hard to break away. The pain of that transition, real or projected, keeps women stuck with assholes or pulls them back to them.

It is important to take the process one day at a time. The overall task of getting out (or resisting the temptation to get involved initially) can seem overwhelming or insurmountable. We acknowledge a debt to Twelve-Step programs when we say that it is possible to get through a day (or an hour or a minute) without succumbing to the lure of an unhealthy relationship. You need to both realize that the immediate emotional pain will subside and have a plan to cope with it when it occurs.

The key to this process is remaining aware daily that your long-term best interests have to supersede your short-term discomfort. It also involves truly understanding how vulnerable you are to a certain type of guy and respecting how reckless that vulnerability can make you if you aren't on the lookout for it.

Use Self-Help Principles

Become aware of your specific personal vulnerabilities and the kinds of men who play into them. Then remain vigilant daily for both of those. You might need to post reminders to yourself and read them every morning: "Watch out for the guy who needs mothering." "Don't find an excuse to call him today." "Remember, 'exciting' guys have usually turned out to be emotional poison."

Read over the categories and signs of problematic men. Get to know them well enough that they become automatic, second-nature parts of your perceptions of guys you meet.

If you are with an asshole and staying with him (even for the short term), remind yourself daily that you can't let your guard down and treat him the way you do everyone else. Become familiar with the specific asshole management strategies that pertain to your situation, and work on making them a habitual part of your interactions with him.

Go Public and Garner Support

Don't let him make you choose between him and your friends and family. It can seem romantic, initially, in a Romeo-and-Juliet kind of way (since a lot of people will probably see him for what he is and you won't), but it isolates you from any reality other than his.

Don't be afraid to confide in friends and family about problems he has or the two of you have, *especially* if he tries to persuade you to keep them a secret. In many dysfunctional, abusive relationships, a conspiracy of silence between the two partners allows the relationship to continue and for people on the outside to still see him as a nice, reasonable guy.

Get regular feedback from your friends and family about your relationship (or budding relationship) and accept it without defensiveness. This is obviously very difficult. They are not always right, and you are ultimately the best judge; you don't have to always agree with whatever your friends think. However, if you argue too much with them when they present their perceptions, they will quickly stop offering them. Remain open to multiple perspectives on your situation, and then decide what is best for you.

Women often confide in friends, but they don't give those friends the tools to really help and wind up getting confusing, conflicting advice from different people. Sympathetic listeners are important to have, but not sufficient. Let a select few friends know what your specific, personalized self-help strategies are. They can then help keep you on track by reinforcing what you yourself are attempting to do.

Be Open to Helping Others with Similar Problems

It is often easier to see problems in, and solutions for, other people than it is to see them in yourself. What you say to other women in similar dilemmas is often what you need to hear yourself say. Also, by helping someone else, you feel strong and effective, rather than stuck, one down and helpless, as you often can in your own relationship. Keep in mind your daily struggle to better deal

with the assholes around you, and don't be afraid to share your weak moments with those you are trying to support.

Are We Being Too Hard on Men?

You would have to comb through this book very carefully to find even a handful of positive references to men. We call them assholes. We accuse them of lying and controlling, and generally avoid highlighting any positive attributes they possess.

Our answer to the question of whether we are being too hard on men is: "Hell, no!" It seems to us that everybody else is being too easy on them. Granted, a lot of self-help books point out men's difficulties in managing relationships, communicating and parenting. But they have a heavy bias toward understanding and remediation. To a large extent we are playing devil's advocate by going to the other extreme. We don't deny that men are shaped by evolutionary, cultural and familial influences. We're just tired of their being used as excuses for unacceptable behavior.

Let us also reiterate one last time that we don't, by any means, intend to imply that all men are assholes. But an alarmingly high proportion are, and even many who aren't have tendencies it would serve them well to be more aware of. It is one thing to criticize and demean disenfranchised segments of our society—minorities, women, the poor. It is quite a different matter to come down on those who dominate society as men do.

Few men will read this book because they are not uncomfortable; they have it made; they have power in government, finance and relationships. People read self-help books when they are hurting. If what women read in this book can be used to help them make certain types of men even a little less comfortable, we will be delighted. When people are uncomfortable, they look for new ways

to do things. Men need to be more uncomfortable.

Are We Too Quick to Advise Women to Leave?

As badly as we talk about men in many parts of this book, it could easily be concluded that we expect (and encourage) most women to leave relationships with difficult men. If that is what you believe, you haven't been paying attention to what we've written.

When we discussed counterbalancing factors such as personal values and commitments, the best interests of the children, financial considerations, and emotional attachments, we were not just paying lip service to them. Everyone has flaws, and the men we've described in this book have more than most. That alone is often not enough to justify ending a relationship. Many times it is easier, from many aspects, to stay than to go. The key is learning how to stay with self-respect and relative comfort and happiness.

That can be achieved. The chapters on coping with the myriad of men laid out a wide variety of uncommon strategies that not only make women more comfortable in their relationship, but also set the stage for the men to change. By coping better, women will do things differently and react to their partners differently. In that context, the men almost *have* to change. It might not be for the better, or enough, or permanent, but it does happen.

We are not contradicting what we said in chapter 1 about difficult men not wanting to change. Most don't. That doesn't mean they don't want to stay in relationships. If you are able to truly change the way you deal with a problematic partner, it is quite likely he will change in spite of himself. Whether or not you like the results is another matter. Having said all that about their capacity for change and women's realistic option to stay with them, we freely admit we don't always believe it is the best option for many women.

It has been a priority of ours to validate women who are in truly unworkable relationships and who feel compelled to stay when it is *not* in their best interests. While not all men are assholes and not all assholes are unchangeable, the worst ones are toxic for women in relationships. We have tried to confirm what many women already know—that unregenerate men do exist. Overall, it is our hope that our ideas serve as a counterpoint to books, articles and "experts" that say you *can* make any relationship work, and should (and, implicitly, that it is the woman's responsibility to do so).

Society places women in one-down positions in many areas. Nowhere does this inequity exist more than in romantic relationships. Given that situation, women need all the skills, knowledge and flexibility they can muster to care for themselves in that environment. When they can see clearly what they are dealing with (a Critic or a Boss, for instance) and the full range of alternative ways to cope, they can then make the best choices and take charge of their lives.

As a final note, let us reiterate that women are, as a rule, far too likely to give guys the benefit of the doubt. They see potential and overlook obvious, glaring shortcomings. Change those attitudes. Hold men accountable. They're grown-ups who are responsible for their behavior and for whom excuses shouldn't count anymore. Expect what you deserve, and recognize as quickly as you can when you are settling for less.

Appendix A

A Quick Guide to Mental Health Mythology

*When money speaks, the
truth keeps silent.*

—Russian proverb

J ust as myths about relationships can limit your
solution possibilities, myths about mental
health can also reduce your options in psychotherapy. Many people, including some therapists,
believe that it is the all-knowing therapist and his
or her all-powerful techniques that cause people to
change—*the myth of the guru.* Belief in this myth
unfortunately diminishes your importance to the
process of change, excludes your perspective and
may influence you to accept treatment that does

291

not seem right for you. Drs. Scott Miller, Barry Duncan and Mark Hubble review forty years of research in their books *Escape from Babel*, *Psychotherapy with "Impossible" Cases* and *The Heart and Soul of Change*, and show that change in therapy does not come from the special powers of any particular therapist or approach. Rather, change principally results from your input and participation—*you are the star of the therapeutic drama*. Research shows that:

a. Change depends far more on your resources and abilities than on the therapist's pet approach. Good therapy utilizes your strengths to create solution possibilities.

b. Change depends far more on your perceptions of the therapist and the relationship formed in therapy than on the therapist's pet approach. If there is not a good fit, find another therapist.

c. Change depends upon addressing *your* goals for therapy as well as fitting your views of the problem and how it may change, instead of what the therapist's model says.

d. Change depends upon the therapist exploring options *with* you rather than imposing a model's "right" way to address a problem.

Another belief widely held by consumers and therapists alike is the seductive idea that psychiatric drugs offer the best available treatment for emotional problems—*the myth of the magic pill*. Belief in this myth undercuts the importance of your participation in changing your life, influences you to do nothing else to address your problems and, if you receive some relief from medication, may encourage you to accept intolerable circumstances in your life or with a difficult partner. In their book *From Placebo to Panacea*, Drs. Roger Greenberg and Seymour Fisher review decades of research and demonstrate that the value of psychiatric drugs is grossly overstated. Research shows that:

a. Drugs are no more effective than short-term therapy in alleviating depression. Therapy has fewer side effects and longer maintenance of gains.

b. Antidepressant drugs are no more effective than placebos in alleviating depression. This *doesn't* mean they are not helpful (they can be), just that they are not as helpful as drug companies say they are. Knowing there is a level playing field opens up more possibilities to consider.

c. Antianxiety drugs actually increase anxiety and panic attacks over time. They are helpful in the short run but encourage dependence and dysfunction in the long run.

d. There is no scientific basis for drugging children with psychiatric medication (except perhaps for Ritalin). Some scientists believe it is unethical.

e. Standard medical textbooks say there is no such thing as a simple "biochemical imbalance" to explain emotional problems. So why do you hear about it everywhere? Because drug companies want to simplify complex human difficulties into problems "cured" by their products. Drugs are big money. "Biochemical imbalance" is a catch phrase like "Did somebody say McDonalds?"

Appendix B

We hope that readers find the following award to be humorous, even helpful. By merely thinking of worthy recipients of the award, women can validate their feelings and leave an indelible impression in their minds about the various types of men to avoid. Like writing a letter they never send, this is a cathartic way for women to validate their experience.

Certified Asshole Award

Because of your dedicated service to your own selfish interests at the expense of many women, blatant disregard for the consequences of your relationship actions, and persistent penchant for making women's lives hell, by the power invested in the grantor of this award by virtue of her completion of the "Let's Face It, Men Are @$$#%\¢$" survival training, this Certified Asshole Award is hereby conferred on:

_____

You are hereby entitled to all the rights and privileges of the title "Certified Asshole,"

Awarded this _____ day of _____, _____.

Please attach this certificate to your forehead so that women may avoid you.

You have been observed to be the following type:

_____

Bibliography

Avis, Judith Myers. "Where Are All the Family Therapists? Abuse and Violence Within Families and Family Therapy's Response." *Journal of Marital and Family Therapy* 18 (1992): 225-232.

Bateson, Gregory, Don Jackson, Jay Haley, and John Weakland. "Toward a Theory of Schizophrenia." *Behavioral Science* 1 (1956): 251-264.

Duncan, Barry L., Mark Hubble, and S. Scott Miller. *Psychotherapy with "Impossible" Cases.* New York: W. W. Norton and Co., 1997.

Duncan, Barry L., and Joseph Rock. *Overcoming Relationship Impasses.* New York: Insight Books, 1991.

Ehrenreich, Barbara. "Whose Gap Is It, Anyway?" *Time.* May 6, 1996.

Farrell, Warren. *Why Men Are the Way They Are.* New York: McGraw-Hill, 1986.

Fisch, Richard, John Weakland, and Lynn Segal. *The Tactics of Change: Doing Therapy Briefly.* San Francisco: Jossey-Bass, 1982.

Fisher, Seymour, and Roger Greenberg, eds. *From Placebo to Panacea: Putting Drugs to the Test*. New York: John Wiley and Sons, 1997.

Gray, John. *Men Are from Mars, Women Are from Venus*. New York: HarperCollins, 1992.

Green, Shelley. "WWW.Sex.Family." In *The Emergence of Families into the Twenty-First Century*, edited by P. Munhall and R. Chenail, in press.

Hollander, Dory. *101 Lies Men Tell Women*. New York: HarperCollins, 1995.

Hubble, Mark, Barry Duncan and Scott Miller. *The Heart and Soul of Change*. Washington, D.C.: APA Books, in press.

Kosinski, Jerzy. *Being There*. New York: Bantam, 1987.

Le Guin, Ursula. *The Left Hand of Darkness*. New York: Ace Books, 1969.

Marin, Rick, and T. Trent Gegax. "Bad Boys." *Newsweek*. Dec. 1996.

Miller, Scott D., and Insoo Berg. *The Miracle Method*. New York: W. W. Norton and Co., 1995.

Miller, Scott D., Barry Duncan, and Mark Hubble. *Escape from Babel: Toward a Unifying Language of Change*. New York: W. W. Norton and Co., 1997.

Peyser, Marc, and Yahlin Chang. "The Queen of Hearts Gives Up Her Throne." *Newsweek*. Aug. 1997.

Vonnegut, Kurt. *Slapstick*. New York: Dell Publishing, 1976.

Watzlawick, Paul, John Weakland, and Richard Fisch. *Change: Principles of Problem Formation and Problem Resolution*. New York: W. W. Norton and Co., 1974.

Wolf, Naomi. *The Beauty Myth*. New York: William Morrow and Co., 1991.

About the Authors

Joseph Rock, a clinical psychologist, received his bachelor's degree from Amherst College, his master's degree from Cleveland State University, and his doctor of psychology (Psy.D.) degree from Wright State University School of Professional Psychology.

He cowrote with Dr. Duncan *Overcoming Relationship Impasses*. Dr. Rock has appeared on national TV and has been featured in *USA Today* and *Psychology Today*. He currently directs a private psychological practice in the Cleveland, Ohio area. With over eighteen years of clinical experience with relationships, he makes regular appearances on a local TV show, *The Morning Exchange*, to discuss relationship issues.

Barry Duncan, a clinical psychologist, received his bachelor's degree from Wright State University (WSU) and his Psy.D. from the WSU School of Professional Psychology, where he met Dr. Rock.

He has authored or coauthored over fifty

professional publications, including eight books, and has been honored by the Ohio division of the American Association for Marriage and Family Therapy for his contributions.

Dr. Duncan has appeared on *Oprah* and other national programs, and has been featured in *The Family Therapy Networker*, *Psychology Today*, *USA Today* and *Glamour*. With over seventeen years of clinical experience, he now is an associate professor in the Department of Family Therapy at Nova Southeastern University.

To share your relationship stories, successes and failures with the authors, write to:

Barry Duncan, Psy.D.
School of Social and Systemic Studies
Nova Southeastern University
3301 College Avenue
Fort Lauderdale, FL 33314

"Let's Face It, Men Are
@$$#%\¢$"